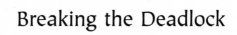

Breaking the Deadlock

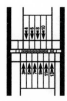

Breaking the Deadlock

The 2000 Election, the Constitution, and the Courts

Richard A. Posner

Princeton University Press

Princeton and Oxford

Published by Princeton University Press,
41 William Street, Princeton, New Jersey 08540

In the United Kingdom: Princeton University Press,
3 Market Place, Woodstock, Oxfordshire OX20 1SY

Library of Congress Cataloging-in-Publication Data

Posner, Richard A.
Breaking the deadlock . the 2000 election, the constitution, and the courts /
Richard A. Posner.
p.   cm.
Includes bibliographical references and index.
ISBN 0-691-09073-4 (cl. : alk. paper)
1. Bush, George W. (George Walker), 1946–   —Trials, litigation, etc.   2. Gore,
Albert, 1948–   —Trials, litigation, etc.   2. Contested elections—United States.
4. Presidents—United States—Election—2000.   5. Law and politics.   I. Title.
KF5074.2 P67   2001
324.973'0929—dc21   2001035078

British Library Cataloging-in-Publication Data is available

This book has been composed in Tiepolo Book and Stone Serif
by Princeton Editorial Associates, Inc.,
Scottsdale, Arizona, and Roosevelt, New Jersey

Printed on acid-free paper. ∞

www.pup.princeton.edu

Printed in the United States of America

1 3 5 7 9 10 8 6 4 2

Contents

Preface   vii
Chronology of the Deadlock   xiii
Glossary of Election Terms   xv

Introduction   1

—— *Chapter 1*
The Road to Florida 2000   12

—— *Chapter 2*
The Deadlocked Election   48

—— *Chapter 3*
The Postelection Struggle in the Courts   92

—— *Chapter 4*
Critiquing the Participants   150

—— *Chapter 5*
Consequences and Reforms   221

Conclusion   252

Index   261

Preface

THE MOST RECENT Presidential election was held on November 7, 2000, and by the morning of November 8 it was apparent that the election would be decided by the popular vote in Florida, with its 25 electoral votes. George W. Bush led in the popular vote in Florida by fewer than 2,000 votes out of almost 6 million cast. A machine recount was automatic under Florida law, given the closeness of the result, unless the loser refused it. Al Gore did not refuse it. By not refusing and—when the machine recount failed to overcome Bush's lead—by demanding hand recounts in four counties, he precipitated an extraordinary legal and political struggle over who would become the 43d President of the United States. The struggle ended (realistically, not technically; technically it did not end until January 6, 2001, when Congress counted the electoral votes) on December 13, when, following his decisive defeat in the U.S. Supreme Court the night before, Gore conceded the election.

The 36-day drama was dense with legal and political maneuvering; clouded with statistical uncertainty; saturated with state and federal law, both statutory and constitutional, with trials and appeals, stays and opinions; rich in issues of constitutional and democratic theory and in practical issues of election administration; revealing in exposing the limitations of appellate judges and professors of constitutional law and the extent of penetration of law by politics; exacerbated by racial politics; and resounding with cries for reform on many levels. Its multifaceted character, its narrative and analytic complexity, its peripeteias, the fierce passions it aroused in the political class, the naked partisanship of intellectuals that it evoked, the sense of crisis, the sense of law stretched to the breaking point, the spectacle of obscure people thrust unwillingly into the limelight—all this was reminiscent of the Clinton-Lewinsky scandal and its aftermath, about which I had written a book that could, I decided, serve as a model for a study of the election deadlock and its aftermath.[1] Of course there were many differences, of which the most important was overlooked: the election crisis involved, so far as appears, no scandal, no crimes—just the rash of mistakes that occur whenever human beings are confronted with something difficult, emotional, and unexpected; mistakes, moreover, susceptible of correction for the future.[2] But one great point in common was that both crises demonstrated the indispensability of pragmatism to the resolution of tumultuous, law-saturated public issues.

The election deadlock alone was one of the great political events of recent times. It and the ensuing litigation—of which the Supreme Court's decision in *Bush v. Gore* that ended the deadlock was just one phase—are as fascinating as they are momentous. Multidisciplinary treatment is needed to do justice to the complicated series of legal and political maneuvers that unfolded in a setting of profound statistical uncertainty and against a complex

---

1. Richard A. Posner, *An Affair of State: The Investigation, Impeachment, and Trial of President Clinton* (1999).

2. The big corrigible mistake of the Clinton impeachment—the independent-counsel law—has been corrected. The law has been allowed to expire, without mourners who might seek to reenact it.

background of constitutional and statutory law and racial and party politics. Such a treatment must cover statistics (was it a real deadlock?); law, constitutional and otherwise, and the legal process; political theory and political science, especially democratic and constitutional theory; racial politics; the role and character of the Supreme Court; and issues of technology and cost in election administration.

My essential purpose is to make the various facets of the election deadlock and its litigation aftermath intelligible. But I also make and defend a number of claims, among them that Gore was not the "real winner" in Florida, although he might have won had a more "user-friendly" voting technology been used throughout the state; that Gore's lawyers did not blunder (nor did Bush's) and therefore should not be blamed for Gore's failure to overturn the result of the election; that the contemporaneous response of the legal professoriat exposed serious deficiencies in the academic practice of constitutional law; that the U.S. Supreme Court's interventions in the postelection struggle were not the outrages that its liberal critics have claimed them to be but, rather, a pragmatically defensible series of responses to a looming political and constitutional crisis; and that radical reforms in the electoral process (such as a national ballot for Presidential elections or the abolition of the Electoral College) are not justifiable, although more limited reforms in election administration may well be. In the last chapter I offer a modest blueprint for feasible reform.

Although it has proved impossible to avoid all technical issues of law and of statistics, the book is written to be accessible to a general audience. For it is intended not only for specialists in election law and constitutional law but also for anyone who is interested in the role that voting plays in a democracy and in the role of courts, particularly the U.S. Supreme Court, in our constitutional system, and for anyone who was captivated by the drama of the 2000 election and its aftermath. I do not apologize for the technical aspects of the book. In the wake of the deadlock the view rapidly took hold in influential quarters that the election had been "stolen" from Gore by an act of judicial usurpation. That is a drastic and misleading oversimplification, in part because it overlooks or misunderstands the legal, statistical, and political complexity of the deadlock.

At first I thought that everything I might be able to say about the subject could be said in an article, and so I wrote "Florida 2000: The Election Deadlock and the Litigation That Ensued."[3] Even before publication, the article attracted an unusual amount of attention.[4] It became apparent that there was a demand for a fuller treatment and that issues essential to an evaluation of the deadlock and its resolution could not be adequately analyzed in an article.

The article was the indispensable beginning, however, and I thank all those who gave me comments on early drafts of it, as well as those who commented on it later and contributed to the refinement of my thinking that is reflected in this book: Jack Balkin, Gary Becker, Christopher DeMuth, John Donohue, Frank Easterbrook, Eldon Eisenach, Einer Elhauge, John Ely, Richard Friedman, Elizabeth Garrett, Howard Gillman, Richard Hasen, Dennis Hutchinson, Pamela Karlan, Michael Klarman, Andrew Koppelman, William Landes, Lash LaRue, Lawrence Lessig, Michael McConnell, Frank Michelman, Edward Morrison, Charlene Posner, Eric Posner, Eric Rasmusen, Stephen Stigler, David Strauss, Cass Sunstein, and Benjamin Wittes. I also thank Benson Dastrup, Boris Kasten, and especially Bryan Dayton, for their very valuable

3. 2000 *Supreme Court Review* 1 (2001). A second, shorter article, entitled *"Bush v. Gore:* Prolegomenon to an Assessment," largely a knockoff of the first but with a few additional points, has been published as a chapter in an electronic book, *The Vote: Bush, Gore & the Supreme Court* (Cass R. Sunstein and Richard A. Epstein eds. 2001), http://www.thevotebook.com, and will also appear, in slightly different form, in the summer issue of volume 68 of the *University of Chicago Law Review* (2001). I cite other essays from *The Vote* in this book, but will spare the reader further reference to the *Review* version.

4. See, for example, Benjamin Wittes, "Maybe the Court Got It Right: A Judge's Defense of the Florida Election Decision," *Washington Post,* Feb. 21, 2001, p. A23.

research assistance; state and local election officers in Florida, voting system vendors, and Jeanne Heffernan, for helpful information; William Landes, Edward Morrison, and Stephen Stigler for helpful suggestions with regard to the statistical analysis in Chapter 2; Richard Friedman and Michael Klarman for very fruitful e-mail exchanges; Ward Farnsworth for his helpful suggestions; Bruce Ackerman for helpful comments on a draft of Chapter 5; participants in a symposium on the election aftermath held at Northwestern University School of Law on January 12, 2001, for their stimulating comments; and Michael Boudin, Eldon Eisenach, Larry Kramer, Thomas LeBien, Eric Posner, and two anonymous readers for Princeton University Press, all of whom commented helpfully on the manuscript; Professor Kramer's generosity in offering extensive expert comments on the legal and historical aspects of the manuscript deserves a special acknowledgment.

Chronology of the Deadlock

November 7, 2000   Presidential election

November 9   Gore protests outcome, demands hand recounts in four counties

November 14   Deadline for counties to submit vote totals to secretary of state

November 18   Deadline for adding overseas votes to totals

November 21   Florida supreme court, ruling in Gore's protest suit, extends November 14 deadline to November 26

November 26   Florida secretary of state certifies Bush as winner of popular election in state

November 27   Gore brings suit to contest certification of Bush as winner

December 4   U.S. Supreme Court vacates and remands Florida supreme court's November 21 decision

December 4   Judge Sauls, confirming his oral ruling of the previous day, throws out Gore's contest suit after two-day trial

December 8   Florida supreme court reverses Judge Sauls, orders statewide hand recount of undervotes

December 9	U.S. Supreme Court stays recount
December 11	Florida supreme court responds to December 4 remand by U.S. Supreme Court
December 12	Safe harbor deadline for appointment of state's Presidential electors
December 12	U.S. Supreme Court reverses Florida supreme court's December 8 decision
December 13	Gore concedes election to Bush
December 18	Electoral College casts its votes
January 6, 2001	Congress meets to count electoral votes; declares Bush winner and next President

Glossary of Election Terms

Chad — A perforated area, usually rectangular, next to a candidate's name in a punchcard ballot, which the voter punches to record a vote.

Hanging chad — A chad attached to the ballot by only one corner.

Swinging chad — A chad attached to the ballot by two corners.

Dangling chad — A hanging or a swinging chad.

Tri-chad — A chad attached to the ballot by three corners.

Dimpled (also known as pregnant) chad — A chad that, while bulging, indented, or marked, remains attached to the ballot by all four corners.

Pierced chad—A dimpled chad that is pierced. (The term "dimpled chad" is sometimes reserved for an unpierced dimpled chad, and when that is done "pregnant chad" becomes the only designation for all chads, pierced or unpierced, that are attached to the ballot by all four corners.)

Overvote (or overvoted ballot) — A ballot that contains more than one vote for the same office.

Undervote (or undervoted ballot) — A ballot that contains no vote for one or more offices.

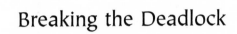

Breaking the Deadlock

Introduction

THE TUMULTUOUS political and legal events (in a word, the "deadlock") that are the subject of this book ran their course in only five weeks—from November 8, 2000, the day after the 2000 Presidential election, to December 13, 2000, the day that Al Gore conceded the election to George Bush. This short period was dense with incident, and the book will be more intelligible if I supplement the chronology at the front of the book with a brief narrative. That is one task of this Introduction; the other, with which I begin, is to outline the book itself.

To understand and appraise the deadlock, and trace out its origins and likely consequences, we need to place it within a broader framework than a blow-by-blow account of the five weeks can provide. (Such accounts are in any event available from journalists.)[1]

---

1. See, for example, Correspondents of the *New York Times, 36 Days: The Complete Chronicle of the 2000 Presidential Election Crisis* (2001); Political Staff of the *Washington Post, Deadlock: The Inside Story of America's Closest Election* (2001). The first of these books, however, is merely a compendium of *New York Times* articles that were published during the deadlock; the second is a lively and balanced narrative written after the deadlock was resolved.

The building of that broader framework, partly historical and partly theoretical, is the project of Chapter 1. I survey the early history of voting, its place in democratic theory, the relevant provisions of the U.S. Constitution (with particular emphasis on the provisions dealing with the election of the President, and hence on the Electoral College), and the evolution of voting from the adoption of the Constitution to the eve of the 2000 election. The last deadlocked Presidential election before 2000—the Hayes-Tilden election of 1876—figures here, along with the other close calls in Presidential election history and the emergence of modern voting law. A number of issues presented by, and responses to, the deadlock, including the racial aspect, cannot be fully understood without reference to history and democratic theory.

Chapter 2 looks at the Florida popular vote and the recount results and asks whether it is possible, through the use of statistical analysis, to determine who the "real" winner was. The answer is no. The election in Florida was an unbreakable statistical tie. And in any case determining the "real" winner of an election is a legal rather than a factual matter. One of the most persistent fallacies in the public, especially political, commentary on the deadlock has been the notion that the winner of an election can be determined without reference to election rules.

The chapter also tries, by means of statistical analysis, to discover why there were so many "spoiled ballots" (that is, ballots that the tabulating machinery did not record as votes, whether because of voter error, machine defects, or other factors) in some Florida counties. The nature of the voting technology, and whether votes are counted at the county or the precinct level, turn out to be important factors, and likewise the correlated factors of literacy, income, and race. The Democrats' belief that Gore would probably have won the popular vote in Florida had more counties used a more user-friendly voting technology is not groundless, but it does not follow that he was the "real"—that is, the legal—winner.

In Chapter 3, I turn to the litigation over the election. The chapter is partly descriptive, an effort both to explain an exceedingly complex series of cases interpreting and applying complicated federal and state statutes and difficult constitutional concepts and to map the likely consequences had the Supreme Court not intervened and stopped the recount on December 12. But the chapter is critical as well. I emphasize the discrepancies between the text, structure, and other clues to the meaning of the Florida election statute, on the one hand, and the interpretation placed on the statute by the Florida supreme court, on the other, and on the possible constitutional significance of such discrepancies. These discrepancies enable me to offer a tentative answer to the question, left open at the end of Chapter 2, of who the *legal* winner of the Florida popular vote for President was, and to offer a preliminary assessment of the soundness of the U.S. Supreme Court's decision of December 12, in *Bush v. Gore,* that ended the deadlock. I argue that the Florida supreme court's abrogation of the discretionary authority that the state legislature had unmistakably vested in state and local election officials furnished a plausible ground for concluding that the state supreme court had violated the requirement of Article II of the U.S. Constitution that each state's Presidential electors be appointed in the manner directed by the state's legislature.

Chapter 4 is a critique of the participants in the litigation—the judges and the lawyers, but also the professors of constitutional law who commented on the litigation either while it was going on or afterwards. There has been a great deal of criticism of the judges, mainly the five-Justice majority of the U.S. Supreme Court. That criticism is largely unjust. The Court was operating under great time pressure—and it shows. But there was no injustice. There has also been much criticism of Gore's legal team for tactical decisions that it made over the course of the litigation. I argue that these criticisms are also unfounded. The critics fail to appreciate that in political litigation, tactics designed solely to increase the probability of winning the lawsuit may be unsound when the political context is given proper weight.

The harshest criticisms, however, have been leveled against the Supreme Court. The Court could have deflected some of them by adopting the ground of decision advocated by three concurring Justices—the ground I have mentioned already—that Article II of the Constitution limits the extent to which a state court can in the name of "interpretation" alter the provisions in the state's election code *after* the Presidential election has taken place. The narrow perspective of the typical legal professional is inadequate for evaluating the performance of the Supreme Court in so "big" a case as *Bush v. Gore*—"big" in the sense of involving a dispute whose consequences seem to dwarf the strictly "legal" considerations bearing on its sound resolution. In Chapter 4 I defend, as I have done in previous books, a conception of constitutional jurisprudence that places pragmatic considerations front and center and that—if my conjectures about what might have happened had the recount ordered by the Florida supreme court continued are correct—provides a substantial basis for the suggested interpretation of Article II's "Manner directed" clause. I relate the pragmatic approach to the Supreme Court's "political questions" doctrine, and I argue that the Article II ground of decision, which unfortunately failed to capture the support of a majority of the Justices, is not only plausible (as I argue in Chapter 3) but also, when a pragmatic approach to law is taken, persuasive. The decision averted what might well have been (though the Pollyannas deny this) a political and constitutional crisis—a crisis precipitated by an interbranch struggle within the Florida government that the "Manner directed" clause could properly be used to prevent.

Among the most vehement critics of *Bush v. Gore* have been professors of law, especially of constitutional law, though other law professors have not hesitated to chime in. The precipitance and shallowness of many of these criticisms cast a shadow over constitutional law as a subject of law school teaching and research. As an academic field, constitutional law is both overpoliticized and underspecialized. The phenomena are related. Professors of constitutional law have little command of the full range of subjects encompassed by modern constitutional law. Their reaction to a subject within that range that eludes their understanding tends to be driven by their politics rather than by their expertise.

Chapter 5 takes up the related topics of the likely consequences of the deadlock and of the ensuing litigation, and the path to reform. The consequences necessarily are speculative at this time. They seem most likely to involve damage to judicial prestige, racial harmony, and Presidential legitimacy, but are likely be short-lived because of the rapidity with which the deadlock was resolved, the complexity of the issues, and the short attention span of a busy populace.

I turn next to an analysis of reforms that might prevent a repetition of the deadlock and of the ensuing crisis narrowly averted. Many of the proposals that have been floated in the wake of the deadlock, including abolition of the Electoral College and the creation of a national ballot for federal elections, seem unwise for a variety of reasons. Others—having to do with reforms in election law (both state and federal, including constitutional and statutory provisions relating to the Electoral College), election administration, and voting technology—are both feasible and desirable, though they may be opposed by incumbents, who have adapted to and are comfortable with the imperfections of the existing system. A particularly delicate question is whether voting should be made easier for people of limited literacy; I argue that it should be.

To make the analysis in the book easier to follow, let me take a moment to remind the reader of the crucial stages of the deadlock.

On the eve of the 2000 Presidential election, Bush was holding a slight lead over Gore in the public opinion polls, as he had been for months; he was generally expected to win. Although neither candidate was from the extreme wing of his party, and the area of agreement between them on the larger issues of domestic and foreign policy was in fact broad, the dynamics of the campaign, and in particular the inroads made by Ralph Nader's third-party candidacy on Gore's base of support, had led to a certain polarization. Gore had increasingly—and, as it seemed to some observers, stridently—sounded liberal themes. Noting Bush's public praise of Supreme Court Justices Antonin Scalia and Clarence Thomas, Gore had made clear that his model Justices were William Brennan and Thurgood Marshall; indeed, he had tried to frighten voters with the prospect that, if elected President, Bush would appoint Justices in the mold of Scalia and Thomas. Gore had striven mightily to increase the turnout of black voters, while Joseph Lieberman, his running mate, had worked hard to increase Jewish turnout in Florida, recognized as a state that might be vital to Gore's chances of winning.

On the night of the election, it became apparent that Florida's 25 electoral votes were indeed the key to victory. At first, as the returns came in and were combined with the results of exit polling to generate projections of the outcome, Gore was thought to have a commanding lead in Florida, and the television networks incautiously announced him the winner. They did this shortly before the polls closed in the Florida panhandle, which is in the Central time zone, and thus may have discouraged some Republicans from bothering to vote. Then the lead swung to Bush, and he was proclaimed the winner; Gore actually called him and conceded. But Bush's lead began to erode, Gore retracted his concession, and the embarrassed networks announced that the election in Florida was too close to call.

When the tabulation of the Florida vote (minus late-arriving overseas ballots, for which the deadline was November 18) was completed on November 8, Bush was ahead of Gore by 1,784 votes.

As this was less than 0.5 percent of the total number of votes tabulated for the Presidency in Florida, a recount was automatic unless Gore refused it.[2] He did not refuse, and the recount was conducted. This was a mechanical recount, designed to correct any errors in the tabulation of the vote by the machines used for tabulation. Within days, Bush's lead dropped to 327 votes.

Already a controversy had arisen over the ballot used in Palm Beach County: the so-called "butterfly ballot," which Gore's supporters claimed was confusing and had led a number of elderly Jewish voters to vote for Patrick Buchanan, the right-wing candidate of the Reform Party, thinking they were voting for Gore. (Not only Jews; but along with blacks they were the demographic group least likely to vote for Buchanan deliberately.) There were calls for a revote in Palm Beach County.

Gore's legal team, however, focused not on the "Jews for Buchanan" issue (which only a revote, quickly dismissed as infeasible and probably unlawful, might have resolved), but rather on the unusual number of "undervotes" (ballots that the tabulating machines had not counted as a vote for any Presidential candidate) in counties that used punchcard voting machines. On November 9, even before the statewide machine recount was completed, Gore demanded a hand recount in four of those counties—Broward, Miami-Dade, Palm Beach, and Volusia, all ones that he had carried by healthy margins. The Republicans denounced the demand, urging the importance of finality ("closure") in a Presidential election.

The voter who votes on a punchcard voting machine uses a stylus or the equivalent to punch out a "chad" (a small perforated rectangle or circle) in a paper ballot that is placed on a tray that has a space between the ballot and the bottom of the tray, to which the chad falls. The punched ballot is placed in a computer that counts the votes in the ballot by shining a light on it. If a chad has been

---

2. Fla. Stat. § 102.141(4).

punched through, the light will shine through the hole, registering a vote for the candidate whose chad it was. If the chad is still clinging to the hole, it may obstruct the beam of light, and so a vote will not be counted. That is an "undervoted" ballot. And if the chads of more than one candidate for the same office have been punched through, or if the chad for one candidate has been punched through and the name of a candidate for that office has been written in the space for a write-in candidate—even if it is the name of the punched candidate—the computer is programmed to record no vote for that office. That is an "overvoted" ballot.

Florida's election statute requires the county canvassing boards to submit their final counts within seven days after the election— thus, in 2000, by November 14—although late-arriving overseas ballots were, as already mentioned, to be counted until November 18. Only Volusia County completed its hand recount by the November 14 deadline. Katherine Harris, who as the secretary of state of Florida is the state's highest election official, refused to extend the statutory deadline for the other counties. Had this refusal stood, Bush would have been certified as the winner of the popular vote in Florida by 930 votes on November 18 after receipt of the last overseas ballots—which, strongly favoring Bush, had boosted his earlier 327-vote margin. But the Broward, Palm Beach, and Miami-Dade canvassing boards sued Harris to extend the deadline, and though she prevailed in the trial court, the Florida supreme court (after granting a stay to prevent her from certifying a winner during the court's consideration of the canvassing boards' appeal) reversed the trial court on November 21. The court ordered the deadline for the recounts, and thus the earliest date for the certification, postponed to November 26.

To the surprise of most observers, only Broward County completed its recount by the newly extended deadline, the Florida supreme court having refused to grant a further extension. Harris refused to include the incomplete totals from the recounts conducted by the other two counties. One, Palm Beach, had worked diligently to complete the recount and did so a few hours after the deadline; but that was too late, Harris ruled. Miami-Dade had abandoned its recount earlier in the week, deciding that it would not be able to make the deadline. (Volusia's recount totals, having been submitted by November 14, had already been included.) After adding in the Broward recount results, Harris on November 26 certified Bush the winner of the popular vote in Florida by 537 votes. Inclusion of the Palm Beach recount totals would have cut down Bush's lead to little more than 300 votes. Although Bush's lead fluctuated throughout the five weeks of the deadlock, at no point did he lose the lead.

Bush had asked the U.S. Supreme Court to review the November 21 decision of the Florida supreme court. The Court had agreed, and on December 4 it vacated (that is, set aside) the Florida court's decision and sent the case back to that court for clarification of its grounds. It wanted to know whether the court had taken forbidden considerations into account in deciding to extend the statutory deadline for recounts (see Chapter 3) and by doing so had usurped the state legislature's authority, conferred by Article II of the U.S. Constitution, to determine the manner in which a state's Presidential electors are appointed.

Meanwhile, on November 27, the day after Harris had certified Bush as the winner of the popular vote in Florida, Gore had brought suit in a Florida state court to contest the certification. Bush had already filed suit in a federal district court to halt the recounts; that suit went nowhere. The trial judge in Gore's case ruled against Gore on December 3 and 4, after a short trial. Gore appealed and on December 8 the Florida supreme court reversed the trial judge and ordered that the untimely Palm Beach recount results and the partial recount results from the interrupted recount in Miami-Dade County be added to the certified totals, thus whittling Bush's lead down to as few as 154 votes. The court also ordered that all the undervotes (some 60,000) statewide be recounted by hand, but it refused to specify criteria for counting undervoted ballots as votes. The counters were left free to pick whatever criteria they wanted, subject however to judicial review at the end of the recount. In the original hand recounts, Broward County apparently had counted all dimpled as well as dangling chads as votes for whichever Presidential candidate had a dimpled or dangling chad. (A dimpled chad is a chad that has an indentation, but is still attached at all four corners to the ballot; see the Glossary of Election Terms.) Palm Beach County's canvassing board had used a somewhat more conservative method of recovering votes from undervoted ballots (see Chapter 2).

Bush immediately sought review of the Florida supreme court's decision in the U.S. Supreme Court and asked the Court to stay (enjoin) the recount pending its review. The Court issued a stay the next day, December 9, by a vote of 5 to 4, with Chief Justice William Rehnquist and Justices Sandra Day O'Connor, Anthony Kennedy, Scalia, and Thomas in the majority and Justices John Paul Stevens, David Souter, Ruth Bader Ginsburg, and Stephen Breyer in the minority. Three days later, on December 12, by the same vote and the same lineup, the Court declared the recount ordered by the Florida supreme court unconstitutional as a denial of the equal protection of the laws, and added that under Florida law December 12 was the outside deadline for a recount in a Presidential election; therefore the recount could not resume.

Actually seven Justices, not five, had agreed that the recount ordered by the Florida court was so standardless as to deny Florida's voters the equal protection of the laws, in violation of the Fourteenth Amendment to the Constitution. But two of the seven, Souter and Breyer, believed that the proper remedy was to send the case back to the Florida supreme court and let that court decide whether, consistent with Florida law, there was time to conduct a recount that would comply with the Constitution. Three of the other five Justices in the majority (Rehnquist, Scalia, and Thomas) concluded in a concurring opinion by Rehnquist that the Florida supreme court had also violated Article II of the Constitution.

There had been other legal challenges to the election results. In particular, supporters of Gore had sought to invalidate thousands of votes for Bush in Seminole and Martin Counties, where Republican campaign workers had been permitted to fill in required information on absentee ballots cast by Republican voters. But the Florida courts had already rejected these challenges when the U.S. Supreme Court decided *Bush v. Gore;* and so, the day after the Court ruled in that case that the recount which the Court had stayed could not resume, Gore, his litigation remedies exhausted, conceded the election. The case was formally dismissed by the Florida supreme court on December 22.

Because of the bitterness in political and minority circles that the election and its aftermath had engendered and the fact that Bush had only one electoral vote more than a bare majority, there was some concern that when the Electoral College electors cast their votes, on December 18, some of Bush's electors might defect to Gore. But this did not happen—though, ironically, one of Gore's electors refused to cast her vote, as a protest against Congress's refusal to grant statehood to the District of Columbia. On January 6, 2001, when Congress met to count the electoral votes, several black members of the House of Representatives objected to counting Florida's electoral votes for Bush. But because no Senator would join in the objection, it was not considered,[3] and Bush was declared the winner of the Presidential election at last.

---

3. Under section 15 of Title III of the U.S. Code, an objection to electoral votes may be considered by Congress only if it is signed by both a Senator and a Representative.

Chapter 1

The Road to Florida 2000

Democratic Theory—Briefly

BEHIND THE 2000 Presidential election in Florida lie thousands of years of thinking about, controversy over, experimentation with, regulation of, and tinkering with the popular vote as the method of political governance deemed central to democratic theory.[1] Not that voting is limited to the political arena, or to democracies. Appellate decisions are determined by judges' votes; one of the jokes that went the rounds after *Bush v. Gore* was decided had Bush saying, "I want to thank those who voted for me for President: Rehnquist, O'Connor, Scalia, Kennedy, and Thomas." And one of the complaints about the punchcard voting machines used in a number of Florida counties was that the machines had been worn down by being lent for use in union elections. Voting is a

---

1. For a taste of the complexity of democratic theory, to which I cannot possibly do justice in this book, see Thomas Christiano, *The Role of the Many: Fundamental Issues in Democratic Theory* (1996); James A. Gardner, "Consent, Legitimacy and Elections: Implementing Popular Sovereignty under the Lockean Constitution," 52 *University of Pittsburgh Law Review* 189 (1990).

highly economical method of aggregating preferences, which is why it is used so widely. But it is also a very crude method.[2] It does not weight preferences by intensity or knowledge, and, partly for that reason, it does not impose a cost on the ignorant, irresponsible, or exploitive exercise of the franchise. Especially when the ballot is secret (which it has to be wherever there is concern about intimidation or other coercion, or undue influence), the voter is insulated from criticism, however just; he is neither rewarded for voting intelligently nor punished for voting stupidly.

I have been speaking thus far of voting in its pure "one person–one vote" sense, however, and often impurities are deliberately introduced. Corporate voting is by share rather than by shareholder; votes are weighted by the voter's financial interest in the outcome of the vote. We shall see that John Stuart Mill thought that in political elections abler individuals should be given additional votes. Even in modern American political elections there are eligibility requirements that, deliberately or not, prevent or discourage the most incompetent, apathetic, and irresponsible elements of the population from voting. Voters must be adults, must register to vote, must not be in jail or prison (often, must not be ex-felons as well), must be residents of the voting district, usually must be citizens. Obviously these are coarse sieves if the objective is to confine voting to intelligent, knowledgeable, civic-minded, politically mature, responsible people with a tangible stake in the outcome of the election.

Why anyone who is eligible *bothers* to vote is a puzzle,[3] especially to economists, who emphasize self-interest as the engine of human action. The puzzle is not why voters do not invest much

---

2. A proposition substantiated in a huge literature; for a glimpse, see Amartya Sen, "How to Judge Voting Schemes," *Journal of Economic Perspectives,* Winter 1995, p. 91. One of the complications is that there is a great variety of potential voting rules, all with different effects. For a lively discussion, see Gordon Tullock, *On Voting: A Public Choice Approach,* ch. 2 (1998).

3. John H. Aldrich, "When Is It Rational to Vote?" in *Perspectives on Public Choice: A Handbook* 373 (Dennis C. Mueller ed. 1997); Anthony Downs, *An Economic Theory of Democracy,* ch. 14 (1957).

time in equipping themselves to vote intelligently (something that many of them would lack the intelligence or education to be able to do, no matter how much time they spent studying the issues and the candidates); obviously they have little to gain from such an investment, since political elections, other than on the most local level, are virtually never decided by a single vote. The puzzle is that people vote at all in a society in which voting is not compulsory, given the lack of instrumental value to which I have just pointed—even the 2000 Presidential election in Florida was not decided by a single vote.

Of course, many Americans who are eligible to vote do not vote. The nationwide turnout in the 2000 Presidential election was only 50 percent of the eligible voters, and it is often much lower in more obscure elections. Yet many do vote. The costs are slight. But what are the benefits? Because a single voter cannot swing the election, voting is less plausibly regarded as an activity yielding instrumental benefits than as a form of consumption, like rooting for one's alma mater at a college football game. Consistent with this suggestion, voter turnout is largely a function of how exciting the election campaign has been; the voter chooses between the candidates much as he would between competing brands of an ordinary product or service.[4] Voting is also a way of constructing and signaling the voter's solidarity with like-minded people. But that is often an element of ordinary consumption too; the choice of brand may be influenced by a desire to signal taste, values, or affluence. Because the benefits of voting are small, however, even modestly high costs of voting can depress turnout significantly. The fact that turnout in U.S. elections is low by international standards is largely explained by mundane factors affecting, however slightly, the cost

4. See, besides the references in note 3, Daniel Hays Lowenstein, *Election Law: Cases and Materials* 54–60 (1995), a good summary of the literature on incentives to vote.

of voting. For example, elections are scheduled on regular workdays in the United States, rather than on holidays or weekends as in a number of other countries. Registering to vote is also more of a bother in the United States, because registration is carried out at the state level; Americans tend to move around a great deal and so have to register more frequently than the citizens of less mobile or more centralized societies.[5]

The popular vote is often thought to be *the* defining element of political democracy, but that is a modern view. The classical view, which originates in the Athenian concept of democracy[6] and contains an insight that we moderns have largely lost sight of, is that filling political offices by popular election rather than by lot conduces to *aristocratic* (in the Aristotelian sense) rather than democratic government. Conduces, in other words, to government by "the best" rather than by the average (as in a system of filling offices by lot) or by "the people" as a whole.[7] Only *representative* democracy is aristocratic in this sense, however. Direct democracy—voting on issues rather than for officials—is not. Although a hallowed part of our tradition in the form of the New England meeting and still employed to a limited extent in some of our states, primarily in the form of the referendum, direct democracy is infeasible in a large, complex polity. Switzerland employs the referendum extensively—and it is exceptional even among small countries in this respect.[8] Moreover, Switzerland is also and primarily a representative democracy, like California and other U.S. states that authorize referenda. In these instances direct democracy merely

---

5. Nelson W. Polsby and Aaron Wildavsky, *Presidential Elections: Strategies and Structures of American Politics* 5–8 (10th ed. 2000).

6. Scott Gordon, *Controlling the State: Constitutionalism from Ancient Athens to Today* 66–80 (1999).

7. Bernard Manin, *The Principles of Representative Government* (1997). Schumpeter's theory of competitive democracy is similar; Joseph A. Schumpeter, *Capitalism, Socialism, and Democracy,* ch. 22 (3d ed. 1950).

8. On direct democracy generally, see Dennis Mueller, *Constitutional Democracy,* ch. 7 (1996).

supplements representative democracy, providing a means of breaking cross-party coalitions of politicians.[9]

The aristocratic character of representative democracy is rooted in the fact that, especially if political parties are weak or nonexistent (the significance of this qualification will become clear shortly), voters will tend to pick the best candidate for each office. The best candidate—which is to say the candidate most likely to occupy the office with distinction—is likely to be a superior person, not at all typical of the voters. And it is the officeholders, the elected officials and the officials whom they appoint, who govern—not the people who elect them.[10] Of course voters may often be deceived about who is the best candidate; even so, an average Joe is unlikely to prevail in electoral competition, just as an average Joe is unlikely to win the world boxing title. The glib, the clever, the shrewd, the handsome, and the charismatic are likely to dominate the electoral competition, occupy the principal offices, and constitute, in short, a political aristocracy. Not that the people are an inert element in representative democracy. The politicians will vie for their favor by advocating policies that command broad support. But these advocates will be drawn from a narrow and unrepresentative segment of the community, and the policies they advocate, or seem to advocate, to win popular support will often not be the policies they implement.

Representative democracy becomes monarchical when the representative is a dictator and there is only one candidate, as in the plebiscites employed by Napoleon and Hitler to cement their rule, or the one-party voting in communist states. But democratic

---

9. Bruno S. Frey, "Direct Democracy: Politico-Economic Lessons from Swiss Experience," 84 *American Economic Review Papers and Proceedings* 338 (May 1994).

10. This assumes that, as in our system of government, the voters are not authorized to issue binding instructions to the successful candidate. If they were, officeholders would be genuine agents, rather than principals; the people would rule, as they do not in our system.

aristocracy, oxymoron as it may seem, best describes our system. The framers of the original Constitution, the Constitution of 1787, decreed that the House of Representatives would be popularly elected, but they had a distinctly aristocratic conception of the Presidency; it is reflected in the device of the Electoral College. In the wake of the 2000 election fiasco, there are renewed calls to abolish the Electoral College. We shall be considering the merits of abolition throughout this book, particularly in the last chapter. The deadlock, and the difficulties of resolving it, were inseparable from that institution. But even if the Electoral College were abolished and the President directly elected by popular vote, our political system would remain aristocratic in Aristotle's sense.

Our political aristocracy is not hereditary, and its direct or indirect dependence on the popular vote, not only for initial appointment but also for reappointment at stated intervals, tends to align its interests more closely with the interests of the population at large than do other systems of government.[11] Nevertheless, representative democracy, democratic self-government, and popular government are misleading descriptions of the system for governing modern "democracies." This is so not only because the people do not rule, and because there are no guaranties that they vote intelligently or even conscientiously, but also because the voters are not the people, but only a fraction (and not necessarily a representative fraction) of the entire population, and also because, as I have noted, voting is a crude method of aggregating preferences. In the 2000 Presidential election, little more than a third of the population actually cast a ballot that was counted as a vote for one of the Presidential candidates, and the winner of the popular vote lost

---

11. In a representative democracy, "elections are part of the system of accountability and control" (Gordon, *Controlling the State,* at 360), along with a host of other mechanisms, as Gordon emphasizes.

the election, because the loser had more electoral votes. Winner and loser, moreover, each had the votes of only about one-sixth of the total population.

Although the Electoral College is controversial, one of the principles that it embodies, that of districted rather than at-large elections, is not; and yet districting drives a further wedge between popular majorities and electoral outcomes. If two parties compete for control of a 100-member state legislature elected by districts of equal population, a party that wins a bare majority of the votes in a bare majority of the districts will end up with control of the legislature, though that party could be the preference of only a shade over 25 percent of the state's voters, who might in turn be only a modest fraction of the population. This paradox is complicated at the Presidential election level by the facts that a state's electoral votes are the sum of the state's Senators and Representatives in Congress and that each state has two Senators regardless of its population. This might be thought to imply that the votes of the voters in the less populous states are weighted more heavily in the Electoral College than those of the voters in the more populous states. Yet we shall see in Chapter 5 that this is an oversimplification, because given the winner-take-all rule that all but two states use for allocating their electoral votes, swing voters in more populous states have more influence in the Presidential election than swing voters in less populous ones.

The only constant is that voting is indeed a crude method of mapping preferences onto policies—and for the further reason that voting for a candidate is voting both for a person and, in effect, for a package of likely policies: the policies the candidate supports, possibly the policies endorsed in his party's platform. So wholly apart from voter ignorance, policies may be adopted that do not actually command majority support, either because a majority of voters prefers the candidate whose policies they do not like (they may consider him an abler leader) or because the majority likes only a subset of those policies. In a two-party system, moreover, the parties have a strong incentive to move to the center of the distribution of political opinion. This may force voters to choose between two candidates who have largely identical views that are not widely supported but that have the support of the median voter. Making a choice between two alternatives is more difficult the harder the alternatives are to distinguish—but it is also more difficult the more alternatives there are, so that a proliferation of candidates does not cure the Tweedledum-Tweedledee problem.[12] And such a proliferation is in any event unlikely because a two-party system is a natural although not inevitable corollary of a Presidential as distinct from a parliamentary system. It is difficult for a third party to mount a credible Presidential campaign—third-party Presidential candidates are invariably just "spoilers"—and so it is difficult to take the party itself seriously as a national force.[13] What really does in third parties, however, is a winner-take-all voting system (as distinct from proportional representation) at the legislative level. For that is likely to prevent a third party from electing any legislators at all, making the party impotent at the legislative as well as the executive level.

When ignorance about issues and candidates,[14] exploitive intentions (voting for the party that you hope will, if it takes

---

12. On both points, see Richard R. Lau and David P. Redlawsk, "Voting Correctly," 91 *American Political Science Review* 585, 592 (1997).

13. Arend Lijphart, *Democracies: Patterns of Majoritarian and Consensus Government in Twenty-One Countries* 130–131, 180 (1984).

14. "Interest in politics is generally weak, discussion is rare, political knowledge on the average is pitifully low, and few people actively participate in politics beyond voting. . . . And what good is even voting if for so many it is based on so little information?" Lau and Redlawsk, "Voting Correctly," at 585. "Individuals are creatures of habit when they vote, as when they work and play. They vote for the same party in the present election as in the last one, unless that decision is perceived to have been unrewarded or punished. Unlike in market transactions, however, the rewards and punishments that follow voting are neither immediate nor often clearly linked to the act of voting. Thus, rational or irrational political beliefs and behavior—like beliefs in the prognostic powers of constellations of stars—are likely to persist even in individuals whose everyday behavior in the market place conforms well to that predicted by rational actor models." Dennis C. Mueller, "Capitalism, Democracy and Rational Individual Behavior," 10 *Journal of Evolutionary Economics* 67, 73 (2000). See also Larry

power, redistribute wealth to you from other people), low turnout, and errors in voting and in tabulating votes are added to the brew, it becomes apparent that voting registers informed public opinion in only the loosest sense and the "popular will," Rousseau's "general will," perhaps not at all. Some of the distortions may be offsetting, but that cannot be assumed. And while it is true that low turnout would not matter if nonvoters had the same interests as voters, they do not. Turnout is disproportionately high among the elderly even after adjustment is made for other influences on it[15]— a factor that, in combination with the disfranchisement of children, creates a strong public policy tilt away from children and toward the elderly.[16] We shall note in Chapter 5 that the expressed political *preferences* of nonvoters tend to be quite similar to those of voters; but those preferences may not correspond very closely to nonvoters' *interests*. As nonparticipants in the electoral system, nonvoters are unlikely to have given much thought to aligning their political views with their interests.

Our actual existing democracy falls so far short of the soaring ideals of the theorists of democracy[17] that some of those theorists might be inclined to deny that our system is democratic. But that is to be unrealistic, as well as to attribute a fixed meaning to a word ("democracy") of notorious plasticity. Representative democracy has decisive *pragmatic* advantages over alternative systems of governing a modern society, and so we can be enthusiasts for democracy without having to prate about self-government or the popular

---

M. Bartels, "Uninformed Voters: Information Effects in Presidential Elections," 40 *American Journal of Political Science* 194 (1996). But not all students of the electoral process believe that voters are seriously uninformed. See, for example, Sam Peltzman, "How Efficient Is the Voting Market?" 33 *Journal of Law and Economics* 27 (1990); with specific reference to Presidential elections, see ibid. at 59–62.

15. John E. Filer, Lawrence W. Kenny, and Rebecca B. Morton, "Redistribution, Income, and Voting," 37 *American Journal of Political Science* 63, 74–75 (tab. 2), 80 (1993).

16. Richard A. Posner, *Aging and Old Age* 148–149, 288–289 (1995).

17. See, for example, David M. Estlund, "Democracy without Preference," 99 *Philosophical Review* 397 (1990).

will. Paradoxically, the advantages of representative democracy emerge most clearly if we eschew pious platitudes about civic virtue and assume that people (including those who live in democratic societies) are, whether as citizens or as officials, self-interested rather than public-interested or altruistic, or that, if they are public-interested or altruistic, the specific beliefs they hold are likely to be distorted by self-interest or ignorance. It is a realistic assumption and implies that people—whether the collective "We the People" of the Constitution's preamble or individual persons— cannot be trusted to exercise power.

That is a worrisome thought. The core function of government has always been to provide services—classically, internal and external security—that the market cannot provide efficiently because the benefits which these services generate could not be appropriated by the private individual or firm that produced them. Imagine trying to finance the national defense by means of voluntary contributions. People who did not contribute would obtain the same benefits from national defense as those who contributed, and so the incentive to contribute would be meager. The same thing is true with regard to the financing of police, prosecutors, judges, and the rest of the law enforcement apparatus.

The effective performance of the core functions of government requires a concentration of physical power—the "monopoly of force" that all governments claim. Force to maintain law and order, force to extract the revenues necessary to pay for that maintenance. As a result, control of the government creates opportunities for expropriation of the citizenry's wealth, and for other abuses, provided there are significant costs of emigrating, as there usually are. Quite apart from the danger of abuse, the mere fact that the basic government services are ones not sold in a market makes the monitoring of their efficient provision difficult. Both the loyalty and the competence of our political fiduciaries must somehow be secured by the institutions of the society.

The key institution in our society is, precisely, representative democracy, and its defining "democratic" feature is that the representatives are elected by the public at large, with each eligible member of the public having a single, nonsalable vote. But why voting? Why majority voting? Why equal voting? And why are votes nonsalable? These turn out to be related questions, and the answers will point us toward the central concerns of this book.

Voting in effect constitutes citizens[18] the "owners" of the government, in much the same way that shareholders are the owners of corporations. But whereas shareholders vote by shares rather than per capita, because their stakes in the corporation may be very unequal, citizens have more or less equal stakes. Not entirely so, of course; people are very differently related to government so far as the costs they bear and the benefits they reap. But because of the great power of government, almost everyone has a significant stake in the government's operation.

Too great a departure from the "one person–one vote" principle (as opposed to corporate democracy's "one share–one vote" principle, under which, were it transposed to the political setting, a share might be a specified percentage of the total wealth of the electoral unit) would make acute the danger of the government's being captured by a minority (I mean an electoral, not an ethnic, minority—a cabal, an oligarchy) bent on expropriating the property or extinguishing the freedom of the majority or of another minority. The reason is that the fewer people who have to be organized in order to achieve a common end, the more likely they are to succeed: transaction costs are lower, a proposition familiar to students of price fixing and other conspiracies.

For the same reason, votes must not be salable,[19] since that would enable the concentration of voting power in the hands of a

18. Here used in a loose, indeed circular, sense, since aliens are sometimes permitted to vote—a permission that constitutes them "citizens" in a meaningful sense, despite their (formal) alienage.

19. See Downs, *An Economic Theory of Democracy*, at 188–194; and for a fuller dis-

relative handful of people or corporations. A market in votes presents a classic free rider problem. If a wealthy individual offered to buy the first million voting rights tendered to him at $25 a vote, he would have little difficulty closing the deal, especially if many voters assumed that others would sell their right to vote for that price.[20] Suppose he wanted to buy a really commanding number of votes, such as 10 million—only a modest percentage, however, of the total number of votes cast in the 2000 election, and an even smaller percentage of the total number of votes potentially buyable, since the half of the electorate that did not bother to vote would be especially eager to sell their voting rights. He might have to pay a much higher price per vote. Suppose it would be $100. Still, many firms and even individuals can plunk down $1 billion in cash for an asset that is worth that much to them. Allowing votes to be bought and sold would, therefore, be practically as well as theoretically inconsistent with the principle of equal voting. Majority voting also follows from that principle, because it is the only method of vote counting that weights each voter's vote equally.

In short, although the people do not rule in a representative democracy—that would be infeasible—they pick the rulers, kick them out when necessary, and provide for an orderly, peaceful succession (although the one in 2000 turned out not to be so orderly) when a vacancy occurs. The last point deserves particular emphasis given the subject of this book. Hereditary monarchy solved the succession problem, but at the sacrifice of both quality assurance and democratic control, sacrifices that representative democracy avoids having to make. Taken all in all, representative democracy not only

---

cussion of the pros and cons of allowing votes to be sold, see Saul Levmore, "Voting with Intensity," 53 *Stanford Law Review* 111 (2000).

20. The theory of the two-tier tender offer. And during the 2000 Presidential campaign a market in votes did emerge, briefly, on the Internet ("voteauction.com"), before being shut down by a reminder of its illegality. The average transaction price was indeed only $24.28. See http://62.116.31.68/end_of_bids.htm. Cf. Pamela S. Karlan, "Politics by Other Means," 85 *Virginia Law Review* 1697, 1713–1714 (1999).

honors the democratic principle but also controls the rulers, and solves the succession problem, better than any alternative system, provided—a qualification to be borne in mind throughout this book—that the procedures for determining the succession are fixed in advance, objective, administrable, and clear, so that succession is according to rules rather than to a power play by the loser.

With such advantages, one may wonder why representative democracy is not the universal system of government, and particularly why it seems to flourish only in wealthy modern countries, with a few exceptions, such as Switzerland even before modernity and a poor India today. (The Roman Republic was an interesting mixture of democracy and oligarchy.) Notice that I did not number the ancient Greek city-states among the exceptions. Direct democracy, the ancient Greek form of democracy, is feasible only in a very small, simple polity, because in a large or complex one the information costs—not to mention the costs of underspecialization and of time—of citizen government are prohibitive. Representative democracy reduces all these costs by enabling a political division of labor between governed and governing without relinquishing popular control over the governors.

But unlike Greek-style democracy, representative democracy requires an elaborate institutional framework to avoid degenerating into oligarchy or dictatorship. Remember that in such a democracy it is officials who rule, not the people. Officials have their own interests, which may not coincide with those of the people. If able to monopolize the information relating to the administration of government, these imperfect agents may be able to perpetuate themselves in office while adopting policies that disserve their constituents. So a reasonably well-informed citizenry—a citizenry that even if not highly educated, or even highly literate, makes at least approximately accurate judgments about candidates and policies—is a prerequisite of democracy. Another prerequisite is a system of property and personal rights, including the right of free speech, enforced by judges who are not beholden to or intimidated by the representatives. For without such a system—that is, without real liberty—the representatives will be able to cow political opponents, steal elections through fraud and through intimidation of voters, and, by thus making reelection an empty formality, perpetuate their rule indefinitely.

So democracy depends on liberty, as well as being in tension with it because liberty curtails the power of the majority to impose its will. The right to vote is not enough; it is really just the tip of an institutional-cultural-juridical iceberg; a competent and independent electorate, which implies a liberty-securing institutional infrastructure, is indispensable to the operation of representative democracy. Since people are self-interested and for that and other reasons untrustworthy, pure democracy—democracy that places no limits on what the majority or its representatives can do[21]—is an extremely dangerous system of government, viable if at all only in tiny polities, where ties of family and friendship may enable voluntary cooperation to be substituted for coercion. Pure democracy is unstable and likely to degenerate into oligarchy or autocracy. Limited democracy is best. Representative democracy is limited democracy, even without judicially protected liberty, because it puts up a screen between citizens and the application to them of state power by other citizens.

It is also a far more efficient and economical system of governance than direct democracy. Not only does it enable specialization in the provision of government services and political goods; in addition, because governance is delegated to the specialists, the elected and other officials, the people at large do not have to

---

21. The term "pure democracy" should not be confused with "direct democracy." The former is democracy, representative or direct, without legal limits on what the democratic majority may do. The latter is governance by the people themselves rather than by representatives whom they elect.

spend all or even much of their time worrying about politics. Some theorists—Hannah Arendt is perhaps the outstanding modern exemplar—are distressed that modern democracy enables the mass of people to redirect their energies from the public to the private sphere.[22] Bonnie Honig would go further, radicalizing Arendt in an effort to restore "politics as a disruptive practice that resists the consolidations and closures of administrative and juridical settlement for the sake of the perpetuity of political contest."[23] For most of us, it is a relief not to have to be jawing all the time in the *agora.*[24] Not for us exhaustive deliberation, life modeled on a faculty seminar. Not only is there much more to life than politics, but a preoccupation with politics is likely to exacerbate social conflict. Political conflicts are not intellectual disagreements, resolvable by deliberation or debate. They are clashes of interests and values. The political class in this country—the class that dwells obsessively on political issues—is more contentious, radical, dogmatic, and polarized than the country as a whole.

Representative democracy is historically and today associated with the market economy, though the correlation is one-sided. Nondemocratic nations often have market economies, but nations that do not have market economies are rarely democratic. A market economy seems therefore to be a necessary but not a sufficient condition for democracy. It is easy to see why it is not sufficient. Free markets are much more effective at generating wealth than non-

---

22. See, for example, Hannah Arendt, *The Human Condition* (2d ed. 1998), esp. pt. 2. "Arendt insists that a person can achieve an identity only through being seen and heard by his equals as they all deliberate the common fate. . . . Authentic politics fills the gap at the heart of the human condition." George Kateb, "Political Action: Its Nature and Advantages," in *The Cambridge Companion to Hannah Arendt* 130, 145–146 (Dana Villa ed. 2000).

23. Bonnie Honig, *Political Theory and the Displacement of Politics* 4, 124 (1993).

24. John Mueller, "Democracy and Ralph's Pretty Good Grocery: Elections, Equality, and the Minimal Human Being," 36 *American Journal of Political Science* 983 (1992). See also Will Kymlicka and Wayne Norman, "Return of the Citizen: A Survey of Recent Work on Citizenship Theory," 104 *Ethics* 352, 361–362, 369 (1994).

market economic systems, and an autocrat generally wants his country to be wealthy in order to keep his subjects happy, finance an effective security apparatus, and become wealthy himself without taking such a large proportion of national wealth that he causes serious unrest. (The qualification "generally" is important, however, as wealth may create pressure for democracy, as we are about to see.)

Three things make a market economy a prerequisite for representative democracy. First, such economies depend on respect for property rights, and the effective enforcement of property rights requires a competent and impartial judiciary, which is also essential to ensure that elections are honest and to protect the personal liberties that democracy, the (potential) "tyranny of the majority," threatens. Judicial protection of property rights is the forerunner of judicial protection of political liberty. Second, market economies generate wealth, and wealth increases the demand for and the supply of education, communications, and leisure. These goods, along with the financial security of living in a prosperous society, create a citizenry that not only is reasonably well informed about political issues and candidates, but also is sufficiently independent economically not to be the pawn of the mighty; relations of patronage and dependence undermine the power-diffusing objective of equal voting. Third, market economies reward and thus encourage commercial values, which are more hospitable than aristocratic or religious ones to the political equality that undergirds a democratic system. Like theocrats, aristocrats (not in the Aristotelian sense, the sense I used earlier, in which aristocracy is rule by the best, but in the more familiar sense of a hereditary caste preoccupied with honor and status and disdainful of commercial pursuits) think the issues involved in government too important to be left to the people They also (the extreme example is Coriolanus) disdain the dependence on the goodwill of *hoi polloi* that a democratic system imposes on officials.[25] Persons engaged in market activities disdain others at their peril, since success in the market involves catering to the preferences of others, namely one's customers and to a lesser extent one's employees and other suppliers.

There are countercurrents. The ideology of the market can foster contempt for voting because of its lack of instrumental value and its failure to weight preferences by willingness to pay, which is how the market weights preferences. The sacralizing of property rights in the name of economic efficiency curtails democratic governance by disqualifying government from intervening in the market. And markets can foster inequalities in income and wealth, which can in turn foster selfish, exploitive voting as the electorate splits into classes that have little in common with each other. But these effects are outweighed by the support that a market economy offers to representative democracy; otherwise having a market economy would not be a necessary condition of a society's being a representative democracy.

The foregoing introduction to the practice of representative democracy, brief as it has been, suggests several points germane to the argument of this book. Representative democracy is a pragmatic institution rather than the instantiation of a theorist's ideal state. Voting is a method of control, not of administration. The people do not rule in a representative democracy; they control the rulers, their delegates. For voting to perform its function of control, voters must have some minimum of political sophistication, along with a measure of independence from other people. Voting is central to the orderly succession of democratic "rulers." "Orderly" implies ordered, and delegation of governance to specialists implies realism and practicality. American democracy is structured, formal,

---

25. Don Herzog, *Happy Slaves: A Critique of Consent Theory* 198–199 (1989), remarks in a similar vein that a contested election "requires candidates to think the prize of election worth the risks of losing honor, of having one's neighbors publicly certify that they prefer someone else. So it requires and reinforces the decay of honor as an organizing principle." George Washington refused to be considered for President until assured that the vote for him in the Electoral College would be unanimous.

practical, realistic, and both supportive of and supported by commercial values. It is not starry-eyed, carnivalesque, or insurrectionary. It is not pure or participatory democracy, and it does not consider political chaos a price worth paying to actualize the popular will. Its spirit is closer to that of Burke than to that of Rousseau. The populism of a Jefferson or a Jackson remains a part of our democratic ideology, but a smaller part than in days of yore. These summary reflections, too, will turn out to be relevant to evaluating the Supreme Court's performance in *Bush v. Gore.*

A History of the Suffrage

The entwinement of democracy with economy will also play a role in our analysis of the Florida election. As we shall see in the next chapter, the deadlock and some of the bitterness sparked by its resolution had economic roots, such as illiteracy, which is linked to poverty, and the financial costs and benefits associated with different systems of voting. There was a subterranean issue of whether literacy should be a voter qualification. Although federal law forbids the use of literacy as a voter qualification in federal elections,[26] the punchcard ballot used in a number of Florida counties (indeed used widely throughout the United States) requires a higher degree of literacy than other common voting technologies.

Poverty fosters ignorance, and also dependence. These are age-old worries about political elections. By the eve of the American Revolution, the idea that an elected legislature was an element of civilized government had taken firm hold in Great Britain and its American colonies. But neither the principle of universal suffrage

---

26. 42 U.S.C. § 1973b(e)(2), upheld against constitutional challenge in *Oregon v. Mitchell,* 400 U.S. 112 (1970). It might be questioned whether Congress has the power to regulate voter qualifications in Presidential elections, since the Constitution assigns the power to determine the manner of appointing Presidential electors to the states. U.S. Const. art II, § 1, cl. 2. But it would be impracticable for a state to fix different qualifications for voters for different offices in the same election. More on congressional power to regulate Presidential elections in subsequent chapters.

so familiar to us (though not fully actualized even today), nor the idea that all legislators (and the executive as well, and maybe even judges) should be elected by the people, had yet taken hold. The suffrage was limited as a matter of course to free adult males who owned property, specifically land. Property ownership was much more widespread in the colonies than in the mother country, with the result that something like two-thirds of free American adult males could vote. But they could vote only for the members of the lower house of the state legislatures. The governor was appointed by the Crown, and the members of the governor's council, corresponding to the Senate in the federal government ordained by the Constitution of 1787, were appointed by the governor.[27]

This basic structure was retained in the Constitution.[28] Article I, section 2, provided that the members of the House of Represen-

---

27. There are minor exceptions to these generalizations about the form of the suffrage—a qualification that should be borne in mind throughout my brief survey of voting history. On that history, see Alexander Keyssar, *The Right to Vote: The Contested History of Democracy in the United States* (2000); Robert J. Dinkin, *Voting in Revolutionary America: A Study of Elections in the Original Thirteen States, 1776–1789*, ch. 2 (1982); Dinkin, *Voting in Provincial America: A Study of Elections in the Thirteen Colonies, 1689–1776*, ch. 2 (1977); Chilton Williamson, *American Suffrage: From Property to Democracy, 1790–1860* (1960); Arnaldo Testi, "The Construction and Deconstruction of the U.S. Electorate in the Age of Manhood Suffrage, 1830s–1920s," in *How Did They Become Voters?* 387 (Raffaele Romanelli ed. 1998); Robert J. Steinfeld, "Property and Suffrage in the Early American Republic," 41 *Stanford Law Review* 335 (1989).

28. Lawrence D. Longley and Neal R. Peirce, *The Electoral College Primer 2000* (1999); Michael J. Glennon, *When No Majority Rules: The Electoral College and Presidential Succession* (1992); Neal R. Peirce and Lawrence D. Longley, *The People's President: The Electoral College in American History and the Direct Vote Alternative* (rev. ed. 1981); Shlomo Slonim, "The Electoral College at Philadelphia: The Evolution of an Ad Hoc Congress for the Selection of a President," 73 *Journal of American History* 35 (1986); L. Kinvin Wroth, "Election Contests and the Electoral Vote," 65 *Dickinson Law Review* 321 (1961). For the most powerful contemporaneous defense of the Electoral College, see *Federalist No. 68* (Hamilton).

Writing in 1999, Longley and Peirce entitled their first chapter "The Election of 2000 Is Not Quite Decided: A Fantasy," and in it sketched a scenario resulting in a deadlocked election and ensuing chaos. The deadlock in their fantasy, however, results from the fact that the electoral vote is split among three candidates (the authors added Colin Powell to Bush and Gore), none of whom has a majority of the electoral votes. The result is fierce politicking, first to get members of the Electoral College to switch, and later, when the election is thrown into the House of Representatives, to woo Congressmen. No one foresaw the form that the 2000 election deadlock would actually take. I am surprised that Longley and Peirce did not, since they discuss a number of challenges to Presidential electors, including one that occurred after the Electoral Count Act was passed in 1887 in an effort to prevent a repetition of

tatives were to be elected by the people of each state. No effort was made to eliminate property qualifications or other limitations on the suffrage; the only stipulation (also in section 2) was that the voters have the same qualifications that the state required of people voting for members of its lower house. Article I, section 3, provided that the Senators from each state would be appointed by the state's legislature. This method of appointing Senators reflected (at a time when states were much more important than they have become) a kind of ambassadorial conception of a Senator. Indeed, state legislatures sometimes instructed "their" Senators with regard to how to vote on specific issues.[29] The state legislatures were authorized to fix the time, place, and manner of choosing Senators and Representatives, though Congress was authorized to alter those regulations—except for the place of choosing Senators, which would be the state legislature itself. Each house of Congress was to be "the Judge of the Elections, Returns and Qualifications of its own Members."

There was little support at the constitutional convention for popular election of the President. Most of the delegates held the aristocratic conception of the Presidency and were dubious about the capacity of the public at large, with the limited filtering provided by gender and property qualifications, to pick the best candidate. There were also concerns about the logistics of conducting a nationwide popular election in a large country with poor transportation and communications. The alternative of having the President elected by Congress was unattractive, as it would make the President unduly dependent on the legislative branch. The ingenious expedient hit upon by the delegates was the Electoral College. Each state would have as many electors, and hence electoral votes, as it had Representatives plus Senators. The Electoral College was

---

the Hayes-Tilden fiasco, which that of 2000 resembled. Longley and Peirce, *Electoral College Primer 2000,* at 122–125.

29. See the discussion of this history in *Cook v. Gralike,* 121 S. Ct. 1029 (2001).

thus to be a kind of ad hoc Congress, its sole function being to elect the President. Its members were to be appointed by each state "in such Manner as the Legislature thereof shall direct" (Article II, section 1, clause 2) and were to meet in their state and vote for the President rather than assemble in one place and confer before voting. Members of Congress, and other high federal officials, were ineligible to be electors. Congress was to fix the time at which the electors would be chosen and the day on which they would cast their votes, provided the day was the same throughout the nation. The state was to transmit its electoral votes to the seat of the federal government, where they were to be counted in the presence of both houses of Congress. If no one received a majority of the votes of the appointed electors, the House of Representatives was to elect the President from among the leading candidates. But in that election, unlike the ordinary procedure of the House, each state delegation would have a single vote.

The framers' insouciance about voting qualifications for the members of the only directly elected branch of the new government, the House of Representatives, was matched by their insouciance about the method of appointing Presidential electors, which was left to the state legislatures to decide. The framers were unperturbed by the possibility that the legislatures might (as most soon did) decide that the electors would be chosen by popular vote. Apparently they thought that the people could be trusted to pick electors good enough to pick the best person as President. Moreover, they expected the contingent election procedure ordained by the Constitution—election of the President by the House of Representatives if no candidate received a majority of electoral votes—to be used frequently, and the House was the most democratic component of the governmental structure created at Philadelphia in 1787, though, since each state's delegation would have only one vote to cast for President, the contingent procedure was not actually very democratic. That was discovered in 1824, the only time the President has been picked by that method. Andrew Jackson lost to John Quincy Adams in the House even though Jackson had the most popular votes[30] *and* the most electoral votes, though not a majority of the latter.

The framers expressed no concern that a popular-vote loser might be an electoral-vote winner, since they had no reason to expect all states to select their Presidential electors by popular election. That such a discrepancy might be anomalous could not even be perceived until it was customary to select Presidential electors by popular vote, as it was, however, by 1824.

The expectation that the President would often be selected by the House of Representatives was related to the framers' failure to foresee the rise of political parties.[31] (Parties in the modern sense were unknown in the eighteenth century.) Without parties to winnow the candidates, electoral votes were likely to be scattered among numerous candidates, reducing the likelihood that anyone would receive a majority, especially as it was doubted that many men had sufficient national reputations to garner a majority of electoral votes. In a two-party system, in contrast, electors would be choosing between just the two candidates chosen by the parties.

The Electoral College was not created to be a deliberative body, since its members would not meet but would, as expressly stated in Article II and the Twelfth Amendment, vote separately in each state.[32] This decision was made partly because of the difficulties of travel, but more because of concern lest the choice of the President be influenced by cabals, agents of foreign powers, other intriguers, or corrupt deals. It was believed that requiring that the electors

30. In those states, 18 out of the then total of 24, in which electors were chosen by popular vote. His popular vote lead over Adams was commanding—42.4 percent versus 31.9 percent; Glennon, *When No Majority Rules,* at 13, 15. By the next election, all but one of the states chose electors by popular vote.

31. See, for example, Jack N. Rakove, *Original Meanings: Politics and Ideas in the Making of the Constitution* 268 (1996).

32. "It was to be a strange college—more like a correspondence school"; Jules Witcover, *No Way to Pick a President* 249 (1999).

vote in their home states rather than congregating to vote, that the electors not be federal officials, and that all electoral votes be cast on the same day would minimize these dangers.[33]

Such was the scheme of representative democracy created by the Constitution of 1787 for the federal government. The history of U.S. representative democracy since that date is a vast subject, but fortunately only three facets of that history are important for my purposes. One is the general though irregular movement to broaden the suffrage. Another is the trend away from indirect election. The third is the evolution of election administration, with particular reference to efforts to avoid (or if necessary resolve) deadlocks and to count votes accurately, which turn out to be related desiderata.

The movement to broaden the suffrage antedates 1787. On the eve of the Revolution, the electorate for the colonial assemblies, following the British model, was generally limited to adult Protestant males who had freeholds (that is, land ownership) of some specified minimum value. The theory behind the limitations was that only propertied men would have sufficient economic independence and political knowledge to be independent and competent voters rather than pawns of the wealthy and knowledgeable, or, in the case of a woman, of her husband, brothers, or father. Though made at least somewhat plausible by the economic and social conditions of the time and by the fact that the ballot generally was not secret, the theory was at best only partial. It did not explain the religious exclusions from the suffrage or the preferred position of owners of real estate compared with owners of other forms of property that might be equally valuable. Religious hostilities, distrust of city folk, and fear of debtors ganging up on credi-

---

33. *The Records of the Federal Convention of 1787,* vol. 2, 500 (Max Farrand ed., rev. ed. 1937); Tadahisa Kuroda, *The Origins of the Twelfth Amendment: The Electoral College in the Early Republic, 1787–1804* 11, 21 (1994); Peirce and Longley, *People's President,* at 22, 27, 29; Slonim, "Electoral College at Philadelphia," at 52–53.

tors and, more generally, of the poor expropriating the rich played a larger role in the restrictions on the suffrage than the incomplete theoretical justifications based on notions of independence and competence. (The most plausible justification for the preference accorded owners of real estate was that they were more vulnerable to expropriation because their wealth was immobile.)[34] Lack of independence was decisive, however, against permitting slaves to vote, since their votes would be controlled by their masters and thus would magnify the political power of slaveholders.[35]

The limitations on the franchise eroded significantly between 1775 and 1787. The causes of this erosion were ideological and practical. The slogan "no taxation without representation" made it difficult to justify the denial of the franchise to people who paid taxes yet happened not to own land, especially since the limitation of the franchise to freeholders had been justified in part by the argument that they paid most of the taxes.[36] The equally influential slogan "all men are created equal" pointed toward universal adult male suffrage. And it was difficult to ask people to join the Continental Army without giving them the rights of a citizen.[37]

Yet when the Constitution was adopted, only Vermont had abandoned all property qualifications for voting,[38] and the framers decided to allow each state to set the qualifications for voters in federal elections conducted in that state. As I have already noted, the qualifications to vote for members of the House of Representatives, the only form of direct election ordained by the Constitution, were

---

34. Dinkin, *Voting in Revolutionary America,* at 29.

35. A similar reason underlies the provision of the Constitution (Article I, section 2, clause 3) that counts a slave as only three-fifths of a free person for purposes of determining the number of members of the House of Representatives and hence of the Electoral College to which a state is entitled.

36. Williamson, *American Suffrage,* at 5–7; see also at 78 and at 79 (rejection of theory of "virtual representation").

37. Ibid. at 80, 82. Later linkages of expansions of the suffrage with wartime exigencies are listed in Testi, "Construction and Deconstruction," at 390. For a more extensive discussion, see Keyssar, *Right to Vote,* at 466 (index references under "War").

38. Williamson, *American Suffrage,* at 135.

to be the same as those for voting for the members of the lower house of the legislature of the voter's state, while Senators were to be appointed by the legislature of each state and Presidential electors by each state in the manner directed by the state legislature.

The trend toward broadening the franchise continued after 1787, powered by democratic sentiment,[39] by (what is not the same thing) a decline of deference, by agitation of the disfranchised for the vote,[40] and by the inherent ratchet effect of changes in the franchise. The franchise is likely to be enlarged whenever the currently dominant political forces in the society believe that the newly franchised voters will support them rather than their opponents,[41] and once a new group is enfranchised it becomes difficult later to withdraw the franchise from it if the political winds change, because the members of the group will vote solidly against the change. By the eve of the Civil War, universal adult (age 21 or older) male suffrage had been achieved in the Northern states,[42] and reinstatement of property qualifications would have been politically infeasible, quite apart from ideological considerations.

But it would be wrong to infer from the ratchet effect that the expansion of the franchise is monotonic. The effect is real, but other forces are also at work. After Reconstruction ended following the election of Rutherford Hayes to the Presidency in 1876, the Southern states, forced by the Fifteenth Amendment to extend the franchise to blacks, nevertheless were able through a variety of devices, ranging from poll taxes and literacy tests to outright intimidation, to disenfranchise most blacks. Moreover, the scope of

---

39. Yet not, oddly, by abolitionism. Although some Southerners linked abolitionism with universal suffrage (ibid. at 288), the voting rights of blacks actually diminished in the North between the Revolution and the Civil War. Keyssar, *Right to Vote*, at 87–93; *Democracy, Liberty, and Property: The State Constitutional Conventions of the 1820s* 137–138 (Merrill D. Peterson ed. 1966).

40. Keyssar, *Right to Vote*, at 35.

41. For examples, see ibid. at 39–42.

42. With the principal exception of blacks, whom only five Northern states allowed to vote.

the franchise can contract merely because of demographic changes occurring against a background of unchanged rules. For example, if aliens are forbidden to vote and they become a larger fraction of the population, the fraction of eligible voters will, if nothing else changes, fall automatically. The same is true if the birth rate increases and as a result a larger fraction of the population is below the voting age. The effect of expansion of the suffrage on actual voting can also be—and in fact to a considerable extent has been— offset by a decline in the turnout of eligible voters.[43]

Aliens are an example of a group that, being unorganized and unpopular, may not be able to take advantage of the ratchet effect. After the Civil War, the flood of immigrants created anxieties about the voting power of these new citizens, and literacy tests were instituted for the first time[44]—along with an effective de facto literacy test that bears a distant resemblance to the punchcard ballot. Until late in the nineteenth century, the government did not supply the ballots for voting in elections. Instead each political party supplied ballots containing a party-line vote for the party's candidates. The voter would simply select one party's ballot and drop it into the ballot box. The party ballot was replaced, largely in the last decade of the century, by the "Australian" ballot: a paper ballot, supplied by the voting authorities, that contained a list of the candidates, on which the voter would mark his preference. (Such a ballot had first been used in Australia; hence the name.) A voter who was not literate would have difficulty using the Australian ballot,[45] a result welcomed by those who feared the voting power of immigrants. At the same time, the heretofore rather

---

43. Testi, "Construction and Deconstruction," at 390–392, 410–413.

44. Keyssar, *Right to Vote,* at 142–146; Testi, "Construction and Deconstruction," at 400. Testi points out that registration requirements, also a late nineteenth-century innovation, had a disenfranchising effect while at the same time reducing vote fraud.

45. This problem is overcome in India, where about half the population is illiterate but illiterates are entitled to vote (as they are in the United States), by printing the party's symbol next to the names of the candidates, so that to vote for a party's candidates the voter has only to learn to recognize the party's symbol.

casual attitude toward voting by aliens[46]—the distinction between citizens and aliens not being strongly marked—gave way to rules excluding aliens from the franchise.[47]

The practical and ideological forces that, despite some back-sliding, led to the enlargement of the franchise in the nineteenth century also led to expanding the categories of officials elected by the people. In the eighteenth century the only popularly elected officials had been the members of the lower houses of the federal and state (or colonial) legislatures. Judges became elected rather than appointed officials in most states in the nineteenth century, as did state governors, members of the upper houses of the state legislatures, and Presidential electors. It has thus become anomalous that the President of the United States is not elected by popular vote. Yet there are only two certain instances in which the popular-vote winner failed to win the electoral vote: the election of 1888, in which Benjamin Harrison lost the popular vote to Grover Cleveland but won the electoral vote and so became President, and, of course, the election of 2000. The controversial elections of 1800, 1824, 1876, and 1960 are distinguishable—some of them, however, only narrowly. Let's consider them briefly.

In 1800 Jefferson and his running mate, Aaron Burr, received the same number of electoral votes, and Jefferson was elected President by the House. The deadlock in the Electoral College had been caused by the fact that Article II of the Constitution, while giving each elector two votes, did not provide for the electors to vote separately for President and Vice President. The theory was that the best man would come in first and become President and the second-best man would come in second and become Vice President. But if the electors thought alike on who should be President

---

46. Keyssar, *Right to Vote*, at 32–33, 38; Williamson, *American Suffrage*, at 277–278; Testi, "Construction and Deconstruction," at 388.

47. Ibid. at 392–393. This change was particularly rough for persons of Asian origin and for American Indians; neither class of persons was eligible for U.S. citizenship until well into the twentieth century.

and who Vice President, and accordingly cast one of their two votes for their preferred Presidential candidate and the other for their preferred Vice Presidential candidate, the two—though candidates for different offices—would end up with the same number of electoral votes, and the designated Vice Presidential candidate might not gracefully withdraw (Aaron Burr did not, and Alexander Hamilton's decision to throw his support to Jefferson was one of the events that lay behind the famous, fatal duel).[48] For that matter, if there was more agreement on who should be Vice President than on who should be President, the Vice Presidential candidate might receive more electoral votes (as almost happened in 1800), and so become President. These sources of deadlock (or worse) were removed by the Twelfth Amendment, adopted in 1804. The amendment required the members of the Electoral College to vote separately for President and for Vice President.

In 1824 Andrew Jackson won both the popular and the electoral vote, but because he did not have a majority of the electoral vote, but only a plurality, the choice of President was made by the House of Representatives, which picked John Quincy Adams.

In 1876 Samuel Tilden was declared the winner of the popular vote, but competing slates of electors in several Southern states (including Florida!) made the outcome of the electoral vote uncertain. An ad hoc commission created by Congress in January 1877 to resolve the dispute over the electors awarded the disputed votes to Hayes, who thus obtained, when objections in Congress to the commission's award failed, a majority in the Electoral College, and so became President.[49] Because of extensive vote fraud by Democrats as well as by Republicans, it is uncertain whether Tilden really did win the popular vote.[50]

---

48. Joseph J. Ellis, *Founding Brothers: The Revolutionary Generation* 40–43 (2000).

49. Asher C. Hinds, *Hinds' Precedents of the House of Representatives of the United States,* vol. 3, §§ 1953, 1954 (1907).

50. See William Josephson and Beverly J. Ross, "Repairing the Electoral College," 22 *Journal of Legislation* 145, 157 n. 77 (1996), and references cited there.

In 1960 John F. Kennedy won the popular vote by only a shade over 100,000 votes. There were serious allegations of fraud by Democratic election officials in Illinois and Texas, but the number of votes affected was not enough either to change the result in the Electoral College vote or to deprive Kennedy of his plurality of the popular vote nationwide. Deciding who won the popular vote in 1960 is clouded, however, by a question unrelated to fraud, namely how to classify the popular votes for the 6 unpledged Democratic electors in Alabama, who, out of a total of 11 Democratic electors in that state, ended up voting for Harry Byrd rather than for Kennedy. If Kennedy is allocated 5/11 of the popular vote in Alabama, then Nixon, not Kennedy, had a plurality of the nationwide popular vote.[51]

In 2000 Al Gore won the popular vote, but George W. Bush obtained a bare electoral-vote majority—thanks to Florida, which many people believe Bush "stole" just as Hayes may have done 124 years earlier. We shall examine that contention in later chapters. Whether it is well founded or not, there is no question that Gore won the nationwide popular vote fair and square.

In short, in five elections (1824, 1876, 1888, 1960, and 2000) the winner of the popular vote for President either was not or may not have been (1876 and 1960) elected President. But the wedge that the Electoral College drives between popular democracy and election to the Presidency is larger. Because Presidential candidates campaign to win the electoral vote rather than the popular vote, they allocate their efforts, their appeals, their choice of running mate, and their policies and appointments when elected differently than they would if the President were chosen by popular vote rather than by the vote of the Electoral College. We shall return to this issue in the last chapter.

---

51. Longley and Peirce, *Electoral College Primer 2000,* at 51; Lawrence D. Longley and Alan G. Braun, *The Politics of Electoral College Reform* 3–6 (1972).

The twentieth century saw further expansions both in the suffrage and in the categories of official appointed by popular vote. The Seventeenth Amendment, ratified in 1913, required the direct election of Senators. The reasons were, in part, intensely practical, such as that elections for state legislators were sometimes overshadowed by concerns over whom a legislator might support for U.S. Senator and that legislatures frequently deadlocked over the choice of Senators.[52] In 1920, the Nineteenth Amendment was adopted, guaranteeing the right to vote to women. Subsequent amendments abolished poll taxes, entitled the District of Columbia to appoint Presidential electors, and guaranteed the right to vote to 18-year-olds. More and more states adopted the primary election as the method of choosing the candidates of the major parties. And legislation designed to make the Fifteenth Amendment a meaningful protection of the franchise of black citizens[53] culminated in the abolition of literacy tests for voters in all federal elections. With universal adult suffrage within reach, attention shifted to subtle issues of voting power, including malapportionment (a conspicuous feature of the U.S. Senate and therefore of the Electoral College as well), gerrymandering, the creation of districts in which minority groups would have a voting majority, restrictions on candidacy, lengthy residency requirements, and campaign financing.

Because it became an issue in the 2000 election deadlock and its aftermath, we should consider the merit of the goal of universal suffrage—especially when it is pressed to the point of insisting that people who cannot read well enough to follow voting instructions should be permitted, perhaps even assisted, to vote. One way to put the question is to ask whether it would be desirable, were it politically feasible (which it is not), to confine the vote to people who

---

52. Congressional Quarterly, Inc., *Guide to U.S. Elections* 447–451 (3d ed. 1994); David A. Strauss, "The Irrelevance of Constitutional Amendments," 114 *Harvard Law Review* 1457, 1496–1499 (2001)

53. Voting Rights Act of 1965, 42 U.S.C. § 1973.

are well informed about the public issues—including issues of leadership, competence, and probity—that are relevant to picking the best representatives. It would be undesirable. The politically well informed are an unrepresentative slice of the population. They differ systematically from the poorly informed along the dimensions of race, income, and education.[54] They have interests as well as opinions, and, since they are not a random draw from the population, their interests differ systematically from those of other groups. If the politically savvy monopolized the vote, their interests would have more weight than those of other people, the politically apathetic, immature, or alienated, unless we indulge the unrealistic assumption that well-informed people can be depended upon to be altruistic rather than self-interested voters. Once that assumption is abandoned, it becomes clear that the interests of any group that lacks the franchise are likely to be undervalued in the political process.[55] It is on this basis that I have urged consideration of giving each parent an extra one-half vote for each of his or her minor children.[56]

Some people, such as small children and the severely retarded, cannot form a competent conception of their own interests. But this is not the case for illiterates, especially in an era in which people get most of their information about public affairs from radio and television rather than from the print media.[57] Literacy tests for

---

54. Michael X. Delli Carpini and Scott Keeter, *What Americans Know about Politics and Why It Matters* (1996).

55. "The interest of the excluded is always in danger of being overlooked"; John Stuart Mill, *Considerations on Representative Government* 66 (1870).

56. Posner, *Aging and Old Age,* at 289.

57. Mill, writing before television, thought a literacy requirement essential. But it is not just television that separates Mill's political culture from ours; the differences between nineteenth-century England and twentieth-century America run much deeper, as is illustrated by his belief that only taxpayers should be permitted to vote ("no taxation without representation" implying, he thought, no representation without taxation), that paupers therefore should be excluded, and that educated people should be given additional votes. Mill, *Considerations on Representative Government,* at 174–186. By "illiterates," I do not mean only, or primarily, people who cannot read at all—cannot read a street sign, for example, or sign their own name. There are, relatively speaking, very few of those. I mean people who have very serious reading difficulties, so that, for example, they cannot read a newspaper with comprehension.

voting have now been outlawed, in major part because of their historical association with the pertinacious efforts of the Southern
states to deny the vote to blacks. But a voting technology that as a
practical matter requires literacy to cast a vote that will be counted
operates in the same direction. Another difference between children and the severely retarded, on the one hand, and illiterates, on
the other, is that children and the severely retarded usually have
someone—a parent or guardian—to look after them, and so are less
needful of the vote to protect their interests; illiterates do not.

There is also a psychological factor to be considered. The right
to vote is a symbol of equality. It dramatizes the principle that
every person is to count for one and no one for more than one, at
least in the political sphere. This may be hokum or sentimentality,
or even a mask for the inequalities of circumstance and opportunity that pervade our (as every) society; but it is a brute fact about
the American political culture. It is one reason why giving additional votes to members of particular groups (say, to blacks, or to
veterans) to reward past services or to compensate for past or to offset present discrimination is out of the question, and why denial of
the suffrage is taken so much more seriously than denial of giving
votes equal weight (as in the Senate and the Electoral College); and
it is why ex-felons are denied the vote in some states—as a symbol
of disapprobation. People are not illiterate by choice, and to deny
them the vote would therefore be a gratuitous insult, as is not the
case with denying the vote to ex-felons.[58]

The psychological effect of denying the vote to people may
have practical consequences. In Mill's words, "whoever, in an otherwise popular government, has no vote, and no prospect of obtaining it, will either be a permanent malcontent, or will feel as one

---

58. With the growth in the number of people who have a felony record, however,
and given that a large and growing percentage of felonies are nonviolent crimes
against willing victims (mainly the sale of illegal drugs, an arbitrary subset of mind-
altering substances) and that the composition of the ex-felon population is disproportionately black, this exclusion too has become controversial.

whom the general affairs of society do not concern."[59] But not too much weight should be placed on the symbolic and psychological dimensions of the right to vote. They are extremely speculative. The important thing is that even people who cross only a very modest threshold of competence and independence ought to be allowed to vote in order to protect their interests, and that illiterates have interests and, in our radio- and television-saturated society, generally cross that threshold.

The dramatic and ultimately successful struggles to broaden the *legal* franchise, plus the increasing preoccupation with subtle issues of voting power (even if everyone has one vote, voting *power*—that is, the power through voting to influence the outcome of an election—may be unequally distributed, as when legislatures are malapportioned), have obscured the mundane issues of election administration that the Florida 2000 Presidential election brought to light. With the successful enforcement of the Voting Rights Act, the abolition of poll taxes and literacy tests, simplified registration, the curtailment of durational residency requirements, and the reduction in the amount of corruption and the hold of machine politics in big cities, the subject of election administration became practical (rather than a matter of theoretical speculation or moral urgency), fragmented (because election administration—as distinct from federal constitutional and statutory regulation of voting—is decentralized to states, counties, and even precincts), and technological. It dipped below the radar screen of constitutional lawyers, and most political scientists as well. Not only the elections of 1824, 1876, and 1888 but also the close and problematic elections of 1960 and 1968 (the former rife

---

59. Mill, *Considerations on Representative Government,* at 172–173. Mill also believed that, independently of all practical considerations, "every one is degraded, whether aware of it or not, when other people, without consulting him, take upon themselves unlimited power to regulate his destiny"; ibid. at 173. Mill made no effort to reconcile this ethical point with his advocacy of excluding paupers and other nontaxpayers, as well as illiterates, from the franchise.

with fraud and the latter almost undone by runaway electors), became "history." Even the much more recent, exceptionally bitter, and absurdly protracted congressional battle over the deadlocked 1984 election in Indiana's Eighth Congressional District was forgotten.[60] Forgotten too was the push in the wake of the 1968 Presidential election to abolish the Electoral College by constitutional amendment, a proposal approved by the House by the requisite two-thirds margin in 1969.

The problematic Presidential elections that I have listed involved or exposed a variety of problems. The 1824 election taught that a President who had lost both the popular and the electoral vote—and who owed his election only to the House of Representatives, because the electoral-vote winner had had only a plurality, and not a majority, of the electoral votes—might not be accepted by the nation as fully legitimate. Adams was defensive about his victory and was soundly trounced by Jackson in their rematch in 1828, though in part this was due to the suspicion that Adams had owed his election to a "corrupt bargain" with Henry Clay, the Speaker of the House, who indeed became Adams's secretary of state[61]—but such suspicions are likely when the election is thrown into the Congress. A similar danger, that the winner of both the popular and the electoral vote might nevertheless not be elected President, loomed in the 1968 Presidential election, because of George Wallace's strong third-party candidacy, since a third-party candidate who won some electoral votes might, by throwing them to the losing major-party candidate, give that candidate a majority in the Electoral College. The problem in the 1960 election was not

---

60. Marie Garber and Abe Frank, *Contested Elections and Recounts*, vol. 1: *Issues and Options in Resolving Disputed Federal Elections* 14–16 (Federal Election Commission, National Clearinghouse on Election Administration, Autumn 1990) ("four months of partisan wrangling . . . that took up more time than almost any other issue the House considered in 1985 . . . left a bitter legacy which has not yet dissipated"). See also Timothy Downs, Chris Sautter, and John Hardin Young, "The Recount Primer" (Aug. 1994, available from Sautter Communications, Washington, D.C.), pp. 39–42.

61. Glennon, *When No Majority Rules*, at 15–16.

only fraud but also, and more seriously, unpledged electors, and it loomed briefly again in 2000 when some Democrats mounted a campaign to persuade Bush electors to switch to Gore. The election of 1888 was a reminder that the popular-vote winner can lose the electoral vote, which of course happened again in 2000, though so far without untoward results. The problem in 2000 was deadlock, and it may actually have had the effect of distracting people from the anomaly of the popular-vote winner's losing the election, though Gore's lack of personal popularity was also a factor.

The 1876 election fiasco was the most ominous portent for 2000. It exposed, as had the 1800 election, an embarrassing gap in the Constitution. The framers had foreseen and provided for the case in which no candidate wins a majority of the electoral votes (though the relevant provision is ambiguous, as we shall see), but not for the case in which there is a dispute over whom a state has appointed to be its Presidential electors. An ad hoc resolution of the dispute over the 1876 election was not achieved until the eve of the inauguration, and it involved Congress's appointing a committee whose deciding member was a Republican Supreme Court Justice who, along with the other Republicans on the committee, voted for the Republican candidate.[62] These events led to the enactment a decade later of the Electoral Count Act, now Title III of the U.S. Code, which specified a procedure for resolving a future such deadlock. We shall see in Chapter 3, however, that the procedure is both incomplete and of uncertain constitutionality.

Completely unforeseen was the possibility that a deadlock in the Presidential election might arise not from skullduggery (as in the 1876 election), not from a failure of any candidate to obtain a majority of the electoral votes, not from runaway electors, and not

---

62. Again there was a suspicion of a corrupt bargain—a promise to end Reconstruction in exchange for the Democrats' accepting Hayes's election. See "The Electoral Commission [Hayes-Tilden Election]," *Great Debates in American History*, vol. 9, ch. 3 (Marian Mills Miller ed. 1970).

from an actual tie in the popular vote in a key state, but from innocent defects in electoral mechanics, whether defects in the design
of a ballot, the staffing of the polling places, or the design, maintenance, or operation of voting and vote-tabulating machines, or
gaps and ambiguities in the state statutes regulating the administration of elections and the resolution of election disputes. Nor was
it foreseen that such shortcomings not only might make it difficult
to determine who had won an election, and thus increase the probability of having to activate some postelection mechanism to
decide who the winner was, but also might selectively disenfranchise voters. It had always been understood that the methods for
counting votes are imperfect; challenges to the outcome of close
elections have not been uncommon and have sometimes resulted
in recounts that changed the outcome. But that this might happen
in a Presidential election, that procedures that function properly in
less momentous and less time-sensitive elections might not serve
for a deadlocked Presidential election, and that the federal constitutional and statutory provisions relating to a contested Presidential election are rickety, were lost to view. These problems achieved
visibility, not only to the public at large but also to scholars of the
electoral process, only with the 2000 election. The gravity of such
problems, and the difficulty of solving them with our existing laws
and institutions, are the themes of the subsequent chapters.

Chapter 2

The Deadlocked Election

The inexact science of divining what the voter intended in the case of a mere indentation or whether the card reader counted a hole that was partly or wholly blocked by a hanging chad has been called "chadology."[1]

FLORIDIANS went to the polls along with the rest of the nation on November 7, 2000. On November 18, after the ballots cast on election day had been counted mechanically and then recounted mechanically, after a few completed hand recounts (mainly in Volusia County) had been factored in, and after late-arriving overseas ballots had been added to the tally, Bush was ahead by only 930 votes out of the almost six million votes that had been cast and counted in Florida for a Presidential candidate.[2]

---

1. Ronnie Dugger, "Annals of Democracy: Counting Votes," *New Yorker,* Nov. 7, 1988, pp. 40, 54.

2. My voting statistics are drawn from the briefs and judicial opinions in the litigation challenging the election results, from the report of the machine count in a table published in the *New York Times* (national ed.), Nov. 27, 2000, p. A15, and from

The secretary of state of Florida, Katherine Harris, wanted to stop there and certify Bush the winner by 930 votes. But as a result of judicial action described in the next chapter, additional hand recounts were conducted that shrank Bush's lead, although they did not eliminate it completely. The hand recounts were stopped by a stay granted by the U.S. Supreme Court on December 9 (by which time Bush's unofficial lead had fallen below 200 votes), and their resumption was precluded by the Court's decision of December 12. Whether hand recounts made sense in the circumstances, and if so how they should have been conducted and with what likely result, are the focus of this chapter. The answers should help us to evaluate the charge that Bush "stole" the election with the aid of the Supreme Court, although they will not tell us whether the Court was right to stop the recounts; that issue is deferred to the next two chapters. The answers also bear on proposed reforms of election administration in Florida and elsewhere, a topic I take up in the final chapter.

A Statistical Tie

Bush's original margin of 930 votes out of six million made the Florida Presidential election a statistical tie. Because the counting of millions of ballots by any method is liable to error, a razor-thin margin of victory such as Bush received establishes merely a probability—and not necessarily or in this case a very high one—that the victor actually received more votes than the vanquished. That is what I mean in calling the vote in Florida a statistical tie. The central question is whether a fair recount would have broken the tie. I think not.[3]

Gwyneth K. Shaw, Jim Leusner, and Sean Holton, "Uncounted Ballots May Add Up to 180,000: Election Officials Said Confusion, Mistakes and Protests All Contributed to Votes Being Thrown Out," *Orlando Sentinel,* Nov. 15, 2000, p. A1.

3. See also David J. Rusin, "Likelihood of Altering the Outcome of the Florida 2000 Presidential Election by Recounting," http://www.math.niu/edu/~rusin/

The initial count of the Florida vote was by vote-tabulating machines, and (at least as corrected by the machine recount) it was fairly accurate, even if the concept of an error in vote tabulation is expanded to include cases in which the machine fails to record a vote because the voter failed to follow the instructions for casting a valid ballot. In Broward County, where the hand recount was conducted in a way calculated to maximize the number of votes missed by the machine count, fewer than 2,000 out of more than half a million votes cast were deemed not to have been recorded for either Gore or Bush as a result of the failure of the tabulating machinery to count an undervote[4] that "should" have been counted as a vote for one of the Presidential candidates. This was fewer than 0.5 percent of the votes cast, a rate that if projected to the state as a whole would mean that only about 30,000 votes statewide had been erroneously not recorded for a Presidential candidate. If those missed votes were representative of the entire Florida vote assumed to be a tie, then counting them accurately would be very unlikely to change (and of course should not change) the result; there would be only a 5 percent probability that the statewide vote for Bush or Gore would change by more than 174 votes.[5] Gore would have needed to pick up approximately 51.75 percent of the 30,000 undervotes to have overtaken Bush's 930-vote lead.

That would not be out of the question. But the 30,000 figure is too large, not only because of Broward County's questionable

---

recount/ (last updated Jan. 5, 2001), an ambitious study by a professional mathematician that reaches a similar conclusion.

4. An undervote is a ballot in which no vote has been recorded for a candidate for a particular office; an overvote is a ballot that contains votes for two or more candidates for the same office. See the Glossary of Election Terms at the beginning of this book. The Broward County canvassing board in its recount may have counted some overvotes, though this is unclear.

5. Imagine flipping a fair coin 30,000 times. There would be a 95 percent probability that the number of heads and tails would be 15,000 plus or minus 174, since any greater deviation would be more than two standard deviations from the mean of 15,000.

method of recovering countable votes from undervoted ballots (of which more shortly) but also because undervotes are much more common in counties that use punchcard voting machines—as do 40 percent of the counties in Florida, containing 63 percent of the state's population. The other counties, with minor exceptions that I shall ignore, use the marksense ("optical scanning") system.[6] The voter marks a paper ballot with a pencil. The ballot is then inserted into an optical scanner (very much like those used for the SAT, the LSAT, and other mass tests), which records the vote—and usually is programmed to reject an overvote.[7] If the scanner is located in the polling place itself, the voter will have an opportunity to revote correctly when the scanner spits back his ballot because it is overvoted. But if the scanner is located in the county election office—

---

6. The more common term nowadays is "optical scanning," or "optical scan," but it is misleading, both because some of the machines use invisible portions of the electromagnetic spectrum and because the computers that tabulate punchcard votes also record them by optical scan. So I shall use "marksense."

The different types of voting system in use in Florida in the 2000 election are shown in the following table (the number of counties using them is in parentheses):

Type of machine	Percent of counties using machine	Percent of population using machine
Datavote	13.43 (9)	1.23
Marksense	64.18 (41)	36.40
Votomatic	22.38 (15)	61.51
Lever	1.49 (1)	0.78
Paper/hand	1.49 (1)	0.08

(The source of these data are two Web pages maintained by Florida's Division of Elections, http://election.dos.state.fl.us/votemeth/table.shtml and http://election.dos .state.fl.us/votemeth/cvs.shtml, both visited on March 27, 2001.) Datavote and Votomatic are two different brands of punchcard system. The former is less prone to produce undervotes, because the voter uses a stapler-like device rather than a stylus to punch out the chads, as a result of which dimpled and dangling chads are less frequent. See Roy G. Saltman, *Accuracy, Integrity, and Security in Computerized Vote-Tallying* § 3.4.2 (National Bureau of Standards Special Publication 500-158, Aug. 1988). To simplify exposition, I lump the two types of punchcard system together in my analysis and also ignore the two counties that use neither a punchcard nor a marksense system. None of the conclusions in this chapter would be altered by distinguishing between the Votomatic and Datavote counties.

7. It can be programmed to reject an undervote as well, but this is less likely to be done, simply because many undervotes are deliberate—the voter didn't want to vote for all the offices on the ballot. What is more common is to program the scanner to reject (besides an overvoted ballot) a ballot that is completely blank, since a voter is unlikely to deliberately cast a ballot in which he has voted for no one for any office, though a few voters may do that as a protest.

that is, if the ballots are county-counted rather than precinct-counted—the voter will not have an opportunity to revote, because his ballot will have been placed in a sealed envelope at the polling place for dispatch to the county election office.

The marksense method reduces, but does not eliminate, the incidence of undervoting, because it is easier to fill in the oval or circle on the marksense ballot than to punch through a chad on a punchcard ballot cleanly. And it solves the overvote problem only when the optical scanner is located in each precinct, which is not always the case.[8] Punchcard votes can be counted at the precinct level as well, but this is less commonly done than when the marksense system is used.[9]

The Florida supreme court eventually ordered some 60,000 ballots recounted—twice my estimate of the number of recoverable undervotes. But the 60,000 figure is an estimate of *all* the Presidential undervotes statewide,[10] and some of them were either deliberate or so inscrutable that no machine tabulator (or for that matter hand counter) could have extracted a vote from them. In addition, however, some fraction of the estimated 110,000 overvotes statewide, which the court decided not to have recounted, were, as we shall see, votes that a fair and competent hand counter, but not a machine, would have awarded to one or another Presidential candidate. Suppose that half the estimated statewide total of 170,000 undervotes and overvotes were votes that such a hand counter

---

8. *Gore v. Harris*, 773 So. 2d 524, 534 n. 26 (Fla. 2000) (concurring opinion); Andres Viglucci, Geoff Dougherty, and William Yardley, "Florida Black Voters Shortchanged," *Pittsburgh Post-Gazette,* Dec. 31, 2000, p. A12; David Damron, Ramsey Campbell, and Roger Roy, "Gore Would Have Gained Votes," *Orlando Sentinel,* Dec. 19, 2000, p. A1; Federal Election Commission, "Marksense (Optical Scan)," http://www.fec.gov/pages/marksnse.htm, visited Feb. 6, 2001.

9. The correlation between county-level (versus precinct-level) vote counting and use of the punchcard method is a highly significant 0.60.

10. Actually, there is a discrepancy here, because the Florida supreme court did not order all undervoted ballots recounted, only those that had not been recounted already, in Broward, Palm Beach, and Volusia Counties. I believe that the total number of all the Presidential undervotes statewide was somewhat greater than 60,000 and the number that would have been recounted pursuant to the court order considerably less.

would have recovered from the ballots (that is, would have awarded to one of the candidates). Again, if those 85,000 votes split evenly between Bush and Gore, Bush would still have won. But Gore would have had to win only a shade over 50.5 percent to have overcome Bush's lead. It is doubtful, however, that a 50 percent recovery rate for undervotes is realistic. It is based on Broward's recount, which as we shall see used inappropriate criteria. And the use of the same recovery rate, indeed of any recovery rate, for the overvotes is complete guesswork, because there was no recount of overvotes—Gore did not want one.

So far—and critically—I have assumed an *infallible* hand counter. Whether the margin of error would have been narrowed by an actual recount of the votes by hand depends in part on the accuracy of hand counting compared with machine counting. Neither method is categorically superior to the other. Machines can be poorly designed, defectively manufactured, inadequately maintained, or poorly operated, and as a result of any or all of these shortcomings make many errors. There is, as we shall see, little evidence that the punchcard voting and tabulating machines in use in Florida are defectively manufactured, inadequately maintained, or poorly operated. But they are unforgiving of human error, and this could be regarded as a defect of design. Human counters can be fatigued, biased, or simply unable to infer the voter's intent with any approach to certainty from a ballot that the machine refused to count; so they can make many errors too—some deliberate, which is beyond a machine's capacity. Republicans were entitled to be concerned about hand recounts by canvassing boards dominated by Democrats, and Democrats about hand recounts by Republican-dominated boards. A further problem is that both machine and hand counting can dislodge chads—this is not just Republican propaganda![11]—which means that the very process of

11. Saltman, *Accuracy, Integrity, and Security,* § 3.4.4; Dugger, "Annals of Democ-

recounting introduces new errors even when the recounters, human or mechanical, are careful, competent, and neutral.

The closeness of the statewide results made it unlikely that hand counting, even if more accurate than machine counting, would break the statistical tie unless it produced a very large margin for one of the candidates. Suppose that hand counting correctly resolves half the errors in the machine count without introducing any new errors, so that the probability of error would shrink from 0.50 to 0.25 percent in a hand recount. (This is still assuming that the Broward County hand recount yielded an accurate estimate of the number of votes missed by the machine, and still defining errors curable by hand recount to include voter errors.) In other words, only about half the 30,000 undervotes statewide that I am assuming were miscounted by the machine would have been accurately counted as a vote for a Presidential candidate. Gore would have had to receive more than 53 percent of these 15,000 recovered votes to overcome Bush's 930-vote lead. (At 53 percent to Bush's 47 percent, Gore would have picked up a net of 900 votes.) Even if the 85,000 figure is used, and it is thus assumed that 42,500 votes would have been accurately counted in a hand recount, Gore would have had to receive more than 51 percent to have prevailed.[12]

This is possible, of course, but unlikely, and not only because of the uncertainties already discussed. The fact that Gore did not request a recount in any counties besides Broward, Palm Beach,

---

racy," at 54; Brian C. Kalt, "The Endless Recount: Some Thoughts on Optimal Recount Strategy and Al Gore's Plan in the 2000 Florida Presidential Race" 26 (Michigan State University-Detroit College of Law, March 2001); Timothy Downs, Chris Sautter, and John Hardin Young, "The Recount Primer" 33, 35, 41 (Aug. 1994, available from Sautter Communications, Washington, D.C.). "The Recount Primer," written by "veteran Democratic trench fighters," was the "bible" of the Gore recount effort in Florida; Political Staff of the *Washington Post, Deadlock: The Inside Story of America's Closest Election* 51, 53 (2001).

12. Assuming the other half of the undervotes or overvotes (those erroneously counted by fallible hand counters) were distributed randomly between the candidates, Gore would have won the election with an even lower percentage; but that would not have been a win based on an *accurate* recount.

Miami-Dade, and Volusia is evidence that he didn't think a re-count in any of those other counties would have yielded net gains. It is true that he offered to agree to a statewide recount if Bush would agree to abide by the results. But he must have known that Bush would refuse, since agreeing would have entailed the surren-der by Bush of options that he possessed to thwart a recount that went against him, notably the option of the Florida legislature's appointing its own slate of Presidential electors pledged to Bush (see Chapter 3).

It is also true that in not seeking a statewide recount initially, Gore may have been concerned with the delay that such a recount would cause. But this would not have been a compelling reason for asking for a recount in just four counties, rather than in five or six or eight or some other number larger than four though well short of 67, the total number of counties in Florida. Since the recounts in the counties in which Gore did not request one would not have produced perfect ties, it is a fair inference that he thought such recounts would have produced a net gain for Bush,[13] though maybe a smaller one than the gains that the recount in the Democratic-selected counties produced for Gore. "Maybe" becomes "probably" if we assume that Bush would have requested a statewide recount had he expected it to favor him; but the assumption may be erro-neous. Bush may not have made such a request because it would have tended to validate the hand-recount method, and he could not be certain how a statewide hand recount would turn out, whereas he was certain that he had won the machine-tabulated vote. From his perspective, he had won the toss and now his oppo-nent wanted to toss again, using a different (but not a more bal-anced) coin.

---

13. An alternative possibility, explored in Chapter 4, is that he may have been confident that a recount limited to the four counties would produce a net gain for him large enough to overcome Bush's lead, so that the delay, even if slight, from requesting additional recounts would not have been offset by benefits.

Still, the possibility that Gore would have received 51 percent of the miscounted votes statewide, or even 53 percent, cannot yet be excluded. Indeed, Gore probably would have overcome Bush's lead had the recounts been confined to the four counties picked by him—but only if those recounts had been administered in accordance with the criteria used by Broward County's board.

A number of alternative criteria for recovering a vote from an undervoted punchcard ballot by a hand recount, that is, by human inspection or interpretation, are possible. Surprisingly, there seems to be no agreement on which are proper. I array the alternatives in ascending order of liberality:[14]

1. Count dangling (that is, hanging or swinging) chads but no dimpled chads.

2. Count any chads if light can be seen through the chad hole.

3. Count dangling chads, plus dimpled chads[15] if but only if none of the chads in the ballot is fully or partly punched through.

4. Count dimpled chads only if there are no fully punched chads.

5. Count dangling chads, plus dimpled chads, provided there are several dimpled chads.

6. Count dangling chads plus all dimpled chads.

7. Count dangling chads plus all dimpled chads plus chads that are near an indentation or other mark (maybe made in pen or pencil rather than with the stylus that the voter is given to vote with) in the ballot, provided the counter feels able to discern the voter's intent from the character or location of the indentation or its relation to other marks on the ballot. This is the heart of "chadology" country.

---

14. Marie Garber and Abe Frank, *Contested Elections and Recounts*, vol. 1: *Issues and Options in Resolving Disputed Federal Elections* 64–65 (Federal Election Commission, National Clearinghouse on Election Administration, Autumn 1990); vol. 2: *A Summary of State Procedures for Resolving Disputed Federal Elections* (Federal Election Commission, National Clearinghouse on Election Administration, Autumn 1990).

15. Remember that a tri-chad is a chad with only one corner severed from the ballot. It is as equivocal as a dimpled chad, and I shall generally discuss the two types of chad together. Nor shall I distinguish between pierced and dimpled chads (the two types of "pregnant" chad), although some pierced chads will pass a light test.

Palm Beach County seems to have moved from (2) to (1) to (5). Broward County used either (6) or (7), probably the latter. It is unclear what criteria Miami-Dade and Volusia Counties used.

Gore's net gain of 582 votes in the Broward County recount represented 0.15 percent of his total votes there. That is, for every 10,000 votes he had received in the machine count (actually the machine recount) in Broward County, the hand recount had netted him 15 more votes over Bush. If the votes that Gore received in the machine count in Palm Beach and Miami-Dade Counties are multiplied by the same percentage and added to his net gain in Broward, his aggregate net gain from hand recounting is 1,480 and overcomes Bush's 930-vote lead.[16]

But the 1,480 figure is unreliable as a guide to who "really" won the election. To begin with, it is based on Gore's recovery of votes in the county in which he had his highest margin (67 percent) and so could be expected to obtain his highest percentage of recovered votes. Next, Democrats dominated the canvassing boards of all four counties. Close calls were therefore likely to favor Gore. Close calls were inevitable if the criteria used by Broward County were used in the other counties as well.[17] The canvassing boards' political complexion also made it likely that they would use criteria (namely the Broward criteria) that maximized the number of votes recovered from the ballots that the machine tabulation had

---

16. Volusia County completed its hand recount before the November 14 statutory deadline for the completion of recounts (see Chapter 3), and as a result the 98-vote net gain that it produced for Gore was included in calculating Bush's 930-vote margin. As we shall see, the Volusia recount probably produced an excessive net gain for Gore.

17. This point helps to place in perspective *Delahunt v. Johnston*, 671 N.E.2d 1241 (Mass. 1996), in which the Supreme Judicial Court of Massachusetts upheld a hand recount of punchcard ballots against the objection that the recount counted dimpled chads as votes. The recount was conducted by a judge, and judges in Massachusetts are not elected. The Supreme Judicial Court's opinion is brief, moreover, and does not explore the full range of potential objections to counting dimples even when the counter's competence and freedom from bias are conceded. Most other cases in which imperfectly punched ballots have been recovered as votes have not involved dimples. See *Pullen v. Mulligan*, 561 N.E.2d 585, 609–613 (Ill. 1990), and cases cited there.

not counted. For as long as the recovered ballots divided in roughly the same proportions as the machine-counted ballots, the more ballots that had been rejected in the machine tabulation that were recovered in the hand recount the greater would be Gore's net gain. Suppose that in some precinct Gore had received 7,000 votes in the machine tabulation and Bush 3,000, and 300 had been rejected in the machine tabulation, so that Gore led Bush in the machine-tabulated vote by 4,000 votes. If now the 300 were counted as votes, and they split in the same proportion as the votes that had been included in the tabulation, Gore would get 210 more votes and Bush 90 more, increasing Gore's lead by 120 votes. This was doubtless one reason why Gore demanded recounts only in counties in which he had received substantially more votes than Bush in the original count.

The Palm Beach County canvassing board refused to use the Broward criteria, and the Miami-Dade board seemed reluctant to do so. Had the Miami-Dade board used Palm Beach rather than Broward criteria, Gore would have gained fewer than 1,480 votes, though probably enough to overtake Bush's lead, as we shall see.

Many of the disputed ballots could not be objectively read as votes, although the Republicans were on weak ground in arguing that *no* hand count of *any* rejected ballot could be so read. Recall how the punchcard voting method works. A card is placed on a tray, and the voter votes by punching a hole (the chad hole) next to the candidate's name. The card is then removed and inserted into a computer that counts votes by beaming light through the holes. A dangling chad may block the light, preventing the machine from recording a vote, yet it is fairly good evidence of an intent to vote for the candidate whose chad was punched, provided the voter didn't also punch the chad of another candidate for the same office.

But inferring a voter's intentions from a merely dimpled chad or, even worse, from indentations next to a candidate's chad (rather than indentations on the chads themselves), is highly questionable. A faint dimple or other slight indentation might be created by the handling of the ballot or by its being repeatedly passed through the vote-counting machines. Or the voter may have started to vote for the candidate but then changed his mind, perhaps realizing he had made a mistake and started to punch the wrong candidate's chad. And of the many undecided voters in the 2000 Presidential election, some may have gone into the voting booth still undecided and, in the end, "decided" they could not make up their minds. And no doubt some voters—probably many more than the undecideds—misunderstood or simply neglected to comply with the ballot instructions, even though they were clear and if followed would ensure that a vote would be registered. In the counties that used punchcard machines, the voter was instructed to punch a clean hole through the ballot (in Broward County, for example, the instruction was to "punch the stylus straight down through the ballot card for the candidates or issues of your choice"). And in the two most populous of those counties, he was also told to turn the ballot over after removing it from the voting machine and make sure there were no bits of paper stuck to it, that is, no dangling chads.[18] But to follow instructions you have to be able to read them, and not all voters are literate. Voters voting on the basis of their recollection of oral instructions received from party activists would be bound often to make mistakes and spoil their ballots.

The punchcard method of voting also requires a minimum of manual dexterity, and some voters lack even that. But emphasis properly falls on "minimum." Since the ballot is softer than an airline boarding pass, the chad is perforated, and there is empty space beneath the ballot, it takes no strength to punch a clean hole, pro-

---

18. That was the instruction in Palm Beach County. In Miami-Dade County the voter was instructed to "pull off any partially punched chads that might be hanging, as shown here [picture]."

vided the machine is not defective, either because chads of previous voters have filled up the tray or because the holes in the lid (called the "template") of the tray are not aligned with the chads in the ballot.

The undervotes and overvotes were together only a small fraction of the total number of ballots cast in Florida. We are talking about the tail of a distribution of voting competence. The average performance in the tail may have been quite different from that in the rest of the distribution. It would not be surprising if a large fraction of the votes cast by the people in the tail had been cast by undecided, confused, clumsy, illiterate or semiliterate, or inexperienced (first-time) voters. The inference of voter error or indecision in casting punchcard ballots is especially compelling in the case of those undervoted ballots in which the voter punched through the chads of candidates for all offices except the Presidency, indicating that the punchcard voting machine itself was not defective. This was the ground on which the Palm Beach County canvassing board eventually decided to exclude such ballots from the recount totals while including those that had several (though apparently the number could be as small as three) dimpled chads.[19] This was also why it would have been wrong for the Miami-Dade County canvassing board, had it decided to count dimpled ballots, to recount only the 10,750 undervotes revealed by the machine count of that county's ballots. Some of the ballots that had been counted for the Presidential candidate whose chad had been punched through may have contained a dangling chad of another Presidential candidate. A hand recount would discover that the voter had voted for two Presidential candidates (had cast, in other words, an overvote), voiding the ballot. We know there were many overvotes,

---

19. Trial Transcript, 2000 WL 1802941, at *104 (Dec. 2, 2000) (testimony of Judge Charles Burton, chairman of the Palm Beach canvassing board), in *Gore v. Harris*, 2000 WL 1790621 (Fla. Cir. Ct. Dec. 4, 2000), affirmed in part and reversed in part, 772 So. 2d 1243 (Fla. 2000) (per curiam).

and a ballot in which the voter punched both Presidential chads[20] yet left one dangling is just as persuasive evidence that the voter voted for both candidates as a dangling chad in an undervote is that the voter tried to vote for that candidate. Not that many people intentionally overvote; but when two chads are punched, the fact that one is still dangling is weak evidence that the voter was intending to vote for the other candidate, the one whose chad he punched through. It would not take a large percentage of overvotes by dangling chads, out of the more than 600,000 cast in Miami-Dade County, to offset defective ballots among the 10,750 undervoted ballots.

According to exit polls, which reflect what voters thought they did in the voting booth, at least 1 percent of the voters in Miami-Dade County voted for other offices but not the Presidency.[21] If we assume that 6,000 (1 percent of the total vote in Miami-Dade) of the 10,750 undervoted ballots are those in which the voter made a deliberate choice not to vote for President, then fewer than 5,000 remain to be allocated between Bush and Gore. But that is also too many. It must include many ballots that were irrevocably spoiled: the voter wanted to vote for President but failed to do so because he made an error that no recount could dispel.[22]

In sum, unless very conservative criteria of vote recovery are used, a hand recount is bound to introduce new errors. And correct old ones? Surprisingly, this is far from certain. We must ask: what exactly is a voting "error" recoverable by a hand recount? A voting

---

20. There were more than two Presidential candidates—in fact there were ten altogether, which was one of the rationales for, and one of the sources of confusion in, the "butterfly ballot" (of which more later). But to keep things simple I shall often pretend that there were just Bush and Gore.

21. One estimate is 1.5 to 2 percent; "Election 2000: The Florida Vote," *CNN Live Event/Special,* Nov. 28, 2000, 10 P.M. E.S.T., Transcript #00112809V54 (remark by Tom Fielder of the *Miami Herald*).

22. The 1 percent estimate that I am using may be too high; inaccuracy in exit polling was apparently one reason for the erroneous projection on the evening of November 7 that Gore had won Florida; Howard Kurtz, "Errors Plagued Election Night Polling Service," *Washington Post,* Dec. 22, 2000, p. A1.

error is not a natural kind, like a star or a penguin or a blade of grass, which are things that exist independently of human cognition. A voting error is a legal category. The belief that it is possible without reference to law to determine who won the popular vote in Florida is the most stubborn fallacy embraced by the critics of the U.S. Supreme Court's intervention to resolve the deadlock.

The legal category "voting error" might be limited to an error in the machine tabulation: the ballot contains a cleanly, completely punched-through vote for Gore and for no other Presidential candidate, yet the counting machine somehow failed to record it as a vote for Gore. There is no evidence that such errors were common or favored either candidate. They make the best fit with the ordinary meaning of an error in tabulating the vote, however, and correcting them is an objective process. You just look for a cleanly, completely punched-through vote for one and only one Presidential candidate. We shall see in the next chapter that probably the best reading of the Florida election statute is that a voter's error is indeed not an error in the tabulation of the vote. If that is right, there is very little doubt that Bush was the winner of the popular vote in Florida.

At the other extreme, a recoverable error might also be any improperly marked ballot that a human counter *thinks* (or says he thinks) contains an indication of whom the voter intended to vote for. That was Broward County's concept, and it is dangerously subjective.

In between is the concept of recoverable errors as including (besides ballots in the first category) improperly marked ballots that nevertheless contain objective indicia of the voter's intention to vote for a particular Presidential candidate. This was the concept the Palm Beach County canvassing board eventually settled on when it decided to count as votes in undervoted ballots all dislodged chads plus dimpled chads in ballots that had at least three dimples. The idea was that three dimples composed a pattern suggestive of a deliberate effort to vote for the dimpled candidates. A more conservative method would have been to count dimples only in ballots in which no chads had been punched through, a pattern more clearly consistent with the voter's having tried to punch through and been thwarted, perhaps by a chad buildup or some other defect in the voting machine. Such a buildup would be more likely to hurt Gore than Bush in counties that Gore carried. There would be more chad buildup under Gore's name than Bush's, making dimpled votes more likely to have been intended for Gore than for Bush.

The methods used by the Palm Beach board produced either 176 or 215 extra votes for Gore; the Florida supreme court declined to decide which number was correct, leaving that question to be answered by the trial court in further proceedings that were interrupted before the question could be answered. Assume, favorably to Gore, that the higher number is correct. That number, 215, was 0.08 percent of the votes that the tabulating machinery had counted for Gore in Palm Beach County. Had the Broward and Miami-Dade canvassing boards used the Palm Beach method and produced the same percentage of additional votes for Gore, he would not have overtaken Bush's lead. His total gain in all three counties would have been only 788 votes (215 in Palm Beach as mentioned, 263 in Miami-Dade, and 310 in Broward). In addition, Gore would have had a net gain of only 78, not 98, votes in Volusia County, reducing his overall net gain from hand recounting in the four counties that he selected from 788 to 768, leaving Bush with a lead of 162.[23]

---

23. Actually more, if the figures are adjusted to reflect the fact that Gore had a larger margin of victory in Broward County than in any of the other three counties. In Broward he won 67 percent of the vote, in Palm Beach 62 percent, and in Miami-Dade and Volusia Counties 53 percent. The figures used in the text are based on Palm Beach County. When they are multiplied by the ratio of Gore's margin in the other counties to his margin in Palm Beach County, he gets the same 215-vote gain in Palm Beach County of course, a 335-vote gain in Broward ($67/62 \times 310$), 225 in Miami-Dade ($53/62 \times 263$), and 67 in Volusia. The result is that Bush retains the lead by a 186-vote margin.

With politically neutral counters (if there are such animals), Gore's net gain would be even smaller, though probably not much smaller, as the Palm Beach counters appear to have been conscientious. (But political neutrals might have adopted a more conservative criterion than the "three dimples" criterion.) The 168 additional votes that Gore netted in Miami-Dade from the first 20 percent or so of the recounted precincts before the recount was interrupted are a meaningless figure, because these precincts are far more heavily Democratic than the county as a whole. Had Miami-Dade completed a hand recount using Palm Beach rules, Gore could have overtaken Bush only if Broward's 582-vote gain for Gore from counting dimples were allowed to stand. Gore's total gain would then have been 1,060 (263 in Miami-Dade, 582 in Broward, and 215 in Palm Beach), and he would have won the election by 130 votes.

Of the disputed votes awarded to either Gore or Bush that yielded Gore's net gain of at most 215 votes in Palm Beach County, 61 percent went to Gore and 39 percent to Bush, compared with a 62/38 percent split of the total machine-counted Palm Beach vote. This suggests that Gore would have received no more than 50 percent of votes recovered in other hand recounts using Palm Beach rules, for that was his total in the machine count; and then of course he would not have overcome Bush's lead. This point also underscores the meaninglessness of the 168-vote gain for Gore from the partial recount in heavily Democratic precincts in Miami-Dade County. He received 70 percent of the additional votes recorded by the recount, though his margin in the county as a whole was only 53 percent. A complete recount might well have reduced the 70 percent margin in the partial count to 53 percent, if the Palm Beach results are representative. The analysis in the next part of this chapter, however, suggests that Gore would have done better than Bush in recovering votes from undervoted ballots.

An alternative method of estimating how many recovered votes each candidate might have received in a completed hand recount in the four counties is to compare Gore's vote gain in Palm Beach County with the number of disputed ballots in that county, 14,500. His maximum net gain of 215 votes from the recount of those ballots was only 1.5 percent of the number of ballots. The same percentage of the 10,750 undervoted ballots in Miami-Dade County would have given him a net gain of only 161 votes in that county, compared with 263 by my earlier method of calculation. And even the 161-vote estimate is inflated. Gore received a lower percentage of the total Gore-Bush vote in Miami-Dade County— 53 percent, compared with 62 percent in Palm Beach County. If a 24 percent margin (62 – 38) would have yielded Gore 161 extra votes over Bush, a 6 percent margin (53 – 47) would have yielded him only 40.

It might make sense to average the machine-count and hand-recount results, since if their errors are independent, averaging the two results will cause many of the errors to cancel out. But averaging Bush's 930-vote machine lead with a smaller but still positive lead for Bush obviously would not swing the election to Gore.

Since the end of the deadlock, there have been several efforts by the media to recount disputed ballots. These recounts cannot reveal who "really" won, because of the subjectivity involved in hand counting punchcard ballots, the biases of counters, and, underlying both points, the fact that what shall count in a hand recount as a vote is a contestable issue, both of law and of judgment.[24] Particularly questionable are the recounts that take as their

---

24. Thus it is misleading to say that because "the ballots may eventually be examined by the press and civic groups, one day we may know who got the most votes in Florida"; Pamela S. Karlan, "Supreme Court's Incursion Was Not Needed," in Correspondents of the *New York Times, 36 Days: The Complete Chronicle of the 2000 Presidential Election Crisis* 291, 292 (2001). To know "who got the most votes in Florida" requires in the first instance a legal judgment as to what marks on what ballots are votes under Florida law.

jumping-off point Bush's official lead of 537 votes,[25] thus allowing Gore to "pocket" the 582-vote net gain that he obtained from the Broward County canvassing board, which used improper criteria.

The most responsible media recount to date has been that conducted by a consortium of newspapers assisted by an accounting firm, BDO Seidman, LLP. (This is usually referred to as "the *Miami Herald* recount," even though other newspapers are involved as well as the Seidman firm.) Its first report, that of its recount of the disputed ballots in Miami-Dade County, showed Gore achieving a net gain of only 49 votes there.[26] About two-thirds of the disputed ballots (which included a small number of overvotes) that the accountants examined contained no hole or mark close enough to the name of a Presidential candidate to be counted as a vote. Some ballots were spoiled in a rather dramatic way. One voter, for example, instead of voting for a candidate, wrote "ELIAN GONZALEZ" in bright green block letters across the top of the ballot.

A subsequent report, on the consortium's statewide recount of undervotes, found that Bush would have won unless *only* fully punched through chads were counted.[27] This is paradoxical in two respects. First, fully punched through ballots are ones the tabulating machines count, and we know that Bush had won the election before any hand recounting began, so how could a hand recount

---

25. As in Michael Crowley, "Media Hounds: GOP v. Recount, Take Two," *New Republic,* March 12, 2001, p. 18. Crowley's article adopts the dubious assumption that Gore could be the "real" winner in Florida on the basis of overvotes even though he opposed any recount of overvoted ballots.

26. Amy Driscoll, "Dade Undervotes Support Bush Win: Review of Ballots by *Herald* Suggests Gore Recount Effort Would Have Failed," *Miami Herald,* Feb. 26, 2001, p. 2. (Ronald Dworkin, a strong supporter of Gore's position in the election controversy, has referred to the "careful unofficial recount" conducted by the *Miami Herald;* Dworkin, "Ronald Dworkin Replies," in "'A Badly Flawed Election': An Exchange [with Charles Fried]," *New York Review of Books,* Feb. 22, 2001, pp. 8, 10.) For details of the methodology, see Geoff Dougherty, "Accounting Firm, Herald Joined in Statewide Effort," *Miami Herald,* Feb. 26, 2001, http://www.miami.com/herald/special/news/flacount/docs/metholodogy.htm; "Herald Ballot Review Information for Punchcard Counties," Feb. 27, 2001, http://www.miami.com/herald/special/news/flacount/extra/instructcontent.htm.

27. Martin Merzer, "But Gore Backers Have Some Points to Argue," *Miami Herald,* April 4, 2001, p. 1A.

that recorded only those votes that the machines had recorded change the result, since the tabulating machines themselves were never challenged as defective? One explanation is that machine recounts of punchcard ballots *always* change the vote totals ("punch card and paper ballot voting provide the greatest chance of change in vote totals"),[28] which means that the original machine recount changed the number of recoverable undervotes. Another explanation is that many ballots have simply disappeared[29]—another example of the sheer shoddiness of U.S. election administration.

The second paradox is the fact that Gore did better in the consortium's recount the more restrictive the criteria that the counters used for recovering undervotes from spoiled ballots. This is the opposite of what everyone believed (and believes) and what the statistical study in the next part of this chapter suggests. There are three possible explanations. One is that Gore would have done better with less restrictive criteria had such criteria been applied by Democratic election officials rather than by Seidman's accountants. Another is that the finding is an artifact of postelection developments, such as the physical changes in the ballots brought about by machine recounting and other handling and the loss of many ballots. A third is that some incompetent voters who wanted to vote for Gore dimpled Bush's chad instead, which the recounters, using liberal criteria, would perforce count as a vote for Bush; errors the other way (Bush voters dimpling Gore's chad by mistake) may have been much less common.

Explaining the Deadlock

The safest conclusion, on the basis of the analysis to this point, is that hand recounts of undervotes using objective criteria would

---

28. Downs, Sautter, and Young, "The Recount Primer," at 33.
29. John M. Broder, "Study Finds Some Ballots Unaccounted for," *N.Y. Times* (national ed.), April 5, 2001 p. A16.

have been unlikely to change the outcome of the election. Further light is cast on the issue of who "really" won—as well as on some of the broader questions of suffrage policy raised in Chapter 1—by a regression analysis of the spoiled ballots in the Florida 2000 election.[30] For readers unfamiliar with the technique, regression analysis is a method of determining correlations between two or more variables. Take the very simple equation $y = a - 2b$, and let us call y the dependent variable, a the constant,[31] and b the independent variable; -2 is the coefficient of the independent variable. The equation says that increasing b by 1 will reduce y by 2. If we make the equation a little more complicated, $y = a - 2b + 3c$, the interpretation is that increasing b by 1 will reduce y by 2 if c is held constant, while increasing c by 1 will increase y by 3 if b is held constant. The equation thus reveals the effect of each independent variable on the dependent variable when the other independent variable is held constant.[32] We know there are more undervotes in Florida counties that use the punchcard ballot than in those that

---

30. I use the word "spoiled" loosely to include undervotes as well as overvotes, cf. Ill. Compiled Stat., ch. 10, 5, § 17-16, though some undervotes are deliberate nonvotes. The source of the demographic data employed in my regressions is U.S. Census Bureau, *Population, Demographic, and Housing Information from the 1990 Census,* http://quickfacts.census.gov/qfd/states/12000.html. These data refer to the population as a whole, not to voters, but are the best I can find. At this writing, I have not been able to obtain final 2000 Census data, which obviously would be more pertinent than the 1990 data. I have, however, obtained the estimated 1990 data, and will indicate the few places in which using them in place of the 1990 data affects my regression results significantly. The source of the literacy data is Florida Literacy Coalition, *The Florida Literacy Data and Statistics Handbook* 7 (Florida Dept. of Education, n.d.) (1992 data). (I have not found more recent county literacy data for Florida.) The literacy measure I use is one minus "the percentage of adults functioning at the lowest level of literacy." The sources of the ballot and counting data are Shaw, Leusner, and Holton, "Uncounted Ballots," and Brooks Jackson, "Fact Check: Examining Florida's Undervote," Nov. 30, 2000, http://www.cnn.com/2000/ALLPOLITICS/stories/11/30/jackson.undervote/index.html and http://www.cnn.com/ELECTION/2000/resources/ballot1.html. The variance across counties in the percentage of spoiled ballots is great, ranging from less than 0.2 percent to more than 12 percent, with a mean of 3.9 percent and a standard deviation of 3.1 percent.

31. If the $a - 2b$ were graphed, it would be a downward sloping line that intersected the vertical axis at a and the horizontal axis at $a/2$.

32. A linear relation between the independent variables and the dependent variable is assumed. (The relation would be nonlinear if, for example, $y = a - 2b + 3c^2$.) Transformation into logs is a method of expressing a nonlinear relation in linear form, and I use it in one set of my regression equations.

do not. But we want to know whether other factors besides the type of ballot might influence the number of undervotes, and, relatedly, how big the effect of the type of ballot is when other factors are accounted for. Taking the frequency of undervotes as the dependent variable, then, we want to see how it changes with changes in variables that might seem likely to influence it, such as the age or income or race of the voter; and if any of these demographic variables are correlated with political preference, we shall have a clue to how different voting systems might have favored one candidate over the other.

Linear regression is a statistical technique for constructing the equation that gives the best fit between the dependent and independent variables. Fitness is measured by the percentage of the variance in the data that the equation explains (R^2); in Table 1 it is 78 percent, which is high.[33] We are also very interested in the statistical significance of the coefficients, that is, the probability that the sign of the coefficient (positive or negative) would be observed even if the coefficient was actually zero. That probability is 5 percent or smaller if the ratio of the coefficient to its standard deviation (that ratio is called the *t*-statistic) is roughly 2 or greater. Coefficients that pass this test are said to be statistically significant at the 5 percent level, and that is the conventional criterion of statistical significance used in social science research. In my regressions, coefficients whose sign is statistically significant at the 5 percent level are in boldface. The size of the coefficients, indicating

---

33. Two other fitness measures are reported in the tables. The "Adjusted R^2" reduces the R^2 to reflect the fact that, as more and more independent variables are added to a regression, the amount of variance accounted for by the regression will generally increase (and will never decrease), regardless of the explanatory value of those variables: in the limit, if there were as many regressors (independent variables) as observations, the R^2 would equal 1. The F-statistic is a measure of whether the equation as a whole has significant explanatory power; stated differently, it is a test of the joint significance of the independent variables. Its significance is shown in the "Probability > F" row of each table; the lower the number following the inequality sign, the greater the significance level. N is of course the number of observations. It is fewer than the number of counties because of missing data for some of them.

the magnitude of the relation between the independent and dependent variables, is also very important.

The salient conclusions that emerge from my regression analysis are the following:

1. The choice of voting technology (punchcard versus other, in Florida generally marksense), and the choice to count votes at the precinct level rather than just at the county level, have a substantial influence on the frequency of undervotes and overvotes, respectively, even after correcting for other factors likely to influence these frequencies.

2. The punchcard ballot increases the frequency of undervotes, and counting votes just at the county level increases the frequency of overvotes. The punchcard ballot may actually reduce the frequency of overvotes.

3. The correlated factors of race and literacy influence the frequency of overvotes, and in the predicted direction, suggesting that a recount of overvotes, though not sought by Gore, might well have yielded a significant net gain for him. Race may also affect the frequency of undervotes, but this is less clear.

4. There is no indication that defects in the punchcard voting machines themselves are responsible for many undervotes or overvotes.

5. The punchcard ballot tends to be the choice of more populous counties, and county-level counting the choice of the poorer counties. The latter correlation reinforces (because income and race are correlated) the likely racial effect of a county's decision to count votes at the county level only. But there is no indication that such choices are racially *motivated*.

6. The butterfly ballot, used in Palm Beach County, does not appear to increase the number of spoiled ballots significantly, although it is confusing, especially to voters with reading problems, and so probably hurt Gore. The distinction that the experience with the butterfly ballot underscores is between a *spoiled* ballot and a clean ballot containing an *unintended* vote.

And now to the analysis itself.

—— Table 1
Explaining the Spoiled Ballots

Independent variable	Coefficient	t-statistic
Punchcard	−0.008	−1.350
County-counted	**0.040**	6.495
Income	0.000	0.258
Hispanic	0.008	0.290
Black	0.039	1.262
Literacy	**−0.230**	−3.077
Over 64	**−0.149**	−3.534
Under 25	−0.159	−1.513
Constant	0.221	4.314

$$R^2 = 0.78$$
$$\text{Adjusted } R^2 = 0.74$$
$$F = 23.35$$
$$\text{Probability} > F = 0.000$$
$$N = 63$$

Table 1 regresses the percentage of spoiled ballots (the dependent variable) on several factors (the independent variables) that might be expected to influence that percentage. In equation form, parallel to $y = a - 2b + 3c$, we would write Table 1 as SpoiledBallots = 0.221 − 0.008Punchcard + 0.040CountyCounted. . . . The tabular form is clearer. Notice that what I am calling "percentages" are actually entered in the regressions as decimals. So the −0.008 coefficient of the punchcard variable signifies that a 1 percent increase in the use of the punchcard ballot reduces the percentage of spoiled ballots by 0.8 percent (four-fifths of 1 percent). Notice also the zero coefficient of the income variable. Actually it is positive, but so small that I have rounded it down to zero.

The variables "punchcard" and "county-counted" are dummy (that is, dichotomous) variables that take, respectively, a value of 1 if the ballot was a punchcard ballot and 0 if it was not, and 1 if the votes are counted at the county's election office and 0 if they are counted at the precinct level and the totals are forwarded to the county office. (Remember that 40 percent of the counties use the punchcard ballot. In 65 percent of the counties, the votes are counted in the county election office rather than at the precinct.) When the vote is counted at the precinct, that is, at the polling place, and the marksense technology is used, the voter has, as explained earlier, a chance to revote if he spoils his first ballot by an overvote. In addition, precinct election workers are more likely to look at the ballot when it is handed to them by the voter than if they are just putting it into a box for shipment to the county office, and they may notice that the ballot is an undervote or an overvote or otherwise incomplete or improperly completed and let the voter revote. This is an irregular practice that compromises the principle of the secret ballot, but it does occur.

For both the reasons I have given, it is no surprise that when the votes are counted at the county level rather than at the precinct level, there is a significantly higher spoilage rate. What is surprising is that when other explanatory variables are taken into account, the punchcard ballot does not generate a higher spoilage rate—and the percentage of elderly residents of a county actually reduces that rate. Income, race, and Hispanic ethnicity are not significant factors, but literacy is significant: the lower the literacy rate in a county, the higher the percentage of spoiled ballots.[34] The effect is substantial; the coefficient of −0.23 implies that a 1 percent increase in literacy reduces the percentage of spoiled ballots by almost one-quarter of 1 percent.

---

34. Some of these variables, however, are highly correlated; for example, the correlation between black and literacy is −0.55 and that between literacy and income 0.73. Not much significance should be attached to the Hispanic variable, because it is highly skewed owing to the concentration of Hispanics in Miami-Dade County. The Hispanic variable is virtually equivalent from a statistical standpoint to a Miami-Dade dummy variable. Another variable that is too skewed to play a constructive role in my regressions is the under-25 variable, included as a possible proxy for inexperienced voters. I have, however, rerun my regressions without the Hispanic and under-25 variables, and the results are virtually identical, with an exception that I mention later.

The lack of significance of the type of voting machine used (that is, whether it is a punchcard machine or a marksense machine) and the significant negative effect of literacy on the percentage of spoiled votes suggest that the undervotes and overvotes are a consequence mainly of voter error rather than of defects in the voting machines. The instructions for voting were clear—if you could read. If you had difficulty reading, you could easily make a mistake that would spoil the ballot. Further evidence in support of this conclusion is provided by the fact that when the Broward, Palm Beach, and Miami-Dade canvassing boards asked for an extension of the deadline for completing the hand recounts and submitting final vote totals to the secretary of state, they did not offer as a reason that any of the punchcard voting machines had been defective—though that would have been the best reason they could have given.

The results in Table 1 change, however, when the percentages of undervotes and of overvotes are regressed separately on the independent variables. That is done in Table 2.[35]

Table 2 suggests that where the ballots are counted is crucial for overvotes but not for undervotes; hence the significant positive sign of the county-counted coefficient in equation (1) but not in equation (2). That makes sense. It is easier for a precinct election worker to spot an overvote as an error and thus invite the voter to vote again than to spot an undervote as an error. An undervote may be deliberate (the voter did not want to vote for President), whereas an overvote, except in the rare case in which it is intended as a protest vote, must be accidental. More important, many undervotes *are* deliberate, are not errors, and so will not be changed even if the voter has an opportunity to revote. More important still, in

---

35. These regressions are not strictly comparable to the regression in Table 1, because of missing data; data for only 52 counties are available, compared to data for 63 counties in Table 1. However, redoing the Table 1 regression with just the data for the 52 counties yields results materially identical to those in that table, showing that the two data sets are indeed comparable.

—— Table 2

Explaining the Overvotes and the Undervotes Separately

Independent variable	(1) Overvotes		(2) Undervotes	
	Coefficient	t-statistic	Coefficient	t-statistic
Punchcard	**−0.014**	−1.971	**0.012**	5.245
County-counted	**0.032**	4.751	0.000	0.216
Income	−0.000	−0.090	−0.000	−1.458
Hispanic	0.031	0.849	−0.013	−1.057
Black	0.085	1.720	0.000	0.017
Literacy	−0.173	−1.673	−0.001	−0.021
Over 64	−0.075	−1.257	−0.024	−1.209
Under 25	−0.146	−0.887	−0.047	−0.843
Constant	0.157	2.130	0.027	1.068

$R^2 = 0.66$ $R^2 = 0.48$

Adjusted $R^2 = 0.59$ Adjusted $R^2 = 0.38$

$F = 10.31$ $F = 4.94$

Probability $> F = 0.000$ Probability $> F = 0.000$

$N = 52$ $N = 52$

marksense counties in which scanners are located in the precincts, an overvoted ballot will be rejected on the spot, giving the voter a chance to revote; an undervoted ballot will not be, unless, perhaps, it is completely blank.

Notice in equation (1) that the punchcard ballot actually *reduces* the percentage of overvotes after correction for the other variables. Equation (2), however, supports the claim that the punchcard ballot increases the incidence of undervotes.[36] None of the other variables besides type of ballot is significant in either

---

36. If the punchcard variable is disaggregated by brand, that is, if Votomatic and Datavote are substituted as independent variables for the punchcard variable, only the Votomatic variable has a statistically significant effect on the frequency of undervotes; the effect of the Datavote variable is positive but not statistically significant, consistent with my original discussion of the difference between the two voting machines. The other results in the regressions are not affected by the disaggregation. And recall from the table in note 6 that only a tiny percentage of Floridians voted on Datavote machines in the 2000 election.

regression at the conventional 5 percent level. Two of them, however, black and literacy, are significant at the 10 percent level in equation (2), and their signs are as expected; the larger the black population and the lower the literacy level, the higher the incidence of undervotes even after other factors are taken into account. Literacy becomes significant at the 5 percent level in the overvote equation if the Hispanic and under-25 variables are omitted, and also if the estimated 2000 Census data are used for the demographic variables in place of final 1990 Census data.

The fact that the coefficient of the county-counted variable in the overvote equation and the coefficient of the punchcard variable in the undervote equation are positive and significant does not reveal the *magnitude* of the effects of these variables on the percentages of undervotes and overvotes, respectively. Yet that magnitude is critical to assessing the impact of the variables on the election. The magnitude is given by the size as distinguished from the sign of the coefficients. The coefficients in Table 2 estimate the number of percentage points that each variable adds to the percentages of undervotes and overvotes (the dependent variables).[37] The average percentage of undervotes in counties that do not use the punchcard ballot is only 0.55 percent, and so the effect of the punchcard variable (the coefficient of which is 1.2 percent) is substantial—it triples the undervote percentage. The average percentage of overvotes in counties that count the votes at the precinct level is 0.28 percent, and the coefficient of the county-counted variable is 3.2 percent, a greater than tenfold increase.

The results in Table 2 lend some (though only weak) support to the Democrats' claim, which they pressed hard in the contest litigation, that the punchcard machines used in the Florida election were defective; they also explain the surprising result (reported in Table 1) that a county's use of the punchcard ballot had no statisti-

---

37. Remember that these percentages are actually decimals in the regressions, as are the coefficients of the independent variables.

cally significant effect on the percentage of spoiled ballots in the county. If, because the punchcard machine is defective, voters have difficulty punching through, this would tend to increase the number of undervotes yet reduce the number of overvotes (and remember that this is what equation (2) showed), so that the net percentage of spoiled ballots might not be greater.

But difficulty punching through might not be the result of a machine defect; instead it might be the result of a failure to follow instructions, lack of manual dexterity, general confusion, or indecision. So let me try another approach, this time transforming the variables (other than the dummies) into natural logarithms in order to reduce the weight of extreme observations, which may be unrepresentative. When this is done, the equation in Table 1 is unchanged, but the equations in Table 2 are changed somewhat, as shown in Table 3.

In the overvote equation, the punchcard variable becomes insignificant but the literacy variable becomes significant (and negative) at the conventional 5 percent significance level. In the undervote equation the only important change is that the county-counted variable becomes statistically significant at the 5 percent level and, as expected, positive: undervotes too are more likely when votes are counted at the county level, as there is then no possibility that a mistake will be caught at the polling place and the voter allowed to revote.[38] Consistent with the earlier point that an overvote is much more likely to be caught and corrected with precinct counting than an undervote, the coefficient of the county-counted variable is substantially greater in the overvote logarithmic regression than in the undervote one.

The magnitudes of the county-counted and punchcard variables remain substantial, though smaller than in the nonlogarith-

---

38. When estimated 2000 Census data are substituted, however, the county-counted variable becomes insignificant in the undervote equation, and the income variable becomes significant and in the predicted direction (that is, negative).

—— Table 3

Natural-Log Regressions of Overvotes and Undervotes

Independent variable	(1) Overvotes		(2) Undervotes	
	Coefficient	t-statistic	Coefficient	t-statistic
Punchcard	0.327	0.714	**1.290**	4.064
County-counted	**1.699**	3.771	**0.639**	2.046
Income	−1.584	−0.946	−1.902	−1.641
Hispanic	−0.061	−0.274	−0.161	−1.050
Black	−0.123	−0.277	0.408	1.324
Literacy	**−9.547**	−2.146	−0.820	−0.266
Over 64	−0.294	−0.320	−0.253	−0.399
Under 25	0.835	0.523	−0.157	−0.142
Constant	8.940	0.510	12.993	1.070

$R^2 = 0.53$	$R^2 = 0.54$
Adjusted $R^2 = 0.44$	Adjusted $R^2 = 0.46$
F = 6.07	F = 6.39
Probability > F = 0.000	Probability > F = 0.000
N = 52	N = 52

mic equations. The county-counted variable increases the percentage of overvotes by 170 percent,[39] while the punchcard variable increases the percentage of undervotes by 129 percent and the county-counted variable increases the percentage of undervotes by an additional 64 percent. The log transformations thus support the main inferences from the original regressions.

The overvote equation in Table 3 also provides some basis for believing that Gore would have won the popular vote in Florida if legal votes could, as a matter of Florida law (a critical issue that I address in the next chapter), be recovered from spoiled ballots. Less

---

39. The coefficients of the natural-logarithm independent variables are percentages of the coefficients of the dependent variables, which are also percentages, whereas in the nonlogarithmic regressions the coefficients of the independent variables, although also percentages, are not percentages *of* the dependent variables. Thus the coefficient of the county-counted variable in Table 2(1) is the additional percentage of overvotes in counties in which votes are counted at the county rather than the precinct level.

literate voters are both more likely to overvote and more likely to vote Democratic. The latter inference is supported by the negative correlation between literacy and being black noted earlier[40] and by exit poll data showing that blacks favored Gore by a margin of 93 percent to 7 percent.[41] An overvote that took the form of punching Gore's chad and then writing his name (or Lieberman's) in the place for a write-in candidate would unambiguously manifest the voter's intention to vote for Gore.

An alternative regression procedure is to weight the observations by the population of each county, rather than to give each county equal weight.[42] The rationale is that the smaller a county's population is, the more likely random factors are to influence the number of spoiled ballots—and the population of Florida counties varies from less than 6,000 to almost two million. Table 4 redoes Table 2 by substituting weighted for unweighted regressions. Although the undervote equation in the new table is virtually identical to that in the old one (except that race now becomes significant at the 5 percent level if the estimated 2000 Census data are substituted for the final 1990 data), the only variable in the overvote equation that is statistically significant at the conventional 5 percent level is race. (Whether the votes are counted at the county

---

40. Illustrative of the problem that difficulty in reading can create, it appears that some voters voted for Gore plus the Libertarian candidate for President (thus producing an overvote), thinking they were voting for Gore and Lieberman; David Damron, "Exposing the Flaws: Language Could Have Tripped Up Some Voters," *Orlando Sentinel*, March 8, 2001, p. A1. Remember too that inexperienced voters have difficulty with complex ballots. Black turnout in Florida rose from 10 percent in 1996 to 16 percent in 2000; Kim Cobb, "Some Blacks Keep Wary Eye on Bush," *Houston Chronicle*, Dec. 17, 2000, p. A1. While some of the greater turnout was of blacks who had voted in other elections, there was probably an unusually large number of new voters. Unexpectedly large turnout would have led to crowding and confusion in the polling places as well—factors that would increase the likelihood of voting errors by new voters and voters who read with difficulty. See also Scott McCabe, "Experts: Lack of Voter Education Added to Problem," *Palm Beach Post* (final ed.), March 11, 2001, p. 15A.

41. This may be an exaggeration. Blacks who vote Republican may be reluctant to acknowledge the fact, because of the strong social pressure on blacks in Florida to vote for Gore in the 2000 Presidential election.

42. An alternative would be to weight by number of votes cast per county, but that turned out to yield materially identical results.

—— *Table 4*

Weighted Regressions of Overvotes and Undervotes

Independent variable	(1) Overvotes		(2) Undervotes	
	Coefficient	t-statistic	Coefficient	t-statistic
Punchcard	0.003	0.370	**0.011**	5.828
County-counted	0.013	1.719	0.001	0.567
Income	0.000	0.419	0.000	0.778
Hispanic	−0.029	−1.597	0.002	0.331
Black	**0.209**	3.426	0.011	0.730
Literacy	−0.095	−0.947	−0.026	−0.977
Over 64	−0.012	−0.169	−0.008	−0.434
Under 25	−0.160	−1.013	−0.014	−0.337
Constant	0.064	0.757	0.019	0.847

$R^2 = 0.53$ $R^2 = 0.73$

Adjusted $R^2 = 0.44$ Adjusted $R^2 = 0.68$

F = 6.02   F = 14.25

Probability > F = 0.000   Probability > F = 0.000

N = 52   N = 52

rather than the precinct level is, however, significant at the 10 percent level—and at the 5 percent level if estimated 2000 Census data are substituted.) This is further evidence that black voters were more likely to cast overvotes than whites, and since we know that black voters heavily favored Gore, recovered overvotes would probably have favored him. We have also seen that at least some overvotes could have been read objectively, by a fair and competent hand counter, as votes for a particular candidate.

It is therefore curious that the Democratic recount efforts were focused entirely on undervotes, leaving Republicans to argue that overvotes should be recounted as well and Democrats to scoff at the argument.[43] It is doubly curious because Gore's team believed

---

43. As late as December 12, 2000, more than a month after the election, Justice Breyer missed the potential significance of overvotes, remarking in his opinion in *Bush v. Gore,* correctly but misleadingly, that "petitioners [that is, Bush] presented no

that readily hand-recoverable overvotes (punching a candidate's chad and then writing in his name in the write-in space) had been cast in Duval County and that their rejection by the tabulating machinery had cost Gore a significant number of votes.[44] Yet it was Bush rather than Gore who complained that to recount undervotes and not overvotes was an unsound procedure and Gore who defended the Florida supreme court's decision to recount only undervotes. Apparently Gore's team did not discover the overvote problem in Duval County in time to request a recount there.[45] Other considerations may have played a role as well, as we shall see in Chapter 4 in discussing the legal strategies of the antagonists.

For completeness, I note that when Table 1 (the regression of spoiled ballots, that is, of undervotes plus overvotes) is redone on a weighted basis, the punchcard ballot variable remains insignificant and the county-counted variable significant, but the literacy variable recedes in significance from the 5 percent to the 10 percent level and the race variable becomes highly significant, both in the predicted direction. Table 4 implies, however, that the racial effect is limited to overvotes. This makes it all the more surprising that Gore did not seek to recount overvotes as well as undervotes.

Emphasis on race is potentially misleading because of the strong negative correlation between race and income and race and literacy. It is surely not because black people in Florida are racially

---

evidence, to this Court or to any Florida court, that a manual recount of overvotes would identify additional legal votes"; *Bush v. Gore,* 121 S. Ct. 525, 551 (2000) (per curiam) (dissenting opinion). He was echoing David Boies, Gore's lawyer, who in the oral argument the day before had told the Court: "There is nothing in the record that suggests that there are such votes" (namely, overvoted ballots in which the punch and the write-in are for the same candidate).

44. Richard T. Cooper, "A Different Florida Vote—In Hindsight," *Los Angeles Times,* Dec. 24, 2000, p. A1. See also Andres Viglucci, Geoff Dougherty, and William Yardley, "Florida Black Voters Shortchanged," *Pittsburgh Post-Gazette,* Dec. 31, 2000, p. A12. Cooper's finding that a not insignificant number of overvotes contained a write-in and a punched vote for the same Presidential candidate is supported in Mickey Kaus, "Almost Everything We Thought about the Florida Recount Is Wrong!" *Slate,* Dec. 28, 2000, http://slate.msn.com/code/kausfiles/kausfiles.asp?Show=12/28/2000&idMessage=6758.

45. Cooper, "A Different Florida Vote."

distinct, but because they are poorer and less literate on average, that they are likely to encounter greater difficulty than whites in coping with user-unfriendly voting systems.

One can get at the problem of correlated variables by rerunning some of the regressions with fewer variables, omitting ones that either had little effect in the earlier regressions or are highly correlated with other variables. This is done in Table 5. Notice that despite the omissions (and tending to validate them), the equations continue to provide a good fit between the dependent and independent variables. Notice, too, how similar the coefficients of the significant variables are to the coefficients of the same variables in Tables 1 and 2.

In the spoiled-ballots equation, the county-counted and literacy variables are significant, along with the over-64 variable—which, being negative, indicates that older voters, presumably because they are more experienced voters, are less likely to spoil their ballots. These effects persist in the separate equation for overvotes, except that the negative coefficient on the punchcard variable is now significant if estimated 2000 Census data are substituted; in the undervote equation only the type of ballot is significant at the 5 percent level (though income is significant at the 6 percent level).[46]

The reader may be dizzy with all these different regression equations! But it is sensible in statistical analysis to experiment with different specifications of the regression equation. Results that are robust to different specifications are more likely to be capturing some underlying reality rather than to be merely accidents or artifacts of the specific form of the equation. The equations in Tables 1-5, taken as a whole, indicate that the punchcard ballot and county counting, together with the correlated factors of low liter-

---

46. Weighting the observations in Table 5 by population, as in Table 4, reduces the significance of the county-counted variable in the overvote equation and the income variable in the punchcard equation.

—— Table 5

Regressions with Omitted Variables

Independent variable	Spoiled		Overvotes		Undervotes	
	Coefficient	t-statistic	Coefficient	t-statistic	Coefficient	t-statistic
Punchcard	−0.008	−1.364	−0.011	−1.170	**0.011**	6.254
County-counted	**0.425**	7.085	**0.036**	5.094	—	—
Literacy	**−0.261**	−6.207	**−0.277**	−5.161	—	—
Income	—	—	—	—	−0.000	−1.971
Over 64	**−0.136**	−4.644	**−0.102**	−2.676	—	—
Constant	0.2378	6.953	0.237	5.456	0.016	2.974

	$R^2 = 0.76$	$R^2 = 0.63$	$R^2 = 0.44$
	Adjusted $R^2 = 0.74$	Adjusted $R^2 = 0.60$	Adjusted $R^2 = 0.42$
	$F = 46.06$	$F = 19.80$	$F = 19.84$
	Probability $> F = 0.000$	Probability $> F = 0.000$	Probability $> F = 0.000$
	$N = 63$	$N = 52$	$N = 54$

acy, low income, and being black, had a significant effect in increasing the frequency of spoiled votes in the 2000 Florida election.

The Butterfly Ballot and a Taxonomy of Voting Error

Some voters in Palm Beach County who cast ballots that the tabulating machines counted as votes were apparently misled by the "butterfly" punchcard ballot used in that county and mistakenly voted for Buchanan when they meant to vote for Gore.[47] The design of the ballot, in which the candidates were listed on both sides of the ballot rather than all on one side, was the brainchild of the Democratic supervisor of elections for the county. Her aim was to enable the candidates' names to be printed in large type, in con-

47. See, for statistical evidence, Kevin Quinn and Mark S. Handcock, "Did Your Vote Count?" http://www.csss.washington.edu/csss-spr01.voting.html, visited March 4, 2001, and studies cited there. The early reports by the media that these were mainly elderly Jewish voters are undermined by my regression results, which suggest that age does not lead to mistakes in voting.

sideration of the number of elderly voters in the county, while at the same time placing before the voter all the candidates for each office on a pair of facing pages; presumably overvotes would be less likely than if there were candidates for the same office on different pages. Another ballot design might thus have disenfranchised some voters who had poor eyesight, who cast their vote before realizing there were additional candidates for the same office on the next page of the ballot, or who cast two votes for candidates for the same office because they failed to realize that the candidates for the same office were on different pages.

Yet although well intentioned, the design of the ballot was, on balance, confusing. As shown in Figure 1, a photograph of the butterfly ballot used in Palm Beach County in the 2000 election, Bush is listed first on the left-hand side of the ballot and Gore second, while Buchanan is listed first on the right-hand side, between Bush and Gore rather than opposite Bush. Since the candidates' chads are in the middle of the ballot, Buchanan's chad is between Bush's and Gore's. A voter who wanted to vote for Gore had to punch the third chad down; if he punched the second, which was almost level with the word "Democratic" above Gore and Lieberman's names, he was voting for Buchanan. This would be an easy mistake to make, especially for an inexperienced voter or one with poor eyesight, even though the butterfly format enables larger type and in that respect helps people with poor eyesight. Some voters probably didn't even realize that the names on the right-hand side of the ballot were names of other Presidential candidates. Looking just at the left-hand side, they saw Bush listed first and Gore second and, if they wanted to vote for Gore, punched the second chad from the top.

The error of the butterfly design was irremediable for purposes of deciding who won the 2000 election. Not only would altering the outcome of an election on the basis of the confusing design of the ballot open a Pandora's box of election challenges; there was

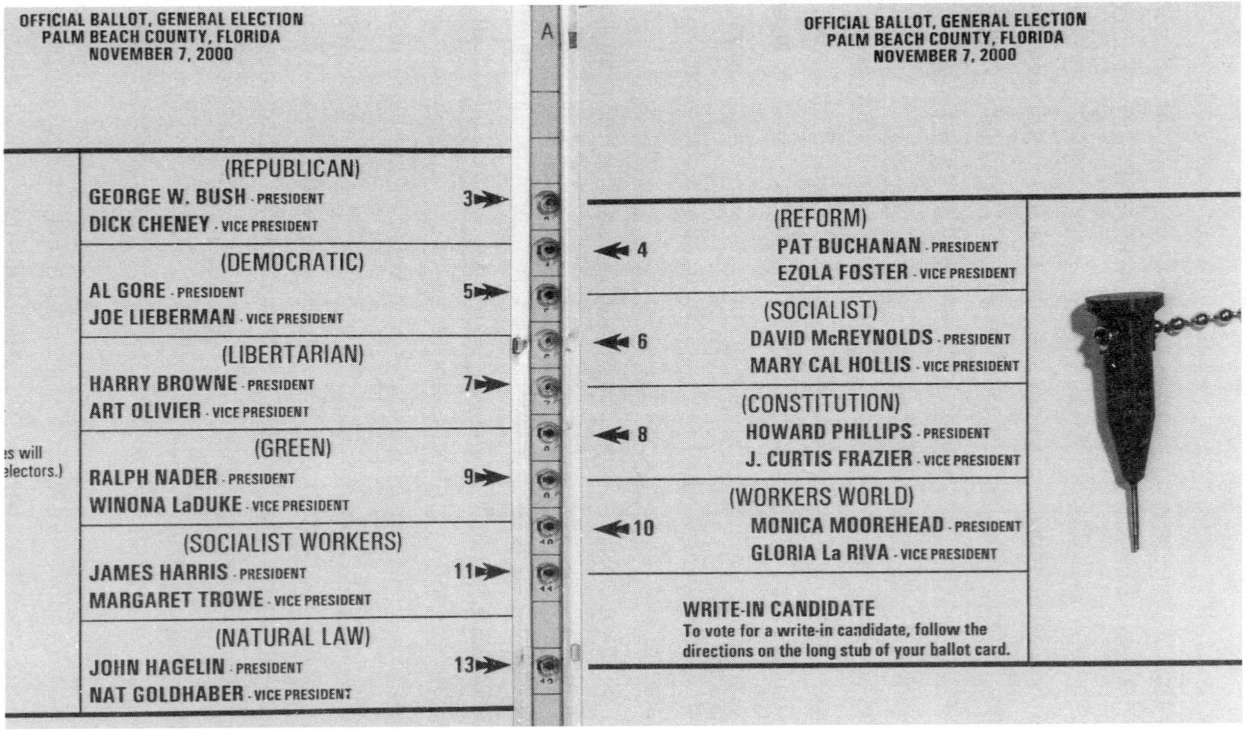

Figure 1 The butterfly ballot. (© Greg Lovett/The *Palm Beach Post*.)

no reliable method of determining within any reasonable deadline for selecting Florida's electors the actual intent of these voters. A new ballot would have had to be designed, approved, and printed, and arrangements made for reopening and restaffing the polling places and retabulating the votes in the new election, all within a few weeks. The holding of a second election would also have required congressional action, because federal law designated November 7 as the day for selecting each state's electors in 2000.[48] We should consider, however, the possibility that the butterfly ballot exacerbated the problem of spoiled ballots. This is far from certain, since the likeliest consequence of its misleading design was simply to produce a "clean" vote for Buchanan, which no hand recount could recover for Gore. But it is possible that its confusing character would increase the rate of spoliation. That possibility is examined in Table 6, a repeat of Table 1 with the addition of a dummy variable that takes a value of 1 if the butterfly ballot was used (or, equivalently, if the vote was cast in Palm Beach County, the only county to use the butterfly ballot) and 0 otherwise.

The results are almost identical to those in Table 1. The butterfly ballot has a positive effect on the percentage of spoiled ballots, but the effect is statistically significant only at the 10 percent level, and it is not a sufficiently large effect to alter the size or significance of the other variables appreciably. In separate regressions for undervotes and overvotes, with or without logarithmic transformations, the butterfly ballot variable is not even significant at the 10 percent level, though in two of the regressions income is, as expected, negatively correlated with the percentage of spoiled ballots at the 10 percent significance level.

The problem with the butterfly ballot underscores the sheer variety of voting-related errors, and it may be helpful to pause for a summary of the different types:

---

48. 3 U.S.C. § 1.

—— *Table 6*

Regression of Spoiled Ballots with
Butterfly Ballot Variable Added

Independent variable	Coefficient	t-statistic
Punchcard	−0.008	−1.494
Butterfly	0.029	1.779
County-counted	**0.040**	6.554
Income	−0.000	−0.098
Hispanic	0.006	0.227
Black	0.038	1.234
Literacy	**−0.220**	−3.005
Over 64	**−0.157**	−3.790
Under 25	−0.165	−1.598
Constant	0.223	4.438

$$R^2 = 0.79$$
$$\text{Adjusted } R^2 = 0.75$$
$$F = 21.94$$
$$\text{Probability} > F = 0.000$$
$$N = 63$$

(1) *Error in Tabulation.* An impeccably completed ballot may fail to be counted as a vote because of a defect in the design, construction, or operation of the tabulating machinery or process (the tabulation might be done by hand). So far as appears, there were few if any errors in the machine tabulation of the Florida Presidential votes, at least after the machine recount. Hand tabulation, as we know, is prone to error.

There is persisting confusion between the *voting* machine, that is, the tray on which the punchcard ballot sits, and the *tabulating* machine, that is, the computer that counts the ballots after they have been voted. Thus Professor Dworkin speaks of "Florida's vote-counting machines, many of which are conceded to be inaccurate, particularly in counties with a high proportion of minority and poor voters."[49] There was nothing wrong with the tabulating machinery. For that matter, most of the spoiled ballots—ballots that properly operated tabulating machinery in perfectly good order would not count—were due to voter error rather than to chad buildup or other defects in the voting machines. Oddly, this is made clear in another article in the same issue of the *New York Review of Books* in which Dworkin's article appears.[50]

(2) *Unspoiled Ballot, Voter Error.* This was the butterfly ballot problem. The ballot was completed and tabulated correctly, but it did not reflect the voter's actual intention. Such errors, it is now agreed, could not have been corrected in time to affect the outcome of the 2000 election.

(3) *Spoiled Ballot, Pure Voter Error.* The voter misread or misapplied the instructions, and as a result cast a ballot that the tabulating machinery would not record as a vote. This was the focus of the hand recounts.

(4) *Spoiled Ballot, Defective Voting Machine.* The voter could not cast a ballot that the tabulating machinery would record as a vote because the voting machine (not the tabulating machine) was defective—for example, cluttered with chads from previous ballots, making it difficult or impossible for later voters to punch their ballots all the way through. It does not appear that many ballots were spoiled because of defects in the voting machines.

Errors of type 1 are neutral, in the sense of being unlikely to hurt either candidate relative to the other. But errors of types 2–4 were all likely to hurt Gore relative to Bush. Type 2 would have this effect because the ballot design was more likely to lead a Gore voter

---

49. Dworkin, "Ronald Dworkin Replies," at 8, 10.

50. Mark Danner, "The Road to Illegitimacy," *New York Review of Books,* Feb. 22, 2001, p. 48.

to vote for Buchanan than a Bush voter to do so, as a consequence of Buchanan's chad being directly beneath Bush's and of Buchanan's name being parallel to the word "Democratic." Types 3 and 4 would have this effect because Democratic voters are more likely than Republican voters to be black and hence to be less literate and so have greater difficulty complying with the voting instructions or realizing that they cannot comply because the voting machine is defective. None of this has anything to do with errors in counting votes; the tabulating machinery operated as it was supposed to. The problem was the use in 40 percent of Florida's counties of a voting technology that, despite the abolition of literacy tests for voting, puts a premium on literacy, and the decision of 65 percent of the counties to count votes in the county election office rather than at the precinct, a procedure that makes it impossible to catch voter errors in time for the voter to revote.

Thus the choice by some counties of punchcard technology, and of those and other counties of centralized vote counting, not only hurt Gore but hurt him through disenfranchising a disproportionate percentage of blacks who were eligible to vote. This was bound to arouse the black community because of the long history of denying the suffrage to blacks, particularly in the South. If punchcard technology had been replaced throughout Florida by marksense technology, if all votes had been counted at the precinct level, if the butterfly ballot had not been used in Palm Beach County (a county in which Gore ran very strongly despite the ballot), and if the polling places had been better staffed and party activists had instructed their voters more carefully,[51] it is quite likely that Gore would have won the popular vote in Florida on November 7 and would thus have become President without any recounting or litigation. To put this differently, if the question is

---

51. See, for example, McCabe, "Experts: Lack of Voter Education Added to Problem."

what percentage of the people who voted in the Florida election thought they were voting for Gore, the probable answer is more than 50 percent. He may therefore have won a moral victory, though it does not follow that he should have won a legal one; the winner of the "what if" or the "might have been" election need not be the winner of the actual election. And we are assuming that the other undoubted irregularities that occurred in the Florida election—including voting by unregistered voters, voters who voted more than once, felons who voted illegally, and nonfelons forbidden to vote under the erroneous belief of election officials that they were felons[52]—did not substantially favor Gore over Bush.

But it is not even certain that Gore should be thought the winner of a moral victory. To speculate responsibly on who would have won a game conducted under different rules requires considering how the players would have adapted their strategies to the different rules. Suppose the populous Democratic-leaning counties in Florida had switched from the punchcard to the marksense voting method *before* the election. Wouldn't Republicans in Florida have warned Bush that there was likely to be a bigger Democratic vote in those counties than if the punchcard method had been retained? And in response to this warning might not Bush have shifted campaign resources from safe Republican states to those counties? Might not this shift have redressed the balance? Unless these ques-

---

52. See, for example, William T. McCauley, Comment, "Florida Absentee Voter Fraud: Fashioning an Appropriate Judicial Remedy," 54 *University of Miami Law Review* 625 (2000); "Florida Voter Fraud Issues: An FDLE Report and Observations" (Florida Department of Law Enforcement, Jan. 5, 1998); Lisa Arthur, Geoff Dougherty, and William Yardley, "452 Felons Cast Votes Illegally in Broward," *Miami Herald* (Broward ed.), Jan. 19, 2001, p. 1A; Manny Garcia and Tom DuBocq, "Unregistered Voters Cast Ballots in Dade," *Miami Herald* (final ed.), Dec. 24, 2000, p. 1A; Adam Smith and Sydney P. Freedberg, "Count Shows Tainted Votes," *St. Petersburg Times*, Dec. 14, 2000, p. 1B; David Kidwell, Phil Long, and Geoff Dougherty, "Hundreds of Felons Cast Votes Illegally," *Miami Herald*, Dec. 1, 2000, p. 1A. These are of course national problems, not ones limited to Florida. See, for example, *Times* Staff Writers, "A 'Modern' Democracy That Can't Count Votes," *Los Angeles Times*, Dec. 11, 2000, p. A1; Dave Umhoeffer and Jessica McBride, "361 Felons Voted Illegally in Milwaukee," *Milwaukee Journal Sentinel*, Jan. 21, 2000, p. 1A; Michael deCourcy Hinds, "Vote-Fraud Ruling Shifts Pennsylvania Senate," *New York Times* (late ed.), Feb. 19, 1994, § 1, p. 1.

tions can be answered, it is impossible to say whether Gore would actually have won if all Florida counties had used marksense voting technology.

The choice of voting technology and counting site cannot be attributed to deliberate racial discrimination or even to indirect discrimination, as might be inferred if the choice were correlated with literacy. Table 7 regresses the ballot and counting-site variables on population and income.[53] The regressions reveal a significant positive correlation between punchcard and population, holding income constant, and a significant negative correlation between county-counted and income, holding population constant.

These results make sense. Poorer counties are more likely to centralize counting because it is more economical than counting at each precinct and then merging the results; smaller staffs and, especially, fewer tabulating machines are required. Why the more populous counties are drawn to the punchcard ballot is less clear, but inquiry of election officials suggests the following reason. When computerized vote tabulation first became feasible in the 1960s, the more populous counties adopted it first because hand counting is slower the more votes there are to be counted, and the only system of computerized vote tabulation available at the time was the punchcard system.[54] The counties that adopted that system were loath to switch later on, when new and better technology

---

53. The probit regression model is used because the dependent variables are dummies. LR (likelihood ratio) corresponds to F in a conventional linear regression, and z-statistic to t-statistic. The population and income variables have been rescaled to avoid zero coefficients. Regressions of the dependent variables on additional independent variables did not produce any significant correlations and so are not shown.

54. National Clearinghouse of Election Administration, *Voting System Standards: A Report on the Feasibility of Developing Voluntary Standards for Voting Equipment* 10–11 (Federal Election Commission 1984); Roy G. Saltman, *Effective Use of Computing Technology in Vote-Tallying* 10–12 (U.S. Department of Commerce, National Bureau of Standards, March 1975); Eric A. Fischer, "Voting Technologies in the United States" (Congressional Research Service, Report for Congress, RL 30773, Jan. 11, 2001), http://www.cnie.org/nle/rsk-55.html. In addition, although this is not mentioned in the literature, more populous counties are likely to have more candidates and offices, and that too would slow down hand counting.

—— *Table 7*

Probit Regression of Ballot and Counting Variables

Independent variable	(1) Punchcard		(2) County-Counted	
	Coefficient	*z-statistic*	*Coefficient*	*z-statistic*
Population (in thousands)	**0.0016**	2.037	0.0011	1.490
Income (in $ thousands)	−0.0210	−0.591	**−0.1000**	−2.775
Constant	0.0718	0.072	5.138	1.473

Pseudo R^2 = 0.07   Pseudo R^2 = 0.10

LR = 6.30   LR = 9.00

Probability > LR = 0.04   Probability > LR = 0.01

N = 65 N = 67

came on the market, because of the cost of buying new equipment when the old was still serviceable. This is an additional reason for believing that any discriminatory effect of the punchcard system, as of county rather than precinct counting, in the Florida 2000 election was unintentional.

Chapter 3

The Postelection Struggle in the Courts

THE LITIGATION that arose out of the deadlocked Florida election and culminated in the Supreme Court's decision in *Bush v. Gore* was hydra-headed, complex, and intricate, despite being highly compressed in time. It involved numerous provisions of state and federal law and encompassed no fewer than eight major judicial decisions and a number of minor ones.[1] We must work

---

1. I count as major the decision by Florida circuit judge Lewis on November 14, 2000, upholding the Florida secretary of state's refusal to extend the statutory deadline for hand recounting beyond that day; the state supreme court's reversal of that decision on November 21, *Palm Beach County Canvassing Board v. Harris*, 772 So. 2d 1220 (Fla. 2000) (hereinafter cited as *Palm Beach County Canvassing Board v. Harris*); the U.S. Supreme Court's vacation of the decision of the state supreme court on December 4, *Bush v. Palm Beach County Canvassing Board*, 121 S. Ct. 471 (2000) (per curiam) (hereinafter cited as *Bush v. Palm Beach County Canvassing Board*); circuit judge Sauls's dismissal of the contest proceeding the same day; the reversal of that dismissal by the Florida supreme court on December 8, *Gore v. Harris*, 772 So. 2d 1243 (Fla. 2000) (per curiam) (hereinafter cited as *Gore v. Harris*); the U.S. Supreme Court's stay of that decision the next day; the Florida supreme court's decision on December 11 purporting to clarify the November 21 decision; and the U.S. Supreme Court's reversal of the Florida supreme court's December 8 decision on December 12, *Bush v. Gore*, 121 S. Ct. 525 (2000) (per curiam) (hereinafter cited as *Bush v. Gore*). Two other decisions should be mentioned. One is the affirmance by the Florida supreme court of the rejection of the challenge to the counting of certain absentee ballots in Seminole and Martin Counties; *Jacobs v. Seminole County Canvassing Board*, 773 So. 2d 519 (Fla. 2000) (per curiam). The other is *Siegel v. LePore*, 234 F.3d 1163 (11th Cir. 2000)

through its stages carefully, beginning with a summary of Florida's election statute, for it was on the meaning of that statute that the entire litigation pivoted.[2]

The Florida Election Statute and *Palm Beach County Canvassing Board v. Harris* (November 21)

Florida's election code requires the counties to submit their vote totals to Florida's secretary of state (in order to enable her to determine the winner of the election) within seven days of the election, which meant, in 2000, by November 14.[3] There is an exception to this deadline: as a consequence of federal law, overseas ballots are to be counted if received up to the tenth day after the election, and the results of the count added to the seventh-day totals.[4]

Up to that seventh day, a candidate may "protest" the result of the election in a county as "being erroneous," and he "may . . . request . . . a manual recount" and the county canvassing board "may authorize" it.[5] This hand recount is of only a sample of precincts. But if it "indicates an error in the vote tabulation which could affect the outcome of the election,"[6] the board must take further corrective action, which can include a hand recount of all the ballots cast in the county.[7] Should this recount not be completed by the seventh day after the election, its results "may be ignored" by the secretary of state.[8]

(en banc) (per curiam), in which a federal court of appeals on December 6, by a divided vote, refused—in a suit similar to *Bush v. Gore* but filed in a federal rather than a state court and by Bush supporters rather than by Gore supporters—to grant a preliminary injunction against the contest proceeding.

2. Fla. Stat. tit. IX, esp. chs. 101, 102.

3. Fla. Stat. § 102.111(1).

4. *Palm Beach County Canvassing Board v. Harris,* 772 So. 2d 1273, 1288 and n. 19 (Fla. 2000) (per curiam).

5. Fla. Stat. §§ 102.112(1), 102.166(1), (4)(a), (4)(c).

6. Fla. Stat. § 102.166(5).

7. Fla. Stat. § 102.166(5)(c).

8. Fla. Stat. § 102.112(1). The preceding section (§ 102.111(1)) says "shall be

Once the secretary of state has received the county totals and certified the winner of the election, the loser can "contest" the outcome by filing a lawsuit against the canvassing board or boards that he contends miscounted ballots. If he can show in the contest suit that enough "legal votes" were rejected in the count on which the secretary of state relied to "change or place in doubt the result of the election," the court can "provide any relief appropriate under such circumstances."[9] The statute does not define "legal vote," but it does say that no vote is to be declared invalid if, though the ballot is "damaged or defective," there is "a clear indication of the intent of the voter as determined by the canvassing board."[10]

None of the hand recounts sought by Gore, except the one in Volusia County, was complete by November 14, and Katherine Harris, the Republican secretary of state, refused to extend the deadline. She interpreted the statute to preclude an extension unless fraud, statutory violations, or some natural disaster (a hurricane, for example) or other catastrophe had interrupted the recount.[11] None of these dire eventualities had occurred. Harris's subordinate, L. Clayton Roberts, the director of the division of elections in the department of state, interpreted (undoubtedly with Harris's concurrence) the statutory term "error in the vote tabulation"—the precondition to a full countywide hand recount—to mean the failure of a tabulating machine to count properly marked ballots, rather than the machine's failing to record a vote because the voter either had not followed the instructions for casting a valid, machine-readable vote or had not complained to a precinct worker

---

ignored," creating a flat inconsistency in the statute. I have no quarrel with the Florida supreme court's preferring "may," which was also the position taken by the secretary of state.

9. Fla. Stat. §§ 102.168(3)(c), (e)(8).

10. Fla. Stat. § 101.5614(5).

11. Her statement is quoted in *Palm Beach County Canvassing Board v. Harris,* 772 So. 2d at 1226 n. 5, the decision the U.S. Supreme Court vacated and remanded under the name *Bush v. Palm Beach County Canvassing Board.*

if the instructions could not be followed because the voting machine was defective.[12] The dimpled and dangling chads discovered in the hand recounts were the result of voters' either failing to follow the instructions or, if the voting machine itself was defective, failing to seek the assistance of one of the precinct election workers.

We must bear in mind that under the Florida election code only errors in the *tabulation* of the vote authorize the canvassing board to order a complete hand recount of the county's votes. If voter error, not being an error in tabulation, is not a valid ground for a complete hand recount, there was no possible justification for extending the statutory deadline for the submission of a county's votes in order to permit an effort to recover votes from ballots rejected because of voter error. The only reason the county canvassing boards needed extra time was to complete the laborious hand recounts necessary to infer the voter's intention from the markings on a ballot that the voter had spoiled—a process of interpretation rather than merely inspection.

Florida's attorney general, Robert A. Butterworth, a Democrat, disagreed with Roberts's interpretation.[13] Yet the attorney general's own Web page states that questions about the election statute should be directed to the division of elections in the department of state. The secretary of state and the attorney general are independently elected officials. The election code gives the former, as we shall see, but not the latter, authority to interpret the election code; and the attorney general is given no authority to override the secretary of state's interpretations. Nevertheless Broward County's canvassing board liberalized its criteria for recovering votes from spoiled ballots after Butterworth chimed in with his broad concep-

---

12. Roberts's interpretation can be found in a letter dated November 13, 2000, printed in the Joint Appendix, at JA 52–58, filed in *Bush v. Palm Beach County Canvassing Board*. In view of his ruling, it is unclear why Harris included the results of Volusia County's hand recount in the statewide vote totals that she certified on November 26.

13. Butterworth's advisory opinion is published in *Bush v. Gore: The Court Cases and the Commentary* 14 (E. J. Dionne Jr. and William Kristol eds. 2001).

tion of error in the vote tabulation, even though he later acknowledged that dimpled chads had never before been counted as votes
in a Florida election.

On November 21 the Florida supreme court reversed the secretary of state and extended the November 14 deadline for protest
recounts to November 26.[14] This decision, the catalyst for the legal
and political broil that ensued, was based on an unreasonable and
not merely unsound interpretation of the statute.

By postponing the certification to November 26, the court
postponed the commencement of the contest proceeding until
then,[15] and this so shortened the time for such a proceeding as to
make completion of it by any realistic deadline—and in particular a
deadline that would avoid throwing the Presidential election into
Congress—infeasible. By moving the boundary between the protest
and contest phases, the court squeezed the contest phase virtually
to death. The unwisdom of such a squeeze argues for Roberts's
statutory interpretation, which was in any event a straightforward
reading of "error in the vote *tabulation*." Voter error is not tabulator
error; the voter is not the tabulator of the vote. An error in the vote
tabulation is most naturally understood as an error made by the
mechanical or human tabulator. More than half the votes cast in
the 2000 election in Florida, including all the votes cast (other
than by absentee ballot) in the four protest counties, were punchcard votes tabulated by computers that are programmed to reject
ballots that are not punched through.[16] So how could the failure of
the machinery to count such ballots be thought an error in tabulation? If you put a steel bar into a meat grinder and hamburger
meat doesn't come out, do you call this an error by the meat
grinder? To classify a "failure" that is built into the design of the

---

14. *Palm Beach County Canvassing Board v. Harris.*
15. Fla. Stat. § 102.168(2).
16. Some dangling-chad ballots are, as it were by happy accident, tabulated as
votes, simply because the chad though not fully dislodged lets enough light through
the chad hole to enable the tabulating machine to register a vote.

tabulating machinery as an error or defect in the tabulation of the vote would make hand recounts mandatory throughout most of the state in all close elections—something the election statute cannot reasonably be read to contemplate.

And if voter error is a proper basis for a recount, why is there no provision for demanding a *statewide* hand recount? Why are recounts county-specific? Voter error, unlike a defect in a particular machine owned by a particular county, does not respect county boundaries.

The election code offers the canvassing board three options if the sample manual recount indicates an error in the vote tabulation that could affect the outcome of the election. The first is to "correct the error and recount the remaining precincts with the vote *tabulation system.*" The second is to "request the Department of State to verify the *tabulation software.*" The third is to "manually recount all ballots."[17] The natural interpretation of this series—which also fits in with the natural interpretation of "error in the vote *tabulation*"—is that the canvassing board will first try to fix the tabulating machinery and only if that fails will it recount the ballots by hand. The hand recount is the if-all-else-fails alternative to the tabulating machine if the machine cannot be fixed, rather than a procedure for curing voter errors. The words "tabulation" and "tabulating" appear throughout the election code, always referring to enumeration or to the counting equipment. Remember, too, that the provision about recording a vote when there is a clear indication of the voter's intent is for cases in which the ballot is damaged or defective, which is different from its being spoiled by the voter, and is indeed a kind of tabulating error. The absence of a postmark on some absentee ballots of military personnel, a defect that the secretary of state did *not* think invalidated those ballots, was also a kind of tabulating error. The voter does not affix the

---

17. Fla. Stat. §§ 102.166(5)(a), (b), (c) (emphases added).

postmark. The overseas voters had followed instructions to the letter and thus had done all they could reasonably have done to cast a legal vote; the error was in the transmission process, which is a step in the overall tabulation.

Accused of being antimilitary, the Democrats decided not to make an issue of the absence of postmarks on military ballots. Another irregularity in the processing of absentee ballots was challenged, however. Republican campaign workers had been permitted to enter the election offices in Seminole and Martin Counties to affix voter identification numbers to absentee ballots that were missing the numbers as a result of a computer glitch. The Florida courts rebuffed the challenge on the ground that the irregularity was harmless.[18] Each party had sent absentee ballots, as permitted by law, to registered members of the party. The computer glitch did not affect the Democratic ballots. As with the military ballots, there was neither voter error nor any ambiguity about the voter's choice.

The difference between voter error and tabulation error blurs only if we forget that a punchcard voting machine does not *tabulate* votes. The machine is just the platform for the ballot, designed to enable the voter to signify his vote by punching holes. After voting he removes the ballot from the machine, and the votes on it are then recorded by another machine, the machine that counts the ballots—the tabulating machine. As I have emphasized, an error in the vote tabulation is an error by the tabulating machine (or ancillary equipment or processes, such as the punchcards themselves or the mail delivery system), or by hand counters if the tabulating machine breaks down and the votes have to be counted by hand instead.

Distinguishing between errors in voting and in tabulation is important because the voter is complicit in the former error whereas the latter error is invisible to the voter. If the punchcard

---

18. *Jacobs v. Seminole County Canvassing Board*, 773 So. 2d 519 (Fla. 2000) (per curiam).

machine does not work and as a result the voter does not emerge with a fully punched-through ballot, he should know, if he has read the directions, that he has a spoiled ballot, and he should request a fresh ballot and a properly operating voting machine. It is easy to understand why a state might not want its canvassing boards to be forced to undergo the bother of hand recounts—let alone the agony of hand recounts protracted beyond the seven-day statutory limit for the submission of a county's votes—merely because voters fail to follow instructions.

Gore's team equivocated skillfully between "counting" a vote and a vote "counting." The team's mantra was that all that Gore was seeking was to have all the votes counted. The 10,750 under-votes in Miami-Dade County had, Senator Lieberman stated, "never once been counted."[19] That made it sound as if there were thousands of ballots that had been cast by voters but never tabulated. In fact all the ballots in question—all the undervoted ballots and all the overvoted ones as well—had been counted (that is, tabulated) twice: once in the original machine count and the second time in the machine recount. Some of the ballots, however, having been spoiled by the voter, had not been counted (recorded) *as votes*. Gore wanted twice-counted, twice-properly-rejected ballots to be inspected by the members of the canvassing boards in the hope that the inspection would enable the recovery of additional votes from ballots that the voters had spoiled because they had failed to follow instructions. We saw in the last chapter what a judgment-laden, subjective, and imprecise process such a recovery effort was likely to be.

I do not suggest that the voters who failed to follow the voting instructions were seriously culpable, or even that voters who are utterly incapable, because of reading deficiencies, to follow simple and clear instructions should be disenfranchised; I argued in Chap-

---

19. *The NewsHour with Jim Lehrer,* Nov. 27, 2000, Transcript #6906.

ter 1 against literacy tests for eligibility to vote. The question rather is the amount of inconvenience that a voter who, however innocently, has failed to follow directions should be entitled to impose upon the election authorities, especially within the compressed timetable of a challenge to a Presidential election. We must keep in mind the role of elections in securing an orderly succession of Presidents and the inutility of absolutes ("every vote must count") as guides to administering the institutions of representative democracy, pragmatically understood.

Florida's election code does not specify the circumstances, if any, in which the secretary of state is required or even permitted to include in her certification of the vote totals the results of a recount not completed by the statutory deadline. For that matter, it does not distinguish between Presidential and other elections. But the statute itself authorizes her to interpret the statute,[20] implying, under settled principles of Florida administrative law as of administrative law generally, that her interpretation, if reasonable, is conclusive.[21] The election division's interpretation, which rejected voter error as a ground for extending the deadline, was reasonable and should therefore have been conclusive on the Florida supreme court. Indeed it was the natural and sensible interpretation of "error in the vote tabulation," which, to repeat, is the only statutory ground for a complete hand recount of a county's votes.

Against this conclusion Michael McConnell, without addressing the question of the secretary of state's interpretive authority, argues that the election statute does not limit the reasons for con-

---

20. Fla. Stat. § 97.012(1).
21. See, for example, *Legal Environmental Assistance Foundation, Inc. v. Board of County Commissioners,* 642 So. 2d 1081 (Fla. 1994); *Krivanek v. The Take Back Tampa Political Committee,* 625 So. 2d 840, 844–845 (Fla. 1993); David M. Greenbaum and Lawrence E. Sellers Jr., "1999 Amendments to the Florida Administrative Procedure Act: Phantom Menace or Much Ado about Nothing?" 27 *Florida State University Law Review* 499, 523–524 (2000); Johnny C. Burris, "The 1989 Survey of Florida Law, Part I: Administrative Law," 14 *Nova Law Review* 583, 636–641 (1990).

ducting a manual recount.[22] That is incorrect. For remember that a full countywide manual recount (as distinct from the initial sample recount) is authorized only if the sample recount "indicates an error in the vote tabulation which could affect the outcome of the election." Professor McConnell cites a provision of the election law which states that if during the manual recount the counters are "unable to determine a voter's intent in casting a ballot, the ballot shall be presented to the county canvassing board for it to determine the voter's intent."[23] The Florida supreme court never cited this provision, and for a good reason: it does not bear on the meaning of "error in the vote tabulation." Once a hand recount is ordered (or in the rare case in which there is no tabulating machinery and the initial vote count is by hand), the counters have to look at each ballot to see whether it contains a vote. The statutory criterion is indeed the "voter's intent." It should be up to the secretary of state to decide, in the exercise of her authority to interpret the election code, whether the "voter's intent" can be discerned from a dimpled chad; but that is beside the point. The canvassing board has no business looking at the ballots unless there has been an error in the vote *tabulation,* that is, in the machine count. And that was never found here. So there should not have been a hand recount; and so the question of what standard to apply to determine the voter's intent when the counter has to look at the ballot rather than just run it through a tabulating machine should never have arisen.

The election statute provides that the secretary of state *may ignore* recount results received after the seventh day following the

---

22. Michael W. McConnell, "Two-and-a-Half Cheers for *Bush v. Gore,*" in *The Vote: Bush, Gore & the Supreme Court* (Cass R. Sunstein and Richard A. Epstein eds. 2001), http://www.thevotebook.com.

23. Fla. Stat. § 102.166(7)(b); McConnell, "Two-and-a-Half Cheers." This had also been the principal basis for Attorney General Butterworth's interpretation of "error in the vote tabulation."

election. This implies that she has discretion to disregard results not barred by the statute (for example, a hand recount conducted because of an error in the vote tabulation that might have affected the outcome of the election) as well as being compelled to ignore those that are barred. That is, there are two separate though related grants of discretionary authority to the secretary of state: to interpret the statute; and, where the statute, properly interpreted, allows for a choice in its application to particular circumstances, to make that choice. As state circuit judge Terry P. Lewis explained in upholding Harris's refusal to include late recount results, "Florida law grants to the Secretary [of State], as the Chief Elections Officer, broad discretionary authority to accept or reject late filed returns. . . . On the limited evidence presented, it appears that the Secretary has exercised her reasoned judgment to determine what relevant factors and criteria should be considered, applied them to the facts and circumstances pertinent to the individual counties involved, and made her decision."[24] Determining the criteria was the interpretive function; applying them to particular circumstances the application function. Both were functions that the election code assigns to the department of state rather than to the judiciary.

The grant of broad discretionary authority to the Florida secretary of state is in stark contrast to the approach of some other election statutes, notably that of Texas, which—as a result of recent amendments much harped on by Gore's team in the Florida litiga-

---

24. *McDermott v. Harris*, 2000 WL 1714590 (Fla. Cir. Ct. Nov. 17, 2000), reversed under the name *Palm Beach County Canvassing Board v. Harris*. As Pamela Karlan, a Gore supporter and election law expert, explained, Harris's decision not to accept late recount results would (in retrospect, "should" would have been more accurate) be reviewed under the "abuse of discretion standard, so that they [the judges] understand that the official may have to make close calls and there may be a lot of complicated circumstances, and they just want the official to act reasonably. They won't substitute their judgment for her judgment. So it's not as if it's a pure question of law[,] which courts review de novo. So although they won't simply substitute their judgment, her judgment has to be reasonable under the circumstances, so if she colors too far outside of the lines, they will overturn her acts as an abuse of discretion." *The NewsHour with Jim Lehrer,* Nov. 15, 2000, Transcript #6898.

tion—grants a candidate protesting the outcome of an election in a punchcard county an absolute right to insist on a hand recount in which the "clearly ascertainable intent of the voter" is the statutory standard. The counting of dimpled ballots is expressly authorized if that standard is met, while the counting of dangling chads, and of chads through which light is visible to the naked eye, is mandatory.[25] In contrast, the Florida law delegates the making of such judgments to the secretary of state and her staff. A surprising failure to recognize this distinction was the cardinal error of the Florida supreme court in the recount litigation.

Even if the secretary of state had erred in her statutory interpretation (erred therefore in thinking her hands tied by the statute), and therefore failed to make a discretionary judgment whether to allow late recount results designed to correct voter error, this would not have entitled the court to make that judgment. Instead the court should have directed her to exercise her discretion; that is the remedy for a failure to exercise discretion.[26] She might then have explained that she didn't want to extend the deadline in a Presidential election because the effect would be to compress the contest period unduly, assuming the desirability of resolving any dispute by December 12, the federal safe harbor deadline (of which more shortly) for the appointment of the state's Presidential electors. This would be a reasonable position for her to take, one that no reasonable court could have deemed an abuse of her discretion.

A court is especially likely to defer to an agency's judgment that draws on the agency's specialized knowledge. When one

---

25. Tex. Code Ann., Election Code, vols. 1–2, §§ 127.130(d)(4), (e), 214.002(b)(2), 214.042(a)(3) (2001 Cumulative Annual Pocket Part).

26. See, for example, *Chathas v. Local 134 IBEW*, 233 F.3d 508, 514 (7th Cir. 2000); *Channel v. Citicorp National Services, Inc.*, 89 F.3d 379, 387 (7th Cir. 1996); *Campanella v. Commerce Exchange Bank*, 137 F.3d 885, 892 (6th Cir. 1998). As the court said in *Channel*, "Because he held that § 1367(a) did not authorize the exercise of supplemental jurisdiction, [the district judge] did not exercise the discretion § 1367(c) confers. It belongs to him rather than to us, so we remand for its exercise." 89 F.3d at 387.

reflects on the considerations bearing on whether to extend a recount deadline—which include how long it takes to do a hand recount in counties of different size and staffing, how fruitful such a recount is likely to be given the vagaries of interpreting spoiled ballots, and how likely it is to alter the outcome of the election, as well as whether enough time will be left for a contest proceeding— it becomes apparent that the judgments that Harris and Roberts were required to make drew centrally on their (or their subordinates') specialized knowledge of election administration.

The fact that Harris and Roberts are Republicans and that their rulings favored Bush's candidacy did not disentitle those rulings to the normal judicial deference granted to determinations that are within the scope of an agency's authority and draw upon its specialized knowledge. Florida had for good or ill made the secretary of state an elected official and entrusted her with broad discretionary authority both to interpret and to apply the election law. It would be a considerable paradox for courts to defer, in the name of democracy, *less* to elected officials than to bureaucrats. Florida law might, it is true, require an elected official to recuse himself or herself in particular circumstances. Harris was not merely a nominal Republican; she had been active in Bush's campaign, just as Attorney General Butterworth had been active in Gore's campaign. But the Democrats never moved to have Harris recused from performing her duties as secretary of state with regard to the 2000 Presidential election, and I have seen no suggestion that there would have been any legal basis for such a motion.

Yet the Florida supreme court reversed Judge Lewis and extended the statutory deadline to November 26, at the same time holding that the recount should include spoiled ballots in which the voter's intent was discernible. The justices thought themselves at liberty to strong-arm the election statute in this way, sweeping aside the discretionary authority of the department of state both to interpret the statute and to decide whether to waive the seven-day deadline for submission of the counties' vote totals, because they considered the statute internally inconsistent. It allows a hand recount to be sought right up to the seventh day after the election, yet a recount requested on the last day could not be completed by the end of that day, the deadline for submission of the vote totals. There is no inconsistency. If the recount is not requested promptly after the election and so cannot be completed by the seventh day, the losing candidate has himself to blame for not having acted faster, and anyway the only consequence is to force him back on his remedy of filing a contest proceeding. The appearance of inconsistency is a result of the court's mistaken interpretation of "error in the vote tabulation." If, as the election officials ruled, this refers only to a breakdown of the tabulating process—unspoiled ballots have not been counted—the hand recount should not take much time at all. It will be obvious at a glance which candidate received the vote on those ballots. Judgment, interpretation, disagreement, objection, challenge, and resulting delay come into play only when, because the ballot was spoiled, the voter's intention is an enigma.

On December 8 the Florida supreme court would, as we shall see, rule in effect that the certification of the election winner by the secretary of state has no presumptive validity. If that is right (it is not, as we shall also see), the disappointed candidate loses little by being hurried through the protest phase and into the contest phase. To allow the deadline for certification to be postponed hands him a Pyrrhic victory by truncating the contest period.[27] But the more important point, since the court's ruling of December 8 *was* erroneous, is, to repeat, that the only thing that could make the seven-day period for the submission of a county's votes unreasonably short (other than extraordinary circumstances such as fraud or some natural disaster) would be a desire to recover

---

27. As McConnell puts it, "the court added twelve days to a phase that had no real legal significance, while shortening the time for obtaining genuine legal relief"; McConnell, "Two-and-a-Half Cheers."

spoiled ballots as votes, a process that is time-consuming because of its subjectivity. In the exercise of her discretion to interpret and apply the statute, the secretary of state was entitled to conclude that wanting to recover votes from ballots spoiled by the voter was not a proper reason for an extension of the statutory deadline—especially in a Presidential election, in which delay in certifying the results of the election could cause chaos.

It can be argued that since the statute regulates all elections in Florida and only the Presidential election is time-sensitive (because of the nature of the office and because of the tight federal statutory and constitutional deadlines for casting and counting electoral votes), to interpret the statute to make it "work" for Presidential elections is to let the tail wag the dog. And it is true that the statute fixes no deadline for the completion of contest proceedings. But it fixes a tight deadline for the certification of the winner after a protest in any election. The tight deadline evinces recognition of the desirability of resolving *all* election disputes as soon as possible, so that the "winner" is not left in limbo during much of his term of office.

Moreover, it is precisely in adapting the statute to the exigencies of a Presidential election that the secretary of state might have been expected to be given a long tether by the courts. The less detail a statute has, the more discretion it necessarily allows the officials who administer it. The statute's failure to deal separately with Presidential elections[28] cried out for administrative supplementation.

For all these reasons having to do with the language and structure of the statute and the principles of administrative law, the secretary of state's decision not to delay the certification of the winner of the Presidential election deserved considerable deference; it received none from the Florida supreme court, which in its

---

28. Compare Cal. Election Code § 16003.

November 21 opinion acknowledged, even boasted, that both in interpreting the statute differently from the secretary of state and in casting aside her discretionary authority it was appealing to a higher law than the Florida election code. It derided "sacred, unyielding adherence to statutory scripture"[29] and "hyper-technical reliance upon statutory provisions."[30] It said that "the abiding principle governing all election law in Florida" is found in the statement in Florida's constitution that "all political power is inherent in the people."[31] It said: "Because the right to vote is the pre-eminent right in the Declaration of Rights of the Florida Constitution, the circumstances under which the Secretary [of State] may exercise her authority to ignore a county's returns after the initial statutory date are limited."[32] The court was using the Florida constitution, or perhaps some principle of natural law, to trim the statute. More likely natural law than the constitution,

---

29. *Palm Beach County Canvassing Board v. Harris,* 772 So. 2d at 1227–28, quoting *Boardman v. Esteva,* 323 So. 2d 259, 263 (Fla. 1975). The court did not, however, quote the following passage from *Boardman:* "the results of elections are to be efficiently, honestly and promptly ascertained by election officials to whom some latitude of judgment is accorded, and . . . courts are to overturn such determinations only for compelling reasons when there are clear, substantial departures from essential requirements of law"; ibid. at 268 n. 5. To the same effect, see the more recent decision in *Krivanek v. The Take Back Tampa Political Committee.* The question in *Boardman*—and in the other decisions from which the Florida supreme court in *Palm Beach County Canvassing Board v. Harris* quoted sonorous right-to-vote language, *Beckstrom v. Volusia County Canvassing Board,* 707 So. 2d 720 (Fla. 1998); *State ex rel. Chappell v. Martinez,* 536 So. 2d 1007 (Fla. 1988); and *State ex rel. Carpenter v. Barber,* 198 So. 49 (Fla. 1940)—was whether substantial compliance with the rules governing voting was sufficient to allow a vote to be counted. The court held that it was, thus presaging its decision regarding irregularities in the absentee ballots challenged in Seminole and Martin Counties in the 2000 election. None of these cases, by the way, involved a Presidential election.

Beckstrom has a further significance, overlooked during the litigation. In a footnote, it defines the statutory term "defective [ballot]," which recall that the head of Florida's division of elections defined as *not* covering voter error, as indeed including a ballot that the voter has marked improperly, and it implies that the canvassing board has a duty to inspect all such ballots. 707 So. 2d at 723 n. 4. This cannot be and apparently never has been taken seriously, Jay Weaver, "Law: Check 'Defective' Ballots," *Miami Herald,* April 4, 2001, p. 18A, and the greater significance of *Beckstrom* may be that it refused to void an election despite significant irregularies, establishing a presumption against recounts that should have been applied to the 2000 election.

30. 772 So. 2d at 1227.

31. Ibid. at 1230, quoting Fla. Const. art I, § 1.

32. Ibid. at 1239.

which, so far as it might be thought to bear on the right to vote, says merely: "All political power is inherent in the people. The enunciation herein of certain rights shall not be construed to deny or impair others retained by the people." (The court did not quote the second sentence.) The article of the constitution from which this "people power" language comes, Article I, captioned "declaration of rights," has 25 sections, but none of them mentions the right to vote. One is mystified, therefore, by the court's statement that "the right to vote is the pre-eminent right in the Declaration of Rights of the Florida Constitution." In any event the court made clear that it was going beyond conventional statutory interpretation: "The will of the people is the paramount consideration. . . . This fundamental principle, *and* our traditional rules of statutory construction, guide our decision today."[33]

The disjunction is emphasized by the structure of the court's opinion, which is divided into ten parts, of which the first four are preliminary, dealing with facts, issues, and so forth. Part V, which begins the legal analysis, is captioned "The Applicable Law" and begins with the "people power" clause of the state constitution. Part VI identifies what the court regards as "Statutory Ambiguity," and this is followed, naturally, by a Part VII captioned "Legislative Intent." But the next part, directly preceding "The Present Case" (which is Part IX, Part X being the conclusion), is captioned "The Right to Vote." There the court returns to the "people power" provision of the constitution, which the court seems to have regarded as paramount to legislative intent in the interpretation of the election code and as the key to its decision.

The court's later claim that it was using that most conservative and formalistic of interpretive principles, the "plain meaning" rule, and that the plain meaning of the statutory term "error in the vote tabulation" encompasses an error resulting from a voter's mis-

---

33. Ibid. at 1228 (emphasis added, footnote omitted).

take that made his ballot unreadable by the machine, rings hollow. The secretary of state's contrary interpretation was the plain meaning of that term.[34] Moreover, had the court really wanted to go the plain meaning route, Gore's contest proceeding would not have gotten off the ground. The Florida statute permits such a proceeding to be filed only by the losing candidate for the office filled by the election (that is, a member of the losing slate of Florida Presidential electors), a voter qualified to vote in that election, or a Florida taxpayer.[35] Gore and Lieberman, the only plaintiffs in the contest proceeding, were none of these.

The Supreme Court Steps Up to Bat:
Bush v. Palm Beach County Canvassing Board (December 4)

Article II of the U.S. Constitution provides that each state shall pick Presidential electors "in such Manner as the Legislature thereof shall direct."[36] Not as the *state* shall direct, but as the state *legislature* shall direct. On this ground, among others, Bush petitioned the U.S. Supreme Court for certiorari to review the Florida

---

34. David A. Strauss, "Not Partisan, but Lawless," in *The Vote*, argues that the Florida supreme court's interpretations of other provisions of the election statute, such as "legal vote," were not "inconsistent with the plain language of the contest statute" and therefore that "there is a plain language defense for the Florida Supreme Court's action." This is a misunderstanding of the "plain meaning" principle of statutory interpretation. The principle is that if statutory language is plain—that is, clear as a linguistic matter, regardless of the real-world context of application, which might expose an ambiguity—the court should apply the statute in accordance with that plain meaning unless the result of doing so would be absurd. See, for example, *Atlantic Mutual Insurance Co. v. Commissioner of Internal Revenue*, 523 U.S. 382, 387 (1998); *U.S. National Bank v. Independent Insurance Agents of America, Inc.*, 508 U.S. 439, 463 n. 11 (1993); *Glaxo Operations UK Ltd. v. Quigg*, 894 F.2d 392, 395 (Fed. Cir. 1990). All that Professor Strauss really means is that some of the statutory language is *not* plain, an observation that has nothing to do with a "plain meaning" defense to a charge that the Florida supreme court's decision was usurpative. In any case, "error in the vote tabulation" happens to be plain in the plain meaning sense, and so it was merely bizarre for the Florida supreme court to have claimed that its interpretation, which flouted the plain meaning of the term, *was* the plain meaning.

35. Fla. Stat. § 103.168(1).

36. U.S. Const. art. II, § 1, cl. 2.

supreme court's decision of November 21. On December 1, the Court granted the petition and thus agreed to review the decision. On December 4, after oral argument, the Court vacated and remanded the Florida court's decision in a unanimous opinion strongly intimating that a state court cannot, by appeal to the state's constitution, limit the power granted the state's legislature by Article II.[37]

The intimation is not, as critics of the decision have argued, that a state court has no legitimate role to play in the selection of electors. The Florida courts could properly decide, for example, whether the election law had actually been adopted by the state legislature. They could resolve genuine ambiguities in the statute not reasonably resolved by the division of elections in the exercise of the division's discretionary interpretive authority. Nor was the U.S. Supreme Court denying that what the Florida supreme court had done was "interpretation," a word of almost infinite plasticity. But Article II may circumscribe (not extinguish) the authority of a state court to interpret state legislation governing the appointment of the state's Presidential electors.

Normally the U.S. Supreme Court defers to a state supreme court's interpretation of the state's statutes. But if Article II grants authority to state legislatures, it may authorize the Supreme Court to protect the prerogative thus granted. The Constitution having appointed a particular organ of state government to be the Presidential election rulemaker, it is a question of federal law whether the state judiciary has allowed the designated organ to determine the manner in which the state shall select its Presidential electors. The power to appoint Presidential electors is not a "reserved" power of the states, that is, a power they had before the Constitu-

---

37. *Bush v. Palm Beach County Canvassing Board.* Twice the Court suggested that the Florida constitution could not, consistent with the "Manner directed" clause, "circumscribe the legislative power"; 121 S. Ct. at 474–475.

tion was adopted and that survived that adoption.[38] There was no Electoral College before then. The power to appoint the electors is a federal power that the states exercise as agents of the federal government. By assigning to state legislatures the task of determining the manner by which federal electors would be picked, Article II may be supposed to have federalized disputes over whether the authority thus granted to those legislatures has been usurped by another branch of state government, including a court that invokes a vague provision of the state's constitution to displace the legislature's authority and in effect write its own election code.

Bush v. Palm Beach County Canvassing Board merely adumbrates the Article II approach to the election deadlock; the majority in *Bush v. Gore* dropped it; and we must reserve final judgment on the merits of the approach until the next chapter. But it is important that the approach be understood, and not rejected out of hand as meaning, for example, that the governor of the state cannot veto a proposed law on the appointment of the state's Presidential electors or that the state's supreme court cannot invalidate an election law as unconstitutional. Article II does not regulate the process by which state legislation is enacted and validated, any more than it precludes interpretation. But once the law governing the appointment of the state's Presidential electors is duly enacted, upheld, and interpreted (so far as interpretation is necessary to fill gaps and dispel ambiguities), the legislature has spoken and the other branches of the state government must back off.[39]

Noting that the provisions of the Florida constitution (like all the amendments to date of the U.S. Constitution) are approved by the legislature before being submitted for ratification, in Florida

---

38. *U.S. Term Limits, Inc. v. Thornton,* 514 U.S. 779, 804–805 (1995).
39. See James C. Kirby Jr., "Limitations on the Power of State Legislatures over Presidential Elections," 27 *Law and Contemporary Problems* 495, 500–504 (1962), where this distinction is emphasized.

by the electorate, critics of the Article II approach have argued that the Florida constitution is just another election statute, which together with the express election code constitutes Florida's election law. That is a strained locution. We do not say that because Congress approves a constitutional amendment before the amendment is ratified, the amendment is a congressional enactment. Statutes must conform to the Constitution but we do not say that they draw their very meaning from the Constitution or that the Constitution is part of every statute. The Constitution is not a brooding omnipresence, or the Supreme Court a council of revision that sits to ensure that every federal statute will reflect the "spirit" of the Constitution. No more does a legislature, by approving a constitutional provision that will be interpreted by the courts, authorize those courts to use the provision to rewrite the legislature's statutes. The courts can invalidate a statute, or interpret it reasonably, but they are not to interpret it unreasonably merely because it does not embody the aspirations that the courts find limned in vague constitutional language. The Florida supreme court is not a third house of the Florida legislature with power to rewrite statutes without the agreement of the other two houses, and the "people power" language in the state's constitution cannot reasonably be understood as a delegation to the state supreme court by the constitution makers of the power to pick the state's Presidential electors after the result of the popular vote is known.

An analogy can be drawn to the law of labor arbitration. In resolving a dispute over the meaning of a collective bargaining agreement, the arbitrator is confined to interpreting the agreement. By this is meant that he may not bring in his own conception of "industrial justice" to resolve the dispute. "The arbitrator's award settling a dispute . . . must draw its essence from the contract and cannot simply reflect the arbitrator's own notions of industrial justice."[40] The cases that elucidate this principle distinguish between a mere misinterpretation and what might be called an imposed interpretation, an interpretation dominated by values that do not reflect the intentions of the contracting parties. When the Florida supreme court drew upon the "people power" clause of the state constitution to construe the state's election code, it was imposing its own populist values; it was not drawing the meaning of the code out of the code itself. The arbitration cases would say that the court was not interpreting the code at all, but dispensing its own brand of justice. The terminology is not important. What is important is recognition that interpretation can be a mask for usurpation. At the point at which a court is not applying but displacing the value choices made by the legislature, judicial interpretation passes over into interbranch struggle, arguably bringing Article II into play. The line is fuzzy, but that is true of many legal distinctions.

In claiming authority to limit a state court's freedom to "interpret" the state's statute governing the manner of appointing Presidential electors, the U.S. Supreme Court in its December 4 opinion quoted from the century-old decision of *McPherson v. Blacker* the statement that the words "in such Manner as the Legislature thereof shall direct" "operat[e] as a limitation upon the State in respect of any attempt to circumscribe the [state's] legislative power."[41] This statement, a dictum uttered in the course of holding that the state legislature could delegate the appointment of elec-

---

40. *United Paperworkers International Union v. Misco, Inc.,* 484 U.S. 29, 38 (1987). See also *Hawaii Teamsters & Allied Workers Union, Local 996 v. United Parcel Service,* 229 F.3d 847 (9th Cir. 2000); *Chicago Typographical Union No. 16 v. Chicago Sun-Times, Inc.,* 935 F.2d 1501, 1506 (7th Cir. 1991); *Ford Motor Co. v. Plant Protection Association National,* 770 F.2d 69, 75–76 (6th Cir. 1985); *Ethyl Corp. v. United Steelworkers of America,* 768 F.2d 180, 184–185 (7th Cir. 1985). Occasionally the Supreme Court has ruled that a state court changed a state statute by purported interpretation. See, for example, *Bouie v. City of Columbia,* 378 U.S. 347, 353–354 (1964).

41. 146 U.S. 1, 25 (1892). The Court in *McPherson* had also quoted with approval a Senate report of 1874 which stated that the power conferred on state legislatures by the "Manner directed" clause "cannot be taken away from them or modified by their

tors to voters in local districts (each district to elect one elector), is not decisive authority for the December 4 decision. But we shall see in the next chapter that the decision can be justified by reference to a role that can legitimately be assigned to the "Manner directed" clause.

The Court sent the case back to the Florida supreme court for clarification not only of the basis of that court's interpretation of the election statute but also of its view on whether the state legislature had wanted to comply with the "safe harbor" provision of Title III of the U.S. Code. Recall from Chapter 1 that Title III, also known as the "Electoral Count Act," is the federal statute adopted in 1887 in the hope of averting a repetition of the Hayes-Tilden electoral fiasco. Section 5, the safe harbor provision, sets a deadline (which for the 2000 election fell on December 12) for the appointment of a state's Presidential electors that, if complied with, precludes any challenge to the appointment when Congress meets in January to count the electoral votes. If the Florida legislature was steering for the safe harbor, this limits the authority of the state's courts to change, through "interpretation" or otherwise, the Florida election code, because the safe harbor is available only if the "final determination of any controversy or contest concerning the appointment of all or any of the electors of such State . . . shall have been made . . . pursuant to such [state] law *existing on said day*," that is, the day of the election, November 7.[42] Changing the

---

State constitutions"; ibid. at 35. And the Court had said that the clause "recognizes that [in the election of a President] the people act through their representatives in the legislature, and leaves it to the legislature exclusively to define the method of effecting the object"; ibid. at 27.

42. 3 U.S.C. § 5 (emphasis added). A further complication is that the safe harbor is not completely safe. Congress might decide to change the law after the election but before the electoral votes were counted; the constitutionality of Title III has never been authoritatively resolved; and while compliance with section 5 precludes a subsequent challenge to the appointment of the state's *electors,* section 15 requires that their electoral *votes* be counted only if "regularly given," whatever that means—no one knows. Michael J. Glennon, *When No Majority Rules: The Electoral College and Presidential Succession* 42 (1992).

existing law would not be a "violation" of the section, as some early accounts of the litigation mistakenly suggested; it would merely forfeit the safe harbor. But if reaching the safe harbor was part of the state's legislative scheme, the Florida supreme court's action in changing the law would compound the court's violation of state law, further violating federal law if Article II, section 1, clause 2 indeed limits a state judiciary's freedom to interpret the statute that prescribes the manner of appointing the state's Presidential electors.

The Florida supreme court dithered. By the time it responded to the U.S. Supreme Court's demand for clarification a week later (December 11),[43] the appeal from the Florida supreme court's second decision—which had been issued on December 8, four days after the remand from the U.S. Supreme Court—had just been argued in the Court. The timing of the clarification was thus curious—it was as if Florida's supreme court justices had waited to see whether the Justices of the U.S. Supreme Court would tip their hand in questioning the lawyers at the oral argument of the appeal from the December 8 decision. (To untangle the confusing chain of events, refer to the Chronology at the beginning of this book and note that on November 21 the Florida supreme court had issued the opinion vacated by the U.S. Supreme Court on December 4; on December 8 the Florida court had issued a new decision; on December 11 the appeal from the December 8 decisions was argued in the U.S. Supreme Court; and on that same day, December 11, shortly after the argument in the Court concluded, the Florida supreme court finally issued the clarifying opinion that the U.S. Supreme Court had directed on December 4.)

The purported clarifying opinion—which recast the original opinion (that of November 21) as an exercise in conventional statu-

---

43. *Palm Beach County Canvassing Board v. Harris,* 772 So. 2d 1273 (Fla. 2000) (per curiam).

tory interpretation and added that therefore the court had not changed the election statute and so had not jeopardized the safe harbor or violated Article II—was suspect for additional reasons besides the timing:

1. The court abandoned reliance on the Florida constitution without comment and specifically without explaining why its original opinion had placed such heavy weight on the constitution if the outcome had been dictated (as the December 11 opinion claims) by conventional principles of statutory interpretation. Usually courts will not base a decision on constitutional grounds when there are adequate statutory grounds for it.

2. The court failed to explain why it had relied in its December 8 decision on the vacated decision of November 21.

3. It stated that the "plain meaning" of the statutory term "error in the vote tabulation" encompasses an error resulting from a voter's mistake that made his ballot unreadable by the machine.[44] I am not a "plain meaning" buff myself, but if that was to be the governing principle of statutory interpretation it supported, as we have seen, the secretary of state's interpretation rather than the court's.

4. By committing itself in its December 8 decision to another adventurous expansion of the election statute, the Florida supreme court had as a practical matter prejudged the propriety of its earlier adventurous expansion. Without looking foolish, it could not have said on December 11—the very day on which the appeal from its December 8 decision was being argued in the U.S. Supreme Court—"Oops, we goofed! The logic of the U.S. Supreme Court's opinion of December 4 requires us to vacate our decision of December 8. Sorry we didn't get around to reading the December 4 decision before we violated Article II again."

In any event the attempt at clarification came too late to allow the lawyers to brief and argue its bearing on the about-to-be-decided appeal to the U.S. Supreme Court.

---

44. Ibid. at 1283.

In defense of the Florida supreme court's delay in responding to the U.S. Supreme Court's demand for clarification, it might be argued that since the case had moved from the protest to the contest phase, it was no longer important whether the Florida court had erred in extending the statutory deadline for the completion of recounts during the protest phase from November 14 to November 26. But it was important. The extension had caused a shrinkage in Bush's lead as certified by the secretary of state, the lead that the contest aimed to reduce further, from 930 votes to 537 votes, by virtue of the inclusion of the results of the Broward recount, which was completed between the fourteenth and the twenty-sixth. The difference might have proved decisive in the recount that the Florida supreme court ordered on December 8 had that recount gone through to completion. Even more important, if voter error provided no basis under Florida law for a recount, it provided no basis under that law for a contest either. It would be odd indeed if a mishap too minor or innocent or difficult to correct to warrant a recount would justify a court, perhaps months after the election, in voiding the election and giving the office at stake to the losing candidate.

The Contest Proceeding: *Gore v. Harris* (December 8)

In speaking of the Florida supreme court's decisions of December 8 and 11, I have gotten ahead of myself. On November 27—the day after the secretary of state had, upon the expiration of the extended deadline for certification following protest, certified Bush as the winner of the Presidential election in Florida, albeit with the diminished lead of 537 votes—Gore had brought suit against Secretary of State Harris and the canvassing boards of Palm Beach and Miami-Dade Counties to contest the election results in those two counties. The suit was tried on December 2 and 3 before state circuit judge N. Sanders Sauls, and on December 4 he issued his decision, throwing out the suit.[45] He ruled that Gore had failed to show that the canvassing boards had abused their discretion, either the Palm Beach board in its methods of recounting or the Miami-Dade board in deciding not to complete the recount that it had begun. Gore's hopes seemed dashed. For even if Sauls was reversed, it seemed impossible that the contest proceeding could be completed by December 12, the safe harbor deadline, now just a week away; after the deadline passed, any subsequently appointed Gore slate of electors was sure to be challenged in Congress. But Gore appealed, and on December 8 the Florida supreme court reversed.[46] This was a surprise not only because it was so late in the day, but also because: the Democrats' efforts to establish at trial that the spoiled ballots were due mainly to defects in the voting machines rather than to pure voter error had failed; the Democrats were attacking decisions by canvassing boards dominated by Democrats and a ruling by a Democratic judge; it had become clear at the trial that no consensus had emerged on an objective standard for recovering votes from a hand count of spoiled ballots; and there was no basis for believing that if an objective standard for counting undervotes were applied, Gore would overcome Bush's lead.[47]

Judge Sauls interpreted the state election statute to make contest proceedings a species of judicial review of administrative action rather than a de novo determination of the lawfulness of the election outcome, that is, a determination that would give no weight to challenged administrative rulings. The purpose of the contest trial in his view was merely to determine whether the canvassing boards, the agencies charged with tabulating election

---

45. *Gore v. Harris,* 2000 WL 1790621 (Fla. Cir. Ct. Dec. 4, 2000), affirmed in part and reversed in part, *Gore v. Harris.* Gore also challenged the certified vote totals in Nassau County, but the court affirmed Judge Sauls's rejection of this challenge; ibid., 772 So. 2d at 1260.

46. *Gore v. Harris.*

47. See, for example, Trial Transcript, 2000 WL 1802941, at *90–104 (Dec. 2, 2000) (testimony of Judge Charles Burton, chairman of the Palm Beach canvassing board), in *Gore v. Harris,* 2000 WL 1790621 (Fla. Cir. Ct. Dec. 4, 2000), affirmed in part and reversed in part, *Gore v. Harris.*

results, had abused their discretion in failing to conduct hand recounts in a certain way (that is, the Broward way, sought by Gore), or at all (the Miami-Dade County canvassing board had begun a hand recount, then changed its mind and stopped). Unless, perhaps, overvotes were recounted—a recount that Gore was not seeking—there was no reason to believe that the result of the election would change in favor of Gore if reasonable recounting protocols were followed. The protocol most favorable to Gore that could be considered within the bounds of reason was Palm Beach's three-dimples procedure, which, as we know from Chapter 2, was unlikely to carry Gore over the top. By reversing Sauls and ruling that the decisions of the canvassing boards on whether to conduct hand recounts were entitled to no deference at all, the Florida supreme court ruled in effect that any doubts that might authorize a canvassing board to conduct a recount at the protest stage *compels* the court at the contest stage to order (in fact to conduct itself or under its supervision) a hand recount.

This ruling made the protest a meaningless preliminary to the contest and expanded, without any basis in the statute, the power of the courts relative to that of the officials—the members of the canvassing boards and the secretary of state—to whom the legislature had assigned the responsibility for the conduct of elections, including election recounts. And while the statute limits the canvassing boards to correcting errors in the vote tabulation, the opinion authorizes judges in contest cases to conduct recounts intended to rectify voter errors as well. Even though they lack staff and experience for counting and interpreting ballots (especially thousands or tens of thousands or millions of ballots), the courts become the primary vote tabulators, rather than the election officials. Hand recounts in close elections would become the rule rather than the exception. This is all upside down.[48]

---

48. As forcefully argued by Florida's chief justice in his dissenting opinion; *Gore v.*

Florida's election code does not, it is true, confine contests, as distinct from protests, to situations in which there has been an error in the vote tabulation. The grounds for a contest include fraud or other misconduct by an election official, bribery of voters or election officials, the counting of illegal votes, and the ineligibility of a candidate.[49] In a contest based on one of these grounds (each far more grave, by the way, than voter error), the court might owe no deference to the election officials, especially if the ground involved misconduct by those officials. But the only ground for Gore's contest was an alleged failure to count "legal votes." And in context that was merely a complaint about the canvassing boards' handling of spoiled ballots. The principles of administrative law required the contest court, as Judge Sauls ruled, to defer to the canvassing boards, as the experts in counting votes, unless their decisions were unreasonable. Given the problems involved in interpreting spoiled ballots, and the looming deadlines, the decisions of the Palm Beach and Miami-Dade boards had been reasonable.[50]

As well as upsetting the balance between court and agency, the Florida supreme court set the threshold for ordering a remedy (whether more recounting or even a new election) in a contest proceeding at an implausibly low level. No human or machine fault in the conduct of the election, and no external circumstances (such as a natural disaster) that might interfere with the conduct of the election or with the tabulation, had to be shown. It was enough that the election had been close and that a hand recount using unspecified criteria might recover enough undervotes to change the outcome.[51] Under this approach, successful contests—in the

---

Harris, 772 So. 2d at 1263–1265. See also Brief of the Florida House of Representatives and Florida Senate as Amici Curiae, Dec. 10, 2000, pp. 3–16, in *Bush v. Gore.*

49. Fla. Stat. § 102.168(3).

50. Cass Sunstein, an expert on administrative law and a strong critic of *Bush v. Gore* (as we shall see in the next chapter), opined that "it was quite reasonable" for Harris "to interpret Florida law as forbidding [her] to receive returns after November 14"; Cass R. Sunstein, "One Fine Mess," *New Republic,* Dec. 11, 2000, p. 15.

51. *Gore v. Harris,* 772 So. 2d at 1255.

sense of contests eventuating in judicial orders for selective or comprehensive hand recounts or even for revotes—would be the norm in close elections.

On November 21 the Florida supreme court had extinguished the secretary of state's discretion. On December 8 it extinguished the canvassing boards' discretion. The court said in effect: if the election is close and we think there were a lot of voter errors, we have carte blanche to order any mode of recount that strikes us as likely to recover a substantial number of the rejected votes.

Turning to remedy, the court ordered that the 215 votes that Gore had gained over Bush in the Palm Beach recount (or 176—the court left it to the trial court to decide which number was correct), plus the 168 that he had gained from the partial recount in Miami-Dade County, be added to his net certified total. The results of Broward County's recount, which had been completed within the extended deadline of November 26, had already yielded Gore a net gain of 582 votes. Other late recounts had netted Bush a few votes, but since his certified lead had already shrunk (mainly because of the Broward recount) to 537 votes,[52] the addition of the partial Palm Beach and Miami-Dade results reduced his lead to 154 votes if the higher figure for Palm Beach (215 rather than 176) was used, and to 193 if the lower figure was used. The court ordered a hand recount of all the remaining undervotes not only in Miami-Dade but throughout the state, estimated at 60,000.[53] No overvotes (estimated to total 110,000 statewide) were to be recounted, however.

---

52. This became, in the end, after the contest proceeding was dismissed by the Florida supreme court in the wake of the U.S. Supreme Court's decision of December 12, Bush's official popular vote margin.

53. This widely reported estimate of how many undervotes would have to be recounted is erroneous, as noted in Chapter 2. The 60,000 figure is an estimate (probably a slight underestimate) of the total number of undervoted ballots statewide. The number *remaining to be recounted* was far fewer, because the undervoted ballots in Broward, Palm Beach, and Volusia Counties had already been recounted by hand and no further recount of them was ordered. The reason, incidentally, that the 60,000 figure exceeds the 30,000 figure that I estimated in Chapter 2 to be the maximum number of machine errors statewide is that 30,000 is an estimate of the number of errors that a hand recount of undervotes would correct, that is, an estimate of the

The trial before Judge Sauls had made clear, if it was not already, that the hand recounts conducted in the wake of the 2000 election in Florida had been neither uniform nor reliable. What had been recounted were ballots that voters had failed to complete correctly, rather than correctly completed ballots that the tabulating machine had failed to count. There were Broward rules for determining the likely intent of the voter who had cast a spoiled ballot (which favored Gore unduly, as I explained in the preceding chapter), and there was a medley of different Palm Beach rules. (It was unclear what rules the Miami-Dade canvassing board had used in its aborted recount.) Palm Beach's three-dimples rule had emerged after the recount had begun; earlier iterations had been a "sunshine rule" (light must be visible through the chad hole) and a "no dimples" rule, the rule followed by the Palm Beach canvassing board in previous election recounts.[54] Yet while acknowledging that "practical difficulties may well end up controlling the outcome of the election"[55]—that is, might terminate the contest proceeding before its completion—the Florida supreme court gave Gore the votes he had gained in Miami-Dade County before the recount was interrupted, even though the precincts counted were unrepresentative. The stunning implication (probably unintended) was that if the recount could not be concluded because of shortness of time, and Gore was ahead in the recount when time ran out, he would be declared the winner of the election even if the disputed ballots in precincts likely to favor Bush had not yet been recounted. For the court had given Gore the votes he had received in Miami-Dade's partial recount even though the full recount might *never* be completed ("practical difficulties may well end up controlling the outcome of the election").

---

number of votes recoverable from the undervoted ballots. Many such ballots remain inscrutable even after the most imaginative inspection.

54. Trial Transcript at *91–104.

55. *Gore v. Harris*, 772 So. 2d at 1261 n. 21.

Without pretending that the hand recounts to date had used uniform or consistent criteria, the court nevertheless failed to prescribe uniform criteria for the statewide recount that it was ordering. It thus was ordering a recount that, as we saw in the previous chapter, would carry no assurance of even minimal accuracy. Critics of the U.S. Supreme Court's intervention in the election deadlock blame this on the Court, which they argue impaled the Florida court on the horns of a dilemma. If that court left "clear indication of the intent of the voter" undefined, it was inviting the equal protection challenge that in fact became the ground on which it was reversed; but if it defined the term, it would be violating Article II as interpreted in the U.S. Supreme Court's first opinion. The argument is unsound. There is a difference between changing the meaning of a statute and filling in empty spaces in the statute. The Florida election law did not specify what type of spoiled ballot might be read as containing a recoverable vote. Here then was a gap in the statute for a court applying normal principles of statutory interpretation to fill—or, better, for the secretary of state, in the exercise of her authority to interpret the statute, to fill, subject to judicial review for reasonableness. She was given no chance to do this. Unwilling to defer to her, the court could on its own have adopted a "no dimples" standard on the ground that since dimpled chads had never before been counted as votes in Florida, the adoption of that standard would ratify rather than alter existing understandings.

The court could also have justified the laying down of precise criteria for recounting by reference to the equal protection clause of the Fourteenth Amendment, the ground later embraced by seven Justices of the U.S. Supreme Court. To conform Florida election law to the requirements of federal constitutional law would not violate Article II. Although *McPherson v. Blacker* had described the power of the state legislatures over the appointment of electors as plenary, a later decision made clear that federal constitutional amendments limit that power.[56] This creates, it is true, a theoretical possibility that by invoking the constitutional jurisprudence of the U.S. Supreme Court concerning voting rights, the Florida supreme court (if nimble) could have reasoned that to save the constitutionality of the state election law it would have to interpret it to require the hand recounting of dimpled and other machine-rejected ballots. But given the vagaries of hand counting spoiled ballots, such reasoning would be untenable. There are limits to the extent to which a court can revise a statute even to save its constitutionality; the power to invalidate an unconstitutional statute is not the power to rewrite it.

An alternative explanation for why the Florida supreme court declined to specify a uniform standard to guide the hand recount that it was ordering is possible, though conjectural: the Broward standard was indefensible, yet if the court rejected it but at the same time included the results of the Broward recount in Gore's vote (as it was obviously minded to do), it would be accepting the results of a standard it had just rejected. Better to say nothing about the standard than to grasp that nettle—or so it may have seemed to the Florida court independently of the U.S. Supreme Court's decision of December 4.

Ordering only undervotes recounted was another indefensible ruling. Gore's gains in the Broward, Palm Beach, Miami-Dade, and Volusia recounts that had already been conducted—gains the court had credited to Gore's account—included recovered (perhaps mistakenly recovered) overvotes, though possibly only a few.[57] The Florida election code states that "if an elector marks more names than there are persons to be elected to an office or if it is impossible to determine the elector's choice, the elector's ballot shall not

---

56. *Williams v. Rhodes*, 393 U.S. 23 (1968). See Glennon, *When No Majority Rules*, at 27–30.

57. Todd J. Gillman, "Recount May Be Adding Up to Confusion," *Dallas Morning News* (3rd ed.), Nov. 11, 2000, p. 10A, confirmed by an e-mail message from Deanie Lowe of the Volusia County election office.

be counted for that office."[58] This is not a bar to recounting over-voted ballots, but rather a direction as to what to do with those ballots when there is a recount. As we saw in Chapter 2, if the chad for one candidate is cleanly punched through and the chad for his rival is slightly dislodged because the voter started to vote for the rival and then realized he was making a mistake, the machine might read the second dislodgement as a vote and void the ballot. Or if the voter both punched a candidate's chad and wrote the candidate's name in the space provided for write-in votes, the machine would automatically reject the ballot, even though the voter's intent in such a case is clear. Recall that Gore's team believed that this type of mistake, which a hand recount would cure, had cost him significant votes in at least one county. With an estimated 110,000 overvotes statewide and the election so close, even a tiny overvote recovery rate could prove decisive.

And so the court's refusal to order the overvotes recounted could not be justified, except possibly by the shortness of time;[59] and subject to the same qualification *all* votes in the four counties in which Gore had picked up additional votes from the hand recount should have been recounted, not just those the machine count had failed to award to one of the Presidential candidates. For some of the votes the machine awarded to a candidate may in fact have been unrecoverable overvotes, in which the voter had punched through the chads for two Presidential candidates but one of the chads had been left dangling and as a result the machine, which cannot be relied upon to count dangling chads as votes, had failed to invalidate the ballot, whereas a hand recounter would have invalidated it.

Yet even the bobtailed recount ordered by the court could not have been completed in time. The court treated the deadline for

---

58. Fla. Stat. § 101.5614(6).

59. Just sorting through the ballots to find the overvotes would probably have taken more time than was available if the recount was to be completed by December 12 or, at the latest, the eighteenth.

recounting the votes and certifying the results as December 12, the safe harbor deadline. No one familiar with judicial processes would believe there was any way in which tens of thousands of votes could be recounted by then, four days from the date of the decision, yet allow time for the contestants' lawyers to challenge, and a judge to review (and his rulings to be appealed and the appeal briefed and argued and decided), the counters' determinations of whether or not to count particular ballots as votes—especially when the counters would be using different criteria of what constituted a "legal vote." One is tempted to speculate that the Florida supreme court was either planning abbreviated judicial review of the recount or expecting the recount to fizzle and wanting to avoid the blame for that.

When time is of the essence, some curtailment of normal procedural rights is excusable. But the lack of time had been caused by the court itself, when in violation of the statute it had extended the deadline for the protest recounts to November 26 and as a result had caused the commencement of the contest proceeding to be postponed from November 15 to November 27. And curtailment and abrogation are not synonyms. I do not share Michael Klarman's preference for "a completed manual recount with uncompleted judicial challenges" over "a machine count that clearly missed thousands of ballots on which the voters' intention could be discerned."[60] That manual recount would have been both standardless and incomplete, and in the absence of judicial review wholly unreliable and in addition tainted with partisanship. Professor Klarman is well aware of the connection between statutory vagueness and political partisanship, remarking that "the genuine indeterminacy of Florida election law probably made it inevitable that the partisan preferences of the Florida court's Democratic jus-

---

60. Michael J. Klarman, "*Bush v. Gore* through the Lens of Constitutional History" (forthcoming in *California Law Review*).

tices would influence their statutory interpretations (in favor of Al Gore)."[61]

If one puts the December 8 opinion of the Florida supreme court side by side with the Florida election code and asks whether the former can be said to derive by a *reasonable* process of interpretation from the latter without (or for that matter with) the assistance of the "people power" provision of the Florida constitution, the answer is "no"—as Florida's chief justice, concluding that the majority had indeed violated Article II, argued in dissent.[62] The "Manner" of appointing Florida's electors prescribed in the majority opinion and in the court's earlier opinion of November 21 was not the manner that the Florida legislature had prescribed when it enacted the election code. The code could have provided that electors are to be picked by the state's supreme court after it knows and maybe does not like the outcome of the election, using a standard of the voter's unclear intent and the principles of natural law even when there is no reason to suppose that an infallible hand recount would reverse the result of the election. The code says nothing like that. The only explicit delegation of authority is to state and local election officials. There is an implicit delegation to the courts to interpret the election law when it is unclear, but what the Florida supreme court did with the statute was so freewheeling as to raise a serious question of conformity with Article II of the U.S. Constitution, which places the authority to determine the manner of appointment of a state's Presidential electors in the state's legislature.

The Florida statute is vague about the relief that the court can order in a contest proceeding. All the statute says on this score is that if the court finds that enough "legal votes" were rejected to "change or place in doubt the result of the election," it can "pro-

---

61. Ibid.
62. *Gore v. Harris*, 772 So. 2d at 1262 (dissenting opinion).

vide any relief appropriate under such circumstances." "Appropriate" is not defined; it has been left to the courts to work out on a case-by-case basis. But even a term as vague as "appropriate" does not give a court carte blanche. If no reasonable person could consider the relief ordered by the Florida supreme court on December 8 appropriate, then once again the court had violated the statute rather than interpreted it reasonably.

Bush v. Gore (December 12): The Holding

When the dispute returned to the U.S. Supreme Court, a majority of seven Justices decided that the recount decreed by the Florida court was indeed unconstitutional. But the ground was not that Article II of the Constitution had been violated; it was that such a recount would deny Florida voters the equal protection of the laws, in violation of the Fourteenth Amendment, because the absence of a precise standard to guide the recounters would inevitably result in different voters' votes being weighted differently. This is not a persuasive ground. The conduct of elections, including federal elections, has been confided to local government—to counties and indeed, to a considerable extent, to precincts. Different counties in the same state often use different equipment, methods, ballots, and instructions, generating different sources and rates of error. Ballots often are counted differently in different precincts, and, what is perhaps more important (as we saw in the preceding chapter), differently when they are counted at the county level rather than at the precinct level. Such differences had not previously been thought to deny equal protection of the laws. If they are now to do so, this portends an ambitious program of federal judicial intervention in the electoral process—a program the Supreme Court seems, given the haste with which it acted, to have undertaken without much forethought about the program's scope and administrability.

The concept of entitlement that underlies the equal protection ground can also be questioned. If my dimple was not counted in the original election and yours was, what exactly is my complaint? Neither dimple should have been counted; both of us disobeyed the voting instructions. For me to complain that the other malefactor (to put it too dramatically) was not punished as I was is like complaining about selective prosecution; and unless based on invidious grounds, selective prosecution is not a denial of equal protection.[63] The differences that influenced the vote count in Florida were not deliberate or invidious; they were the accidents of long-established—if careless and chintzy and ramshackle, even thoughtless and insensitive—local voting practices. An irrational distinction in the government's treatment of different voters could be a denial of equal protection of the laws even if the distinction was not invidious in the sense of being motivated by race, religion, or other forbidden criteria for treating people differently.[64] But it would have to be deliberate,[65] and it was not. An innocent law that just happens to have an unequal impact is not actionable as a denial of equal protection.[66]

Or if I was a good boy and punched my chad clean through, and you only dimpled your chad, what is my complaint if your dimple is counted as a vote, when, if the county had used a superior voting technology from the standpoint of minimizing rejections or even had counted votes at the precinct level rather than at the county level, you would have had no difficulty casting a clearly legal vote? To the extent that the inclusion of the Broward recount totals in Gore's vote could be thought a partisan act akin to vote fraud, the equal protection argument is stronger. But if all the

---

63. *Wayte v. United States*, 470 U.S. 598 (1985).

64. *Village of Willowbrook v. Olech*, 120 S. Ct. 1073 (2000) (per curiam); *Hilton v. City of Wheeling*, 209 F.3d 1005, 1007–1008 (7th Cir. 2000).

65. And maybe even vindictive, as held in the *Hilton* case 209 F.3d at 1008. See also *Willowbrook v. Olech* 120 S. Ct. at 1075 (concurring opinion).

66. *Personnel Administrator v. Feeney*, 442 U.S. 256 (1979).

recounts were conducted by neutrals, the lack of standards to guide the counters, while anarchic, would not be invidious. On this theory, the main and maybe the only thing wrong, from the standpoint of equal protection, with the Florida supreme court's opinion of December 8 was the inclusion of the Broward County recount results.

A better Fourteenth Amendment argument is that an irrational method of determining the outcome of an election is a denial of due process of law.[67] The Florida supreme court's refusal to establish a precise standard to guide the recounters—at the same time that it accepted both the Broward and the Palm Beach recount results, though they had been based on inconsistent methodologies—ensured that there would be arbitrary gross differences across counties in whether ballots were counted as votes. These differences, moreover, might be due to the varying political sympathies of the different counters, in which event the merely arbitrary would become invidious. One can argue, indeed, that such differences would be *bound* to be due to varying political sympathies. Discerning intent is something we do all the time, of course. But usually we have a lot more evidence from which to infer intent than a piece of paper with scratches on it. If two counters look at the same dimpled chad, and one infers an intent to vote and the other does not—a difference the Democrats conceded was possible, even likely, in the recount decreed by the Florida supreme court— what is a more plausible explanation for the difference than that one counter wanted the candidate whose chad was scratched to win and the other did not? This approach to recovering votes turns the concept of the "double blind" experiment on its head, and is condemned by the judicial decisions that condemn vague criteria for the grant or denial of a permit for a march or other demonstration on the ground that the vagueness creates a serious

---

67. As held in *Roe v. Alabama*, 43 F.3d 574, 580–581 (11th Cir. 1995), and *Griffin v. Burns*, 570 F.2d 1065 (1st Cir. 1978).

risk that forbidden political motives will influence the decision on the application for the permit.[68]

Maybe, then, the differences in the treatment of otherwise identically situated voters that the Florida supreme court's order brought about can fairly be described as irrational, even invidious, or at least potentially invidious (for on this theory the only violation of due process or equal protection that had already occurred was the addition of the Broward County recount results to Gore's vote totals). Maybe future cases will read *Bush v. Gore* as standing for little more than that. Yet even that would not be an inconsequential doctrinal step: the creation of a federal duty to use uniform *precise* criteria in a recount in order to avoid arbitrary differences, possibly if unprovably of a partisan political hue, in the treatment of voters. The statutory criterion of "clear indication of the intent of the voter,"[69] which the Florida supreme court refused to elaborate, is uniform as stated. It just is too vague to ensure uniformity of application. Its vagueness creates a risk of political abuse. But since precise rules for the recovery of votes from spoiled ballots are almost certain to recover fewer votes than a vague standard, the interest in preventing arbitrary differences in treatment ought, before it is decided that the differences are unconstitutional, to be weighed against the interest in enabling every voter to cast a vote that counts.

Moreover, to establish a violation of the due process clause requires more than proof of a denial of due process; it is only the deprivation of life, liberty, or property without due process of law that the clause forbids. There is no difficulty in classifying the right to vote—about which the Supreme Court has said that "no right is

---

68. For example, *Baggett v. Bullitt,* 377 U.S. 360, 372 (1964); *Edwards v. South Carolina,* 372 U.S. 229, 236 (1963).

69. This is actually, as I noted earlier, the standard for recovering a vote from a damaged or defective ballot, as distinct from a ballot spoiled by the voter. If votes are to be recovered from spoiled ballots, presumably no more lax a standard would be appropriate.

more precious in a free country than that of having a voice in the election of those who make the laws under which, as good citizens, we must live"[70]—as an aspect of the "liberty" that the Fourteenth Amendment protects against deprivation without due process of law. But in what sense is recounting votes under inconsistent standards, even within a single county, a deprivation of the right to vote? This question returns us to the infirmities of the equal protection argument. In what sense am I denied my right to vote when another voter's spoiled ballot is counted but my spoiled ballot is not, or when that other voter's ballot is counted along with my perfect one, though his would not have been spoiled had his county used a better voting technology?

Bush v. Gore: The Remedy and the "What Ifs"

Having found that the Florida supreme court had acted unconstitutionally, the Court had next to decide on the remedy. Five Justices (Rehnquist, O'Connor, Scalia, Kennedy, and Thomas) held that because the Florida court had indicated repeatedly that Florida's legislature would have wanted the state to enjoy the advantage of the safe harbor for electors appointed no later than December 12, that was the deadline and so no further recount was permissible under Florida law.[71] The Florida supreme court had hinted broadly that it indeed regarded December 12 as the deadline for the recount.[72] "Hinted broadly" may be too weak; the court said that the secretary of state can ignore late-submitted county vote totals if waiting for them would "result in Florida voters not participating fully in the federal electoral process, as provided in

---

70. *Reynolds v. Sims,* 377 U.S. 533, 560 (1964).

71. In accordance with this ruling, the Florida supreme court dismissed Gore's suit; *Gore v. Harris,* 773 So. 2d 524 (Fla. 2000) (per curiam).

72. For example, *Gore v. Harris,* 772 So. 2d at 1261–1262 and nn. 21–22; ibid. at 1268 (dissenting opinion); *Palm Beach County Canvassing Board v. Harris,* 772 So. 2d 1273, 1281–1282, 1289–1291 (Fla. 2000) (per curiam).

3 U.S.C. § 5"[73]—the safe harbor provision. David Boies, in his oral argument to the Florida supreme court in *Palm Beach County Canvassing Board v. Harris,* which led that court to extend the deadline for the counties to submit their vote totals to the secretary of state to November 26, had repeatedly described December 12 as the deadline.

The Court in *Bush v. Gore* might have said that no further recount was feasible given the Florida legislature's undoubted desire that Florida have a slate of electors in the Electoral College— a desire that, as we shall see, could not as a practical matter have been realized by December 18, the date prescribed by federal law for the electors to vote.[74] Whether electoral votes that are cast later can be or must be counted is unclear, as we are about to see. It would be up to Congress, the electoral vote counter, to decide in the first instance whether to count them, and it might decide to count instead the votes cast by a rival slate appointed by the Florida legislature. A section of Title III first enacted in 1845 provides that if the state fails to make a choice for electors on the day prescribed by law ("election day," November 7, 2000), the legislature can appoint them later.[75] Failing to make a choice and uncertainty about what choice has been made are not the same thing; the outcome of a close election is often not known on election day.[76] But at some point continued uncertainty about the outcome of the November 7 election might be deemed a failure to have chosen electors on that day, in which event the Florida legislature could select its own slate, which, given the composition of the legislature, would have been a slate pledged to Bush.

We have entered the domain of "what ifs." Because the Supreme Court halted the recount for good on December 12, we do

---

73. Ibid. at 1289.
74. 3 U.S.C. § 7.
75. Act of 1845, 5 Stat. 721, 3 U.S.C. § 2.
76. See Richard D. Friedman, "Trying to Make Peace with *Bush v. Gore*" 4 (Michigan Law School, April 2001).

not know what would have ensued had the Court allowed it to resume. We know only what *could* have ensued—and what could have ensued is fairly described as chaos, providing a practical argument in defense of the Court's remedy.[77]

One possibility, if Florida missed the safe harbor, is, we have just seen, that the Florida legislature would select its own slate of Presidential electors. The state supreme court might invalidate the selection, however, on the ground that electors had been appointed on November 7—only no one yet knew which electors. Congress might therefore be faced with rival slates of electors in January, one selected by the legislature and another deemed authentic by the state supreme court. The choice between them would be up to Congress because Florida would have missed the safe harbor.

Another possibility, however, if Florida missed the safe harbor, is that Congress might decide to count *no* electoral votes from Florida. Such a decision would raise the unresolved question of whether "a majority of the whole number of Electors appointed" in the Twelfth Amendment means a majority of the electoral votes counted or an absolute majority of electoral votes. (Florida would have appointed electors—in fact two sets of them!) If the former meaning were adopted and Florida's electoral votes were not counted because they were cast after December 18, Gore would be the President-elect. But if the latter meaning were adopted, then no candidate would have an Electoral College majority and so the House of Representatives would pick the President-elect, and Bush would win, because a majority of the state delegations to the House of Representatives are dominated by Republicans. Congress would have to decide the interpretive issue, but an effort might be made to appeal its decision to the Supreme Court. The interpretation that the Twelfth Amendment requires an absolute majority of elec-

---

77. As acknowledged by one of the academic critics of *Bush v. Gore.* See Cass R. Sunstein, "Order without Law," in *The Vote.*

toral votes seems to me preferable, for imagine a disaster that prevented all but 10 of the electors from casting their votes on December 18: could 6 of the 10 elect the President?

Title III provides that if a state's electoral votes are not received in Washington by the fourth Wednesday in December (December 27, in 2000), inquiry is to be made of the state. This might seem to imply that electoral votes can be cast after December 18 and so we would not have to worry too much if Florida were unable to get its act together by then. But the relevant provision is captioned "Failure of certificates of electors to *reach* President of the Senate or Archivist of the United States."[78] That is a failure of delivery, not a failure to vote. The electors cast their votes in their home states and mail the results to Washington, rather than going to Washington to vote. The provision in question dates back to 1887, when transcontinental mail service was not fully dependable.

If read to permit electoral votes to be cast after December 18, Title III may well violate Article II, section 1, clause 4 of the Constitution, which provides that the day on which the electors vote "shall be the same throughout the United States." December 18 was Electoral College election day in 2000.[79] A voter who does not vote on election day loses his right to vote in the election. It is true that in 1960 Hawaii, as the result of a recount, appointed its electors after the statutory deadline yet its votes were still counted. But as they had no effect on the outcome of the election, there was no

---

78. 3 U.S.C. § 12 (emphasis added).

79. Each state must appoint its electors on the first Tuesday after the first Monday in November of the fourth year following a Presidential election (3 U.S.C. § 1)—in other words, on "election day" in the popular sense (November 7, 2000, for example). The constitutional basis for this provision is Article II, section 1, clause 4. See *Foster v. Love,* 522 U.S. 67, 69–70 (1997). But to infer that the only temporal uniformity required is in the appointment of the electors would be an error. Clause 4 reads in its entirety: "The Congress may determine the Time of chusing the Electors, and the Day on which they shall give their Votes; which Day shall be the same throughout the United States." Section 1 of Title III derives from the "Time of chusing the Electors" provision. The same-day requirement applies to the casting of the electoral votes by the electors, not to the appointment of the electors. William Josephson and Beverly J. Ross, "Repairing the Electoral College," 22 *Journal of Legislation* 145, 168–169 (1996).

reason to make an issue of the state's tardiness. Critics of *Bush v. Gore* who cite the Hawaii "precedent" as a reason for thinking there was no urgency about resolving the election deadlock overlook the statement by then Vice President Nixon, presiding over the counting of the electoral votes, that "in order not to delay the further count of the electoral vote here, the Chair, *without the intent of establishing a precedent,* suggests that the electors named in the certificate of the Governor of Hawaii dated January 4, 1961, be considered as the lawful electors from the State of Hawaii."[80]

So December 18, 2000, may have been the final deadline after all for Florida to pick its Presidential electors. A responsible recount could not have been concluded by then. We must imagine the U.S. Supreme Court on December 12 ordering the Florida supreme court to conduct the recount in a manner soberly designed, in conformity with Florida's election law, to identify ballots containing a clear indication of the voter's intent. The court would have required several days to establish criteria. Would they be Broward rules? Palm Beach rules? Which Palm Beach rules? The court would have had to ask for briefs on the question, the parties having been notably unhelpful with respect to the recount criteria—the Democrats because they were avid for Broward rules (without which Gore would be unlikely to overtake Bush) yet reluctant to make an issue of so questionable a standard, and the Republicans because they were adamant against any form of hand recount.

Had criteria for the recount been adopted by December 15 and the recount restarted that day and completed the next, only two days before December 18 would have remained for the courts to evaluate what would undoubtedly have been hundreds, maybe thousands, of challenges to the decisions of particular counters. *All* 60,000 undervoted ballots would have had to be recounted, since the previous hand recounts of some of them had used varying

---

80. *Deschler's Precedents of the United States House of Representatives,* vol. 3, ch. 10, § 3.5 (Lewis Deschler ed. 1979) (emphasis added). See also ibid. §§ 1.1, 1.2.

standards. (Maybe overvoted ballots too, since their exclusion from the recount ordered by the Florida supreme court had been arbitrary.) The counting itself was to be done at the county level, with judicial review of all the recount results by Judge Terry Lewis in Tallahassee, doubtless followed by appellate review by the Florida supreme court and perhaps the U.S. Supreme Court. The process could not have been completed in three days! Think only of the time required for packing, shipping, and unpacking challenged ballots from distant parts of the state. The U.S. Supreme Court, an abler group of judges than the Florida supreme court and with better staff support, was under such time pressure that the opinions the Court issued concerning the Florida deadlock have not satisfied even those commentators who agree with the decisions.

Even if the recount had been completed and new totals certified by December 18 without concern for the niceties of judicial review and due process of law, the infirmity of the process would have ensured a rancorous struggle in Congress when a Gore slate (assuming the recount resulted in the Florida supreme court's ordering the secretary of state to certify Gore's slate) was challenged. Florida's legislature would by then have appointed a Bush slate. Congress was required by federal law to meet to count the electoral votes on January 6.[81] Its choice of whose slate to accept if there were competing slates (or what to do if it rejected both slates) might have led to further proceedings in the Supreme Court, though this might depend on the "political questions" doctrine, consideration of which I postpone to the next chapter.

Had the wrangle in Congress dragged on for two weeks,[82] the Speaker of the House, Dennis Hastert, or, if the Speaker refused to

---

81. 3 U.S.C. § 15.

82. As it could have; although 3 U.S.C. § 17 sets a tight limit on debates over objections to electors, who could enforce it against the Congress? Section 20 in fact envisages indefinite delays, by prohibiting recesses after January 11; and protracted sessions without recesses could give rise to quorum problems. See Gary C. Leedes, "The Presidential Election Case: Remembering Safe Harbor Day," 35 *University of Richmond Law Review* 237, 257, and n. 105 (2001).

resign from the House, the President pro Tempore of the Senate (with the same qualification), 98-year-old Strom Thurmond, would have become acting President on January 20, serving until the winner of the 2000 Presidential election was somehow determined. Next in line, if Hastert and Thurmond both refused the crown, would be the Secretary of State, followed by the Secretary of the Treasury. But the Secretary of State, Madeleine Albright, being foreign-born, was not eligible for the Presidency; and so Lawrence Summers would have become the acting President if, the election still unresolved on January 20, Hastert and Thurmond passed.[83] Hastert would surely have passed, rather than give up both the speakership and his seat in Congress. Thurmond no doubt would have passed too, less because of his age or his desire to remain a Senator (in light of his age, he cannot expect to remain a Senator very much longer) than because if he resigned, control of the Senate would pass to the Democrats. With Thurmond, the Senate was split 50–50, and the governor of South Carolina, who would have appointed Thurmond's successor, is a Democrat. So Summers would have become acting President, for some undetermined time. Eventually, with the nation's patience completely exhausted, either Bush or Gore—probably Bush—would have been elected by the House of Representatives. The new President would have started behind the eight ball, with an irregular and disputed accession, an abbreviated term of office, and no transition.

Now it is true that the path which leads to Summers as acting President would have been open only if, the Presidency having become vacant on January 20, the Senate had not picked a Vice President-elect by then. Section 3 of the Twentieth Amendment provides that if there is no President-elect when the current Presi-

---

83. 3 U.S.C. §§ 19(a), (b), (d). It is not, however, altogether certain that Madeleine Albright, by virtue of being ineligible to be President, could not have become acting President. The Twentieth Amendment speaks of *acting* as the President rather than *being* the President, and maybe one can act as President without being eligible to be President.

dent's term expires, the Vice President–elect shall become acting President. Only if there is not yet a Vice President–elect do the succession provisions of Title III come into play, as expressly authorized by section 3 of the Twentieth Amendment. The procedure for choosing a Vice President–elect is set forth in the Twelfth Amendment, which provides for his election by the Senate if the absence of an Electoral College majority throws the election of the President-elect into the House. With the Senate split down the middle, this was not a promising route to the selection of an acting President. Although the Vice President can vote to break a tie in a Senate vote, the Twelfth Amendment provides that a majority of "the whole number of Senators . . . shall be necessary for a choice" of the Vice President–elect, and the Vice President is not a Senator. So the Senate could not have elected a Vice President who would have become acting President on January 20, and so the path that could lead to Summers as acting President was indeed open.

Lawrence Summers is Jewish,[84] and had he become acting President it would have meant that our first Jewish President had not been nominated by any party for the Presidency or the Vice Presidency. A delicious irony to some (though to semitophobes merely further evidence of Jewish deviousness), it well illustrates the bizarre potential of the election standoff, had the Supreme Court not stepped in.

The outcome of the Presidential election of November 8, 1876, was not determined until March 2, 1877, four months later and only two days before the inauguration.[85] Since then the inauguration has been moved up to January, so had it taken four months to resolve the 2000 Presidential election we would have had an acting President for six weeks. It could be, of course, that the Hayes-Tilden

---

84. For that matter, Madeleine Albright's parents were Jewish, which would make her Jewish under some definitions (Hitler's for example), though she is a Christian.

85. Paul Leland Haworth, *The Hayes-Tilden Disputed Presidential Election of 1876* 280–281 (1966).

dispute was resolved *because* only two days remained to Inauguration Day, and that, with that day now moved up by almost six weeks, Congress would have resolved a Bush-Gore dispute by January 18. But who knows? How many people thought the Clinton-Lewinsky imbroglio would go all the way to a trial in the Senate a year after the scandal first broke?

The dispute over the 1876 election was resolved by an ad hoc commission appointed by Congress, because the Constitution is silent on disputes over the legality of electors; all it says to the point is that the electoral votes shall be counted in the presence of both houses of Congress.[86] The Electoral Count Act, now Title III, was passed eleven years after the Hayes-Tilden election in an effort to head off a future such dispute. But it is unclear whether it would have been of any use in resolving the dispute arising from the 2000 election deadlock. Title III provides that Congress shall resolve such disputes, but it also—and for present purposes unhelpfully—provides that if the Senate and the House of Representatives fail to agree on which electoral votes to count, "the votes of the electors whose appointment shall have been certified by the executive of the State, under the seal thereof, shall be counted."[87] A deadlock of houses was likely with respect to the 2000 election, since the House of Representatives in the Congress that met on January 6 was controlled by the Republicans, and the Senate in effect by the Democrats because Vice President Gore presided over the Senate until January 20 and thus would cast votes to break ties. If, with the houses deadlocked, Florida's governor ("the executive of the State") had certified the Bush slate but the Florida supreme court had declared his certification a nullity and ordered him to certify the Gore slate, and he refused, which

---

86. U.S. Const. art. II, § 1, cl. 3. This clause in the original Constitution was superseded by the Twelfth Amendment, adopted in 1804, but the language about the counting of electoral votes was not altered.

87. 3 U.S.C. § 15.

slate would be the legitimate one? Title III is silent on this as on other critical issues.[88]

To try to head off a collision between court and governor, the Florida legislature might between the election and January 6 have passed a statute withdrawing judicial jurisdiction over the appointment of the state's Presidential electors. But the legislature might not think of this way of sealing a Bush slate and so averting a congressional donnybrook. Anyway the Florida supreme court might invalidate such a statute, perhaps by appeal once again to the Rousseauan "people power" provision of the state constitution. And even if such a statute survived challenge, the circumstances that would make George W. Bush the President under this scenario —circumstances that would include the fact that the governor of Florida was the brother of Presidential candidate Bush and that Gore would by hypothesis have prevailed in the popular vote in Florida as well as nationally—would have poisoned Bush's tenure as President from the beginning, in much the same way that Congress's selection of Adams over Jackson in 1824 poisoned Adams's Presidency and the selection of Hayes over Tilden in 1876 poisoned Hayes's Presidency. In both instances there were charges of a "corrupt deal" that had given the wrong man the office (a promise to make Henry Clay, the Speaker of the House, secretary of state, in the first case, and a promise to end Reconstruction, in the second[89]), and we could have expected similar charges had Bush wrested the Presidency from Gore in Congress.

There are also the unresolved doubts about the constitutionality of Title III to be reckoned with, specifically but not only about

---

88. Well before the 2000 election, the procedure in 3 U.S.C. § 15 for resolving disputes over the election of a President had been described as "a constitutional minefield"; Glennon, *When No Majority Rules,* at 36. For a detailed exegesis of the maddeningly complex Electoral Count Act, see Josephson and Ross, "Repairing the Electoral College," at 158–184.

89. Glennon, *When No Majority Rules,* at 15–16 (1824 election); "The Electoral Commission [Hayes-Tilden Election]," *Great Debates in American History,* vol. 9, ch. 3 (Marian Mills Miller ed. 1970) (1876 election).

whether Congress can authorize electoral votes to be counted that were cast after Electoral College election day, December 18, when Article II decrees that that election day "shall be the same throughout the United States." The broader question is how far Congress can go in regulating Presidential elections. A prohibition against bribery in such elections was upheld against constitutional challenge in *Burroughs v. United States,* but the Court pointed out that the legislation did not "interfere with the power of a state to appoint electors or the manner in which their appointment shall be made."[90] Imagine on the other side of possibility the legitimacy of a Gore Presidency secured by Gore's own vote as presiding officer of the Senate or by the counting of dimpled ballots ("President Dimples") under the supervision of a partisan state supreme court that had flouted the state's election code and against a preelection background of hints and more than hints of corruption, immorality, unscrupulous campaign tactics, and recourse to lawyers' trickery by the Clinton-Gore administration.

Consideration of the practical consequences of continued recounting, the confused yet not implausible scenarios just sketched, is notable by its absence from the opinions of the dissenting Justices in *Bush v. Gore.* They seemed content to leave the matter to be resolved by Congress in January—or later, for that matter—by allowing the recount to continue past the twelfth, or for that matter past the eighteenth. They thought that the democratic way. That is not the usual line that liberal judges take when asked to decide a constitutional question. Judicial liberalism has long signified a distrust of democratic processes. The expansion of constitutional rights brought about by the Supreme Court in a series of adventurous decisions during the chief justiceships of Earl Warren and Warren Burger involved for the most part rights

---

90. 290 U.S. 534, 544–547 (1934). See also U.S. General Accounting Office, "Elections: The Scope of Congressional Authority in Election Administration" 7–9 (Report to Congress, GAO-01-470, March 2001).

against legislatures, the legislatures of the states but also Congress. The democratic character of Congress was not a trump. And one thing we know for certain about the deliberations at the constitutional convention of 1787 is that the framers did not want Congress to pick the President, though it did want the House of Representatives to do so in the event that no candidate had a majority of the lawfully cast electoral votes. And I shall argue in the next chapter that in any case *Bush v. Gore* did *not* prevent Congress from resolving the dispute over Florida's electoral votes in any way that Congress in January might have seen fit to do. This is part of the answer to the criticism of *Bush v. Gore* that the framers of the Constitution did not want the courts to pick the President either, and another part is that the Court was not picking the President but was merely enforcing the Constitution—and still another that for the Florida supreme court to pick the President of the United States is even weirder than for the U.S. Supreme Court to do so.

Had the responsibility for determining who would be President fallen to Congress in January, there would have been a competition in indignation between the parties' supporters, with each side accusing the other of having stolen the election. Whatever Congress did would have been regarded as the product of raw politics, with no tincture of justice. The new President would have been deprived of a transition period in which to organize his administration and would have taken office against a background of unprecedented bitterness. (Even the relatively brief delay in resolving the election deadlock delayed the formation of Bush's administration.)[91] His "victory" would have been an empty one; he could not have governed effectively. The scenario that produces this dismal result is conjectural. But that there was a real and disturbing *potential* for disorder and temporary paralysis (I do not want to exaggerate) seems undeniable. That is why the Supreme Court's

91. Jim VandeHei and Laurie McGinley, "Bush Team Falls behind Schedule in Its Nominations," *Wall Street Journal,* March 22, 2001, p. A24.

decision was greeted with relief by many people, not all of them Republicans.

Not that the decision dispelled all bitterness. Blacks and white liberals will not soon forgive the Supreme Court for dashing Gore's hopes. But the bitterness that lingers may be slight compared with what it would have been had the election outcome not been resolved until January, or later, by unruly congressional process with possibly frequent recourse to the courts. Justice Breyer's claim that "the legislative history of the [Electoral Count] Act makes clear its intent to commit the power to resolve such disputes to Congress, rather than the courts,"[92] while an accurate para-phrase,[93] cannot be taken to mean that the Act actually withdrew jurisdiction over electoral count disputes from the federal courts; nothing in the Act itself purports to do such a thing. The Supreme Court might very well have invoked the political questions doc-trine and refused to intervene in a January dispute in Congress (see the next chapter), leaving it a free-for-all. But then again it might not have. And then what? Think only of the bitter struggle over the deadlocked 1984 election for Representative from the Eighth Congressional District of Indiana. "Four months of partisan wran-gling . . . that took up more time than almost any other issue the House considered in 1985 . . . left a bitter legacy which has not yet [as of 1990] dissipated."[94] That might have turned out to be a por-tent, in miniature, of what would have happened had the Supreme Court not intervened to break the 2000 election deadlock. Because the deadlock was broken by that intervention after five weeks rather than three months, and because the American public has a short attention span and no historical memory, the wounds opened by the deadlock closed quickly for most people outside the

92. 121 S. Ct. at 555 (dissenting opinion).
93. Of H.R. Rep. No. 1638, 49th Cong., 1st Sess. 2 (1886).
94. Marie Garber and Abe Frank, *Contested Elections and Recounts*, vol. 1: *Issues and Options in Resolving Disputed Federal Elections* 14–16 (Federal Election Commission, National Clearinghouse on Election Administration, Autumn 1990).

political class. The longer the deadlock had persisted, the deeper and longer lasting the wounds would have been.

Another problem with Justice Breyer's suggestion to commit "the power to resolve such disputes to Congress, rather than the courts" is that Congress is not a competent forum for resolving such disputes. Legislatures resolve conflicts and clashes all the time, of course; that is what the legislative process is mainly about. But disputes over the lawfulness of competing slates of Presidential electors call for legal-type judgments rather than for raw exercises of political power. Title III is a statute, indeed a difficult and intricate one, and unless Congress simply jettisoned it, congressional resolution of a dispute over electors would be a process of statutory (and constitutional) interpretation and application, the sort of thing that courts are equipped to do but Congress most emphatically not. We learned recently that the elaborate constitutional provisions governing the impeachment and trial of a President—provisions that assign a judicial role to Congress—do not work very well because legislatures are not courts and legislators are not judges. But at least those provisions divide responsibilities between the House and the Senate, establishing an orderly sequence of indictment and trial and eschewing a tight deadline. The Twelfth Amendment and Title III do not. A hurry-up congressional trial of Bush Florida electors versus Gore Florida electors in January 2001 would have been a travesty of dispute resolution.

The dissenters in *Bush v. Gore* may have had a simpler and sunnier expectation than that Congress would resolve the deadlock. They may have thought that remanding the case to the Florida supreme court on December 12 for the continuation of the recount *if that court wished* would have had the same effect as terminating the recount, because the Florida court would quickly have realized that there was not enough time to establish a precise, uniform standard for the recount in order to comply with the Supreme Court's ruling on equal protection, conduct the recount, and still preserve a reasonable opportunity for judicial review. But there would have been three dangers in relying on the Florida court to take the hint. First, it might not have done so, having already turned down the opportunity to end the agony when it reviewed Judge Sauls's decision. It might have endeavored to rush the process through to completion, somehow, by December 18, or even let it continue past that date. It might even, by analogy to what it had done with the partial recount results in Miami-Dade County, have certified a winner on the basis of an incomplete statewide recount of the undervotes.

Second, the Florida court might have terminated the contest proceeding after the recount but before the completion of judicial review. Had the unreviewed recount shown Gore ahead, it would have done substantial and unjustified political harm to Bush. He would have had no opportunity to challenge the result of the recount, however meritorious the basis of his challenge might have been; the case would have become moot. One suspects that by December 12, even before the Supreme Court's decision, most Democratic activists had lost hope that Gore would be President, and their objective had become to cast enough doubt on the legitimacy of Bush's election to undermine his Presidency and weaken the Republican Party.

Third, the U.S. Supreme Court would have lost the credit it earned from the general public for having brought the election deadlock to a prompt and welcome end. It might instead have been accused of playing cat and mouse with the Florida supreme court— remanding, a second time, for a process that it knew to be futile.

Dissenters have the luxury of not having to bear any responsibility for the consequences of the position they are advocating. Their position, having been rejected, has no consequences. The dissenting Justices in *Bush v. Gore* could be casual about the likely consequences of allowing the recount to go forward, because they knew it was not going to go forward. I worry about those consequences. I do not see what the point would have been of risking precipitating a political and constitutional crisis merely in order to fuss with a statistical tie that—given the inherent subjectivity involved in hand counting spoiled ballots—can never be untied.

Was There an Injustice?

I have not finished with my evaluation of the Supreme Court's decision in *Bush v. Gore;* it is continued in the next chapter. Thus far all I have tried to show is that the Florida supreme court acted unreasonably and that the U.S. Supreme Court did not—which is not the same thing as saying that the Court's decision was correct. That is a close question, perhaps unanswerable, and so the possibility that the Court's critics are right and the Court lacked adequate grounds for halting the recount ordered by the Florida supreme court cannot be gainsaid. It is natural to think that, if so, an injustice was done. That is not clear. To begin with, even with Bush's lead whittled down to as few as 154 votes by the Florida supreme court's decision of December 8, it is unclear whether Gore would have prevailed in the recount ordered by that court. It is true that all he needed was to pick up one more than that number of votes from the 9,000 not yet recounted in Miami-Dade County, assuming the other undervotes statewide that had not yet been recounted would have split evenly, as they might well have done, for Bush had won a substantial majority of the votes outside the four counties in which Gore had filed a protest. We do not know what rule the Miami-Dade canvassing board would have used had it resumed recounting. But it is unlikely that it would have used one particularly favorable to Gore, for had it been that well disposed toward him it would not have abandoned the hand recount before the November 26 deadline. Recall from Chapter 2 that if Palm Beach's three-dimples rule had been used to guide the recount of the 10,750 disputed ballots in Miami-Dade County,

Gore probably would not have picked up more than 225 additional votes—only 57 votes more than the 168-vote gain that the Florida supreme court had already given him in its December 8 opinion. Had he gained only 57 more votes in the recount ordered in that opinion, Bush would still have won the election.

Still, Gore *might* have prevailed in the recount—but only by virtue of the Florida supreme court's having butchered the state's election statute. Whether that court misinterpreted the state's election law, and whether the U.S. Supreme Court should have intervened to correct the interpretation, are separate questions; and the answer to the first question is simpler than the answer to the second. The Florida supreme court did misinterpret the Florida election code. Indeed, the court's decisions of November 21 and December 8 made a hash of it. Maybe the U.S. Supreme Court should have kept its nose out of the dispute, either as a matter of prudence or because a substantial basis for the Court's intervening was wanting. But the fact that a decision may be immunized from further review does not make it correct. Abstention by the federal judiciary would not have erased the fact that the Florida supreme court had erred grievously in interpreting the state's election code. That court should not have extended the deadline for hand recounting that had been fixed by the secretary of state, or interpreted "error in the vote tabulation" to include a voter's error in voting, or reversed Judge Sauls's dismissal of the contest proceeding, or ignored the discretionary authority that the election code gives state and local election officials, or authorized relief in a contest proceeding on the basis merely that the election was close and there were a number of undervotes, or credited Gore with the Broward and the partial Miami-Dade recount results, or ordered a statewide recount of undervotes but not overvotes, or condoned inconsistent and subjective criteria in hand recounting. In all these respects it was flouting the state's election code. Had Gore been declared the winner on the basis of the recount ordered by the Florida court on December 8, he would have owed his victory to legal error (whether or not legal error that the U.S. Supreme Court should have corrected). What the Court wrought was, at the least, a kind of rough justice; it may have been legal justice as well.

Chapter 4

Critiquing the Participants

THE ARMCHAIR generals have been busy criticizing the participants in the deadlock drama, notably the judges (especially the Justices of the Supreme Court) who decided the cases discussed in the preceding chapter, and the lawyers for the parties to those cases. These criticisms seem to me largely misplaced. The participants most deserving of criticism, though as yet largely spared it, are the law professors who offered public comments on the unfolding drama.

The Judges

As we saw in the previous chapter, the Supreme Court took the pragmatic route in *Bush v. Gore,* cut the Gordian knot, and let Bush get on with the transition and with governing. But there can be such a thing as an excess of pragmatism. The remedy decreed by the five-Justice majority, cutting off the recount on the ground that Florida law made December 12 the outside deadline, has a "Gotcha!" flavor, as if the U.S. Supreme Court had outsmarted the

Florida supreme court by nailing that court with its perhaps unconsidered suggestion that December 12 was indeed the deadline under Florida law for designation of the state's electors; there is no suggestion of such a deadline in the election code itself. There was an air of non sequitur to ruling that the Florida supreme court had violated the Constitution by failing to prescribe uniform criteria for a recount, yet terminating the recount rather than permitting it to go forward under proper criteria. And by terminating the recount when it did, the Supreme Court was providing no relief to voters whose votes had not been counted but would have been under constitutionally adequate uniform criteria. Yet such voters were as much victims of the denial of equal protection that the Court had just found as those whose valid votes were diluted by the improper recovery of spoiled ballots cast by other voters.

The seeeming illogicality of the Court's remedy has reinforced, in critics not disposed to give the Court's most conservative Justices the benefit of the doubt, doubts about these Justices' impartiality. These doubts have been fueled by a number of other factors as well, including but not limited to the staying of the recount on December 9 by a vote of five to four, the fact that both splits ranged the five most conservative Justices against the four most liberal ones, and the undoubted interest that judges have in who their colleagues and successors will be—an interest that in the case of the Supreme Court is affected by the outcome of a Presidential election.

We must consider whether these doubts—which are distinct from, though closely related to, those discussed in the preceding chapter (and further in this one) concerning the soundness of the Court's ruling that the Florida supreme court had violated the Constitution—are well founded. We must also consider how far doubts about judicial impartiality extend to the members of the Florida judiciary.

The vulnerability of the Supreme Court's remedy arises from the Court's having based its decision on the equal protection clause of the Fourteenth Amendment rather than the "Manner directed" clause of Article II. If the vice of the Florida supreme court's decision of December 8 was the standardless character of the recount that it ordered, the logical remedy was to direct that court to adopt standards; if under Florida law time did not permit this, the Florida court could be expected to dismiss the suit. Or could it? Not having shown itself to be a model of prudence, that court might not have dismissed the suit, and by pressing on with it might have precipitated a national crisis. The dilemma of what remedy to order in these circumstances would have been avoided by ruling that Article II barred the recount because the state supreme court had no statutory basis for ordering it, whatever the criteria to be used in it. In other words, under Article II, as distinct from the equal protection clause, the appropriate judicial remedy was to bar the recount—period.

Even apart from remedial considerations, there is more to be said in favor of the Article II ground for reversing the Florida court than was said by the three concurring Justices who embraced that ground. Not enough to make it conclusive but enough to make it respectable, as well as to confirm its superior fit with the relief ordered—these being relevant considerations in light of the vilification (the word is not too strong) of the Court's decision by its liberal critics.[1]

But there is a threshold question whether the Court's decision can be defended on a ground that did not command the support of the majority. It can be. A decision is not lawless merely because the majority opinion is weak, especially when pressure of time made it

---

1. See, for example, Jeffrey Rosen, "Disgrace: The Supreme Court Commits Suicide," *New Republic*, Dec. 25, 2000, p. 18, and the editorial in the same issue of the *New Republic* entitled "Unsafe Harbor," in which we read of "the Republican larcenists, in and out of robes, who arranged to suppress the truth about the vote in Florida and thereby to make off with the election of 2000. . . . Morally and historically speaking, we have witnessed an outrage." *New Republic*, Dec. 25, 2000, p. 9. See also "We Dissent," http://www.igc.org/gadfly/politics/dissent.htm, visited March 23, 2001, a collection of hysterical denunciations of *Bush v. Gore*. I give more examples of intemperate criticism of the decision later.

impossible for merely human judges to do a good job. Almost every competent professional believes both that the majority opinion in *Roe v. Wade* is weak and that if a decent rationale could be found for the central holding (that the Constitution limits state regulation of abortions)—not necessarily a rationale based on the same constitutional doctrine relied on in *Roe* (substantive due process)—then the decision would be fine, would be rehabilitated, and certainly would not be lawless.

The best rationale for *Bush v. Gore,* as I began to suggest in the previous chapter, is found in the word "Legislature" in section 1, clause 2, of Article II of the Constitution, the "Manner directed" clause that was the nub of the Supreme Court's first opinion, that of December 4, 2000. One of the most hotly debated issues at the constitutional convention in 1787 was how to select the President. Popular vote, appointment by Congress, appointment by state legislatures, appointment by state governors—all these possibilities were discussed and rejected before the idea of selection by electors came into the picture, and then there was debate over how the electors should be appointed. A number of the delegates favored appointment by popular election, but in the end the convention left the matter to the states by the "Manner directed" clause.[2] It is unclear why the clause says "Legislature" rather than "State." One possibility is that the draftsmen wanted to negate any inference that the states were required to select electors by means of a popular vote; it would be up to each state legislature to decide what method to use.[3] Another possibility is that the choice of the word had no more intended force than the choice of the same word in Article I, section 4 ("The Times, Places and Manner of holding Elections for Senators and Representatives, shall be prescribed in each

2. The pertinent debates are summarized in Tadahisa Kuroda, *The Origins of the Twelfth Amendment: The Electoral College in the Early Republic, 1787–1804,* ch. 1 (1994).

3. For a hint of this interpretation, see David A. McKnight, *The Electoral System of the United States: A Critical and Historical Exposition of Its Fundamental Principles* 42 (1878).

State by the Legislature thereof"), where it seems to have been chosen simply because the legislature is the branch of government that makes laws. We cannot be certain that the choice of the word in the "Manner directed" clause was as casual as this, however. Article V, which establishes the methods for amending the Constitution, specifies state conventions or state legislatures as the ratifying bodies; these can hardly be synonyms for "states." Likewise the provision (now superseded) providing for the appointment of Senators by state legislatures.[4] The Seventeenth Amendment authorizes a state legislature to empower the executive of the state to make a temporary appointment to fill a Senate vacancy—is it to be believed that the state legislature could make the appointment itself or could delegate the power to do so to the courts?

It is true that the Constitution nowhere explicitly requires a state to *have* a legislature, though such a requirement may be implicit in the clause that guarantees to each state a republican form of government.[5] Perhaps if a state vested the lawmaking function in courts, and, taking seriously the notion of the "imperial" judiciary, decided to do without a legislature altogether, the courts would become the "legislature" for the purpose of applying the clauses in the federal Constitution that assign duties to state legislatures. But we can cross that bridge when we come to it; as of now, every state has a legislature.

We need not break our shovels trying to excavate the original intent behind the choice of the word "Legislature" in the "Manner directed" clause. One thing courts do all the time is find contemporary functions for old legal categories, pouring new legal wine into old wineskins. Think of the Supreme Court's interpretation of the Eleventh Amendment—the text of which simply forbids a citizen of one state to bring a suit in *federal* court against *another*

---

4. And other provisions as well. See *Barlotti v. Lyons,* 189 Pac. 282 (Cal. 1920).

5. "The United States shall guarantee to every State in this Union a Republican Form of Government"; U.S. Const. art. IV, § 4.

state—to create a comprehensive state sovereign immunity from federal regulation; or the interpretation of the provision of the Constitution that merely authorizes Congress to regulate interstate and foreign commerce as forbidding states to interfere with such commerce; or, coming closer to home, the discovery of a constitutional right to vote in the equal protection clause of the Fourteenth Amendment, which does not mention voting.

A lesson of the 2000 election deadlock is that the word "Legislature" may be the key to heading off future such fiascoes by unequivocally denoting the site within state government of the power to appoint electors. The potential crisis that the Supreme Court's decision averted was a product of uncertainty about which branch of Florida's government had the last word in fixing the rules for the appointment of the electors. Was it the legislature, subject to the normal judicial power to fill statutory gaps and resolve statutory ambiguities, or the courts, exercising a plenary power of "interpretation"? If "Legislature" in Article II, section 1, clause 2 means what it seems to mean, an interbranch struggle over the appointment of Presidential electors, which might spill over into Congress, can be averted by federal judicial decree. Had the U.S. Supreme Court not intervened and had Gore won the recount and had the Florida supreme court ordered the governor of Florida to cast Florida's electoral votes for Gore, Congress in January would have been faced with two slates of electors—unless the governor defied the court; and that was possible too.

If I am right that this would have been a miserable dénouement—not provided for in the Constitution,[6] unreliably addressed

---

6. Article II, section 1, as amended by the Twelfth Amendment, makes provision for the situation in which no candidate receives a majority vote of the electors, but it makes no provision for resolving disputes over the appointment of electors. Title III provides for resolution of such disputes by Congress (if the safe harbor provision is inapplicable) (3 U.S.C. § 15), but of course it is not part of the Constitution. Whether Congress even has the power to resolve disputes over electoral votes has been doubted because there is no express grant of such power in the Constitution, though David P. Currie, *The Constitution in Congress: The Federalist Period, 1789-1801* 137-139,

by Title III, yet imperative to avert—there is much to be said for an interpretation of "Legislature" in Article II that by forbidding gubernatorial and state judicial involvement in the selection of electors, except insofar as the legislature expressly delegates a role in that selection to the governor or the courts, minimizes the risk of an interbranch dispute over the selection of electors that might spill over into January. Had this been the Court's ground, the remedy of stopping a recount that flouted Florida's election law would have followed naturally.

The interpretation that I am suggesting is not compelled by case law, legislative history, or constitutional language. But neither is it blocked by any of these conventional interpretive guides. Indeed it is supported by the few cases on point[7] (although they are state rather than federal cases) and by the only scholarly commentary that I have found on the issue before the 2000 litigation.[8] And it is consistent with the concern expressed at the constitutional convention and in the ratifying debates with preventing the choice of the President by cabals, intrigue, corruption, or agents of foreign powers. That concern informs the provisions of Article II that require the members of the Electoral College to vote in their home states rather than congregating to vote and that require all the electoral votes to be cast on the same day.[9] Interpreting the "Manner

---

288–291 (1997), argues persuasively that Congress does have the power, as a necessary and proper incident to its express power to count the votes.

7. Cited and summarized in James C. Kirby Jr., "Limitations on the Power of State Legislatures over Presidential Elections," 27 *Law and Contemporary Problems* 495, 504 (1962). See, for example, *State ex rel. Beeson v. Marsh,* 34 N.W.2d 279 (Neb. 1948).

8. Kirby, "Limitations on the Power of State Legislatures," at 504 ("state constitutional provisions concerning suffrage qualifications and the manner of choosing electors do not limit the substantive terms of [state] legislation [governing the manner of appointment of the state's Presidential electors]").

9. U.S. Const. art. II, § 1, cls. 2, 4. See *The Records of the Federal Convention of 1787,* vol. 2, p. 500 (Max Farrand ed., rev. ed. 1937); Kuroda, *Origins of the Twelfth Amendment,* at 11, 21; Neal R. Peirce and Lawrence D. Longley, *The People's President: The Electoral College in American History and the Direct Vote Alternative* 22, 27, 29 (rev. ed. 1981); Shlomo Slonim, "The Electoral College at Philadelphia: The Evolution of an Ad Hoc Congress for the Selection of a President," 73 *Journal of American History* 35, 52–53 (1986).

directed" clause to forbid a state's governor or courts to change the electoral rules laid down by the legislature likewise operates to reduce malign influences on the selection of electors. But the principle is more important than the application. If the Florida legislature wants to lengthen the interpretive reach of the state's supreme court, it can do so (it can, for that matter, if it wants, authorize the court to appoint the state's electors); but it must make clear that it is doing this and act in advance of the Presidential election. There will always be room for debate in particular cases over whether, in the absence of such a delegation of authority, the state supreme court has engaged in statutory interpretation so free as to amount to changing the rules laid down by the legislature.

There is undoubted irony in interpreting the Constitution broadly to force state courts to interpret their election laws narrowly. But critics of the Court's decision should ask themselves whether they are willing to acknowledge that the Florida supreme court would have been violating Article II had that court said that because the state's election law did not provide a satisfactory resolution of the deadlock, the judges were going to appoint the state's electors.[10] If so—and the Supreme Court's first opinion, that of December 4, remanding the case to the Florida supreme court, suggests that all nine Justices would think it is so—the only question is whether what the Florida supreme court did do was sufficiently close to my hypothetical example to justify the U.S. Supreme Court in reversing that court.

We need not lose sleep over the possibility that since the statute applies indifferently to Presidential elections and to all other elections, the Florida courts might apply different interpretive principles to protests and contests of Presidential elections from those it applies to protests and contests of other elections

---

10. Some of the critics are willing to acknowledge this. See, for example, Richard D. Friedman, "Trying to Make Peace with *Bush v. Gore*" 25 (Michigan Law School, April 2001).

(including other federal elections), to which Article II, section 1, clause 2 does not apply. That would be nothing new. A state court faced with a vague state statute regulating access to public property may interpret the statute broadly when the use for which access is sought does not involve conduct potentially protected by the First Amendment, but narrowly (if by doing so the court can save the statute's constitutionality) when the use does involve such conduct, for example the use of a public park for a political demonstration.

Had the Florida supreme court, whether under compulsion of Article II or otherwise, upheld the secretary of the state and later (when the contest proceeding was conducted) managed to find a ground for reversing Judge Sauls that was consistent with the Florida election statute, the Republican-dominated state legislature might still have appointed a slate of electors pledged to Bush if Gore had prevailed in the recount. And then there would have been a January crisis. But the scenario I have just sketched was unlikely for a reason that provides additional support for reversing the Florida supreme court on the basis of Article II. What would have given the Florida legislature a colorable, or at least a politically defensible, ground for appointing a Bush slate had the U.S. Supreme Court not cut off the recount was the fact that a court composed of Democrats (the Florida supreme court) had changed the election rules after the election. By doing so the court had challenged the Republican legislature, and a response could be expected. The "Manner directed" clause can head off Presidential election crises by preventing one branch of state government, disappointed perhaps by the outcome of the election, from changing the outcome by altering the election rules after the result is known, provoking an interbranch struggle that is a recipe for chaos. This interpretation derives further support of a practical character from the provision of Title III that requires the governor of the state to transmit the list of the state's electors to Washington.[11] Unless the governor is bound by the rules laid down by the state legislature, there is again the spectre of competing slates of electors and no certain method of choosing between them.

If, moreover, the Florida court did *not* change the rules in violation of Article II, the appointment of a slate of electors by the state legislature might be unlawful. Remember that Title III authorizes such appointment if the state "has held an election for the purpose of choosing electors" but the election has "failed to make a choice."[12] That is an apt description of the situation in which the outcome of the election is mired in controversy when the safe harbor deadline for choosing the state's electors passes. Title III provides the mechanism (appointment of the state's electors by the state legislature) by which the controversy can be bypassed and the new President elected by the Electoral College without the intervention of Congress. If, however, the state's electors have been appointed in the manner directed by the legislature (namely, in the case of Florida, by popular election, not election by the legislature), then a subsequent attempt by the legislature to appoint the electors could be thought inconsistent with Article II and therefore enjoined. Again an interbranch conflict would be averted—though this assumes the constitutionality of Title III.

The imperative of heading off an interbranch struggle over the appointment of a state's Presidential electors does not in itself determine which branch should be supreme. But there is really only one choice, and it is the choice made by Article II. Nothing is more infuriating than changing the election rules after the outcome of the election, conducted under the existing rules, is known. That is what a banana republic might do. If we set to one side the appointment of electors by a legislature dissatisfied with the outcome of the popular election (an improper step if the election was conducted under the preexisting rules), we see that the

---

11. 3 U.S.C. § 6.
12. 3 U.S.C. § 2.

"Manner directed" clause of Article II can be used to curb such abuses by confining the authority to make the rules for the appointment of the state's Presidential electors to the organ of government that operates prospectively, which is the legislature. Courts operate retrospectively. The Florida courts were asked not to set new standards for future elections but to determine the outcome of the 2000 election. The state's highest court assumed the power to change the rules for that election laid down by the legislature. Once the outcome of a close election is known, the choice of a method of recounting likely to change the outcome is all too easy. The U.S. Supreme Court was criticized for intervening when it knew what effect its intervention would have on the outcome of the election. But it would not have intervened had the same principle discouraged the Florida supreme court from intervening when it knew that the effect of its intervention could only be to increase the likelihood that Gore would become President. Legalities aside, if there was one critical misstep—one avoidable precipitant of the postelection crisis (fortunately later averted) but also of the damage to the prestige of the U.S. Supreme Court—it was the Florida supreme court's decision of November 21, which by displacing the secretary of state's discretionary authority invaded the legislative prerogative of establishing the rules for selecting Presidential electors.

Two of the more interesting academic critiques of *Bush v. Gore* are marred by the failure of the authors to assign a function to the "Manner directed" clause; this may be because the critics are fixated on what the Justices said, rather than what they could have said, and might have said had they had more time. Professor Strauss calls the decision "lawless" but acknowledges the possibility that the Court was trying to counteract lawlessness on the part of the Florida supreme court.[13] Professor Sunstein thinks the Court

---

13. David A. Strauss, "Not Partisan, but Lawless," in *The Vote: Bush, Gore & the*

may have avoided a genuine constitutional crisis. "From the standpoint of constitutional order, the Court might well have done the nation a service. From the standpoint of legal reasoning, the Court's decision was very bad. In short, the Court's decision produced order without law."[14] For Strauss the lawlessness of the Florida court, and for Sunstein the avoidance of a genuine constitutional crisis, are not considerations that have any legal standing in Supreme Court adjudication. But they do; they are the considerations that can be used to interpret the "Manner directed" clause in a way that makes it a useful part of the constitutional structure. It is a function of law in general, and the "Manner directed" clause in particular, to *produce* order.

Even if everything I have said so far is accepted, the critics of the Supreme Court's decision will not be stilled, and not only because the Court did not adopt the Article II ground of decision and the concurring Justices who did embrace the ground did not defend it very cogently. The latter failure may be attributed to the sheer pressure of time, and the former to the strategic objective of getting some of the liberal Justices on board—an objective only partially achieved, to be sure. Three criticisms of the U.S. Supreme Court's decisions would be untouched by these points. The first is that the Court should have avoided entanglement in a partisan struggle, and so preserved its image of being above the political fray, by taking advantage of its right to decline to take a case without giving any reason and thus not have intervened at all. (The jurisdiction of most appellate courts is mandatory, but that of the Supreme Court is discretionary.) But if I am right that the Florida supreme court may well have been violating the Constitution, and if, as seems likely, without the Court's intervention the deadlock would have mushroomed into a genuine crisis, the Court's refusal

---

Supreme Court (Cass R. Sunstein and Richard A. Epstein eds. 2001), http://www .thevotebook.com.

14. Cass R. Sunstein, "Order without Law"; ibid.).

to intervene might have prompted the question: what exactly is the Supreme Court good for if it refuses to examine a likely constitutional error that if uncorrected may engender a national crisis? We might call this the reverse political questions doctrine. Political considerations in a broad, nonpartisan sense will sometimes counsel the Court to abstain, but sometimes to intervene. It is not an ordinary court, however much it may pretend to be one in an effort to insulate itself from political criticism.

Judges worry about expending their political capital, which is to say narrowing the margin of protection from other branches of government that they obtain by being thought by the public to personify the judicial virtues and thus (of distinct relevance in an election case) to be "above" politics. Judges seem not to worry *that* much about spending down their capital, if one may judge from the frequency with which they accuse each other of being "result-oriented," tendentious, disingenuous, and downright lawless;[15] we shall encounter this rhetoric in *Bush v. Gore* itself. Still, it is a concern, particularly at the highest level of the judiciary. But before criticizing a judge for spending down his political capital, or more bluntly for deliberately courting a loss of prestige, we should ask what he bought with his expenditure. We should also ask whether it isn't a natural tendency of judges to exaggerate the importance of their prestige to the nation's well-being. *Bush v. Gore* may have done less harm to the nation by reducing the Supreme Court's prestige than it did good by heading off a significant probability of a Presidential selection process that would have undermined the Presidency and embittered American politics more than the decision itself did or is likely to do. Judges unwilling to sacrifice some of their prestige for the greater good of the nation might be thought selfish. The trade-offs become particularly favorable to intervention if one believes that, had the Court abstained in

---

15. Richard A. Posner, *The Federal Courts: Challenge and Reform* 353–354 (1996).

December, it might well have been dragged back into the Presidential selection process in January, facing multiple appeals from rulings in cases brought to challenge the tumultuous proceedings in Congress that might have followed a completed recount. Had the Court ducked *then*—as it would have been quite likely to do (and probably rightly so, as we shall see)—it would have invited comparison to Nero fiddling while Rome burned.

The second criticism that is somewhat to one side of the soundness of the Court's decision is of its action in staying the recount on December 9.[16] A stay is proper only if the party seeking it would suffer irreparable harm were it denied. Critics say the only harm to Bush was the embarrassment he would have suffered had the recount continued and showed Gore overcoming his lead, a merely "political" harm against which courts do not grant a remedy, and that in any event the irreparable harm to Gore from the interruption of the recount was greater. The first point (that denial of the stay would have inflicted no irreparable harm on Bush) is unsound and the second (that the irreparable harm to Gore from the grant of the stay was greater) is misleading. In a political contest, the harm from allowing an unconstitutional recount to continue is bound to be political; what other harm could there be? There is no closed category of harms that a court may consider in acting on an application for a stay pending decision of an appeal. Why then can't a court be realistic about the stakes in a political contest? It was concern with the political impact of Bush's having a lead in the certified vote count that led Gore's forces to press to delay the certification, even though by doing so they compressed the time for waging a contest. Had they not objected to the secretary of state's insistence on adhering to the statutory deadline of November 14, they could have filed the contest proceeding on the fifteenth rather than, by virtue of the Florida supreme court's hav-

---

16. *Bush v. Gore*, 121 S. Ct. 512 (2000) (per curiam).

ing extended the deadline to November 26, on the twenty-seventh, with time quickly running out.

Cases involving voting rights have recognized political harm as irreparable harm for purposes of preliminary relief, such as a stay or a preliminary injunction. "It is well-settled that the claimed deprivation of a constitutional right such as the right to a meaningful vote or to the full and effective participation in the political process is in and of itself irreparable harm."[17] It is arguable (though a bit of a stretch, and not directly supported by any previous case that I have found) that candidate Bush's participation in the political process would not have been "full and effective" had a recount at once unlawful and arbitrarily truncated been permitted to cast a shadow over the legitimacy of his election.

And while Gore indeed suffered more harm from the grant of the stay than Bush would have suffered from a denial of it, the decision whether to grant or deny a stay does not depend only on the balance of harms (a technical point generally overlooked in the initial commentary on the decision). It depends also on the likely outcome of the appeal.[18] If it was certain that the Florida supreme

---

17. *Puerto Rican Legal Defense & Education Fund, Inc. v. City of New York,* 769 F. Supp. 74, 79 (E.D.N.Y. 1991). To the same effect see *Peel v. Crew,* 1996 U.S. Dist. Lexis 18525, at *20 (S.D.N.Y. 1996). Cf. *Stewart v. Taylor,* 104 F.3d 965, 969 (7th Cir. 1997).

18. For example, *Hilton v. Braunskill,* 481 U.S. 770, 776 (1987); *California v. American Stores Co.,* 492 U.S. 1301 (1989) (O'Connor, J., in chambers); *McClendon v. City of Albuquerque,* 79 F.3d 1014, 1020 (10th Cir. 1996); *Michigan Coalition of Radioactive Material Users, Inc. v. Griepentrog,* 945 F.2d 150, 153 (6th Cir. 1991), reversed on other grounds, 954 F.2d 1174 (1992) (en banc); *Cuomo v. Nuclear Regulatory Commission,* 772 F.2d 972, 974 (D.C. Cir. 1985). Cases dealing with the standard for the grant or denial of a preliminary injunction (which is closely analogous to a stay pending appeal) make clear that a "sliding scale" is to be used under which the greater the movant's showing of likelihood of success on the merits, the less showing he need make that the balance of harms favors his position. *Gentala v. City of Tucson,* 213 F.3d 1055, 1061 (9th Cir. 2000); *Sofinet v. INS,* 188 F.3d 703, 707 (7th Cir. 1999); *Serono Laboratories, Inc. v. Shalala,* 158 F.3d 1313, 1318 (D.C. Cir. 1998); *Ross-Simons of Warwick, Inc. v. Baccarat, Inc.,* 102 F.3d 12, 19 (1st Cir. 1996); *Roland Machinery Co. v. Dresser Industries,* 749 F.2d 380, 387 (7th Cir. 1984). The *Griepentrog* and *Cuomo* decisions explicitly apply the sliding scale approach to stays. It would be absurd to say that a party that had a 99 percent chance of prevailing when its appeal was heard should not be entitled to a stay just because the irreparable harm to him from the denial of the stay would be exceeded, perhaps slightly, by the irreparable harm to his opponent from the grant of the stay.

court would be reversed, the harm to Gore from stopping the recount was irrelevant. By December 9, the Supreme Court Justices had undoubtedly immersed themselves in the case. It had already been before them once, in the appeal filed the previous month from the Florida supreme court's decision of November 21. They knew that in all likelihood it would soon be back. Another round of briefs and oral argument by lawyers on the point of exhaustion was unlikely to change the Justices' views. The idea that the outcome of a momentous case is much influenced by lawyers' arguments is naïve. If Gore's defeat was thus a foregone conclusion on December 9, he had no legal interest for a stay to protect.

The harm to Bush from the denial of a stay would have been particularly difficult to justify if the likeliest effect of remanding the case to the Florida supreme court would have been the termination of the contest proceeding short of decision. For that would have opened up the possibility of a recount favoring Gore yet impossible for Bush to challenge, however compelling his grounds, because as soon as the contest proceeding was dismissed any challenge to the results of the recounts would have become moot. Suppose the first few thousand ballots to be recounted had happened to come from Democratic precincts and had given Gore a large enough net gain to overcome Bush's lead, whereupon the Florida courts called "Time!" (maybe because it was December 18) and so the recounts were never completed. The contest proceeding having become moot, Bush could not have challenged the results of the recount. But try explaining that to the American public! Bush would have been compared to John Quincy Adams, the man who became President while losing both the Electoral College vote and the popular vote. Once more: if being thought by the public to have lost the popular vote is not real harm, then Gore committed a fearful blunder in filing protests to the election results rather than moving directly to the contest phase. I shall argue in the next part of this chapter that it was not a blunder, because the political impact of Bush's being declared the winner by 930 votes on November 18 would have been devastating to Gore's chances.

The grant of a stay, as of an injunction (of which indeed a stay is a form), is an exercise of equitable discretion, and the court is not limited to considering the harm to the parties from granting or denying it. It was not only political harm to Bush that the stay averted, but harm to the nation, if we assume that the legitimacy of a President (which an unlawful recount would gratuitously have undermined) is a social good. Granted, it was not the only social good at stake. There was the good of avoiding the assumption of the Presidency by the candidate who had not in fact won the popular election in Florida and so the electoral vote in that state. But there was no way in which the recount ordered by the Florida supreme court was going to determine the "real" winner. The ground rules of the recount were illegal and absurd, and the time insufficient.

The stay may also have averted harm to the Supreme Court, notwithstanding the indignation that the stay aroused in some quarters. Suppose the recount had gone ahead and shown Gore the "real" winner of the popular vote in Florida, and *then* the Court had stepped in, perhaps to break a deadlock in Congress over rival slates of electors, and ruled in favor of Bush. There would then have been no ambiguity about the Court's being responsible for the selection of the 43rd President, whereas now there is, since no one can be sure what the recount would have shown. The media recounts now under way cannot credibly declare a winner; but should they declare Bush the winner, credibly or not, the Supreme Court will be off the hook, because of ever-diminishing public interest in the fine points of the election deadlock and its litigation aftermath. So maybe the Court minimized the damage to its political capital by granting the stay. Maybe the Justices are better politicians than their critics.

But Justice Scalia was, I think, ill advised to go public with his ground for voting for the stay. First, no doubt because of the shortness of time, he did not defend the stay effectively in his very brief opinion. Second, because he was the only Justice who wrote in defense of the stay, he was widely assumed to be the "leader" of the Justices who favored it, and he was of course part of the five-Justice majority in the December 12 decision. Since Scalia is one of the two most conservative members of the Supreme Court—the other being Thomas—and along with Thomas had been described by Bush as a model Justice and by Gore as a scary foretaste of the type of Justice that Bush might appoint if he became President[19]— Scalia's playing point man for the five-Justice conservative majority was bound to bring charges of partisanship to a boil.

A third criticism of the Supreme Court is that in embracing the equal protection ground for reversing the Florida court in *Bush v. Gore,* the Court's five-Justice majority was going against the grain, and this shows that the decision was partisan. The five Justices are conservative, and conservative judges are not supposed to "like" the equal protection clause, unless perhaps when it is invoked by railroads complaining about unequal tax burdens. This is a caricature, but let me for argument's sake accept its validity. These Justices might have preferred to base their decision on Article II; three of them, in a concurrence, embraced it as an alternative ground. There was a public relations advantage, however, to adopting a ground that would attract two of the liberal Justices, creating a solid bipartisan majority for the bedrock proposition that the Florida supreme court had acted unconstitutionally and could not continue with the recount along the lines it had laid down.

The concurring Justices—Rehnquist, Scalia, and Thomas—have

---

19. In his October 3, 2000, debate with Bush, Gore stated: "Governor Bush has declared to the anti-choice group that he will appoint justices in the mold of Scalia and Clarence Thomas, who are known for being the most vigorous opponents of a woman's right to choose. . . . When the names of Scalia and Thomas are used as the benchmarks for who would be appointed, those are code words, and nobody should mistake this, for saying the governor would appoint people who would overturn *Roe v. Wade.* It's very clear to me. I would appoint people that have a philosophy that I think will be quite likely would uphold *Roe v. Wade.*"

been fiercely criticized for joining the equal protection ground of decision, an action thought to be *particularly* out of character for them. But they had no real choice. Had they not joined the equal protection ground, the outcome of the case would have been no different—a reversal terminating the recount—but there would have been a majority to reject *both* possible grounds for that reversal, the equal protection ground (which by hypothesis the three concurring Justices plus Stevens and Ginsburg would have voted against) and the Article II ground (which all but the three concurring Justices would have refused—in fact did refuse—to join).[20] What a field day the critics of *Bush v. Gore* would then have had! The puzzle is why Justices O'Connor and Kennedy did not join the concurrence.

The conservative Justices were not the only ones on the spot. The Court's two most liberal ones (Stevens and Ginsburg), who dissented from the ruling that equal protection had been denied, were put in the uncomfortable position of rejecting an equal protection claim—and, as liberals, they are supposed to "like" the equal protection clause. The two other liberal Justices (Souter and Breyer), who dissented from the remedy while agreeing that the Florida supreme court had acted unconstitutionally,[21] were put in the uncomfortable position of being unwilling to avert a potential political and constitutional crisis, by allowing the deadlock to continue past December 12 and probably past December 18 as well, or even January 6. In a case so politically fraught, a bit of *Realpolitik*

---

20. Michael Abramowicz and Maxwell L. Stearns, "Beyond Counting Votes: The Political Economy of *Bush v. Gore*" (Law and Economics Research Papers Series No. 01-09, 2001, George Mason University School of Law).

21. Because Souter and Breyer described their separate opinions as dissents, some doubt has been expressed whether they really agreed that the Florida supreme court had violated the Constitution. There is no doubt they did. The per curiam majority opinion states: "Seven Justices of the Court agree that there are constitutional problems with the recount ordered by the Florida Supreme Court *that demand a remedy.* The only disagreement is as to the remedy"; *Bush v. Gore,* 121 S. Ct. 525, 533 (2000) (per curiam) (emphasis added, citations omitted). The majority would not have said this without the authorization of Justices Souter and Breyer.

affecting only the ground of decision and not the decision itself should be tolerable to anyone who takes a pragmatic approach to adjudication,[22] as Breyer in particular is known to do. "Fiat iustitia ruat caelum" is not a workable motto for the Supreme Court; and one had not thought it Justice Breyer's slogan either.

There is an old saying of lawyers and judges that "hard cases make bad law." The word "hard" here does not mean difficult. It refers to a tug at the heartstrings. The idea is that the tug may deflect the judges from following the straight and narrow path of the law. But maybe this reflects a crabbed view of what law is. Maybe law is supposed to reflect, to some extent anyway, the pressure exerted by extralegal concerns. Maybe, indeed, courts are not lawless when they "treat the Constitution and the common law, and to a lesser extent bodies of statute law, as a kind of putty that can be used to fill embarrassing holes in the legal and political framework of society"[23] (such as, perhaps, the embarrassing hole dug by the constitutional and statutory provisions relating to Presidential elections). Liberals believe this sort of thing when the extralegal interests clamoring for judicial succor have a liberal cast, when they have to do with abortion rights or affirmative action or school prayer. They draw up short only when the concerns are the sort that conservatives are more likely to voice.

In a fierce attack on *Bush v. Gore*, left-liberal law professor Jack Balkin acknowledges with rare candor for a legal professional that "my [Balkin's] sense of what is possible and plausible, what is competent legal reasoning and what is simply made up out of whole cloth is probably mired in an older vision of the Constitution that owes much to the Warren and Burger courts as well as to the predominantly liberal legal academy in which I was educated and

---

22. I have defended that approach in a number of my previous writings. See, for example, *Overcoming Law* (1995) and *The Problematics of Moral and Legal Theory*, ch. 4 (1999).

23. Ibid. at 258.

trained and now teach."[24] In other words—and we should keep this in mind when considering other criticisms of *Bush v. Gore* by the liberal legal professoriat—what is perceived as "sound" or "lawful" or "competent" or "professional" in constitutional adjudication may often be a matter more of one's personal political values—the product of upbringing and temperament and life experience and all sorts of nonlegal knowledge and opinion—than of a rigorous and impartial professional judgment. So liberals applaud *Roe v. Wade,* as they do the "[Warren] Court's aggressive willingness to implement liberal values,"[25] but they denounce, from the safe distance of half a century, *Korematsu v. United States,*[26] the decision that upheld a military order issued in March 1942 (shortly after the Japanese attack on Pearl Harbor and consequent U.S. declaration of war against Japan) that excluded persons of Japanese ancestry, even if they were U.S. citizens, from the west coast of the United States. The Supreme Court held that the order, though unquestionably a species of racial discrimination, was a permissible exercise of the warmaking powers that the Constitution grants to Congress and the President, and noted that the fear of possible sabotage by persons affected by the order was supported by the reported refusal of thousands of American citizens of Japanese ancestry to swear unqualified allegiance to the United States.

Justice Jackson dissented in an eloquent but strange opinion in which he said that because a court is in no position to determine the reasonableness of a military order, the order's reasonableness cannot be a defense to a charge of racial discrimination: "a civil court cannot be made to enforce an order which violates constitutional limitations even if it is a reasonable exercise of military authority."[27] This is the same Justice who famously said that the

---

24. Jack M. Balkin, *"Bush v. Gore* and the Boundary between Law and Politics" (forthcoming in *Yale Law Journal*).

25. Lucas A. Powe Jr., *The Warren Court and American Politics* 498 (2000).

26. 323 U.S. 214 (1944).

27. Ibid. at 247 (dissenting opinion).

Constitution is not a suicide pact.[28] In his dissent in *Korematsu,* while stating that "defense measures will not, and often should not, be held within the limits that bind civil authority in peace,"[29] he would have forbidden the courts to back up the military order by convicting Korematsu for violating it, pursuant to a statute that made such violations criminal. But if the statute punishing violations of the order were unenforceable, the efficacy of the order, and of "defense measures" taken in time of war generally, would be weakened.

Modern liberals consider the decision in *Korematsu* an outrage, just like *Bush v. Gore.* Yet they believe that the prohibition against racial discrimination can be bent, without violation of the Constitution, if the race discriminated against, under the rubric of affirmative action, is white rather than yellow. The cases may of course be distinguishable, but only because the facts are different. They are analytically symmetrical—*Bush v. Gore* to *Korematsu,* and *Korematsu* to cases allowing affirmative action—showing that powerful norms of legal justice, such as the nondiscrimination principle, can bend to practical exigencies, whether it is winning a war or improving race relations. These pairings suggest that Professor Sunstein is wrong to put "law" and "order" in separate boxes, rather than seeing the good of order as raw material for the fashioning of law.

Few liberal lawyers are disposed to question the legitimacy of the Emancipation Proclamation. Yet its legality is as dubious as that of the exclusion order in *Korematsu.*[30] It was arguably as high-handed an act from a narrowly legal standpoint as President Truman's seizure of the steel mills during the Korean War, which the Supreme Court slapped down.[31] What *Korematsu* and the Emanci-

---

28. *Terminiello v. City of Chicago,* 337 U.S. 1, 37 (1949) (dissenting opinion).

29. 323 U.S. at 244.

30. Sanford Levinson, "Was the Emancipation Proclamation Constitutional? Do We Care What the Answer Is?" (forthcoming in *University of Illinois Law Forum*).

31. *Youngstown Sheet & Tube Co. v. Sawyer,* 343 U.S. 579 (1952).

pation Proclamation have in common, and what distinguishes them from the steel seizure case, is nothing more or less, it seems to me, than the difference in menace between the Civil War and World War II, on the one hand, and the Korean War, on the other. The scope of the President's constitutional power as the commander in chief of the armed forces of the United States is relative to the threat facing the nation. In January 1863, before the Union victory in the Battle of Gettysburg and the surrender of Vicksburg to Grant, the threat was very great. And so was Japan's threat to the nation perceived to be (though in hindsight we know that the perception was exaggerated) in March 1942, when the exclusion order at issue in *Korematsu* was issued. For Lincoln to have refrained from issuing the Emancipation Proclamation because of a belief that it was unconstitutional would have given real meaning to the idea that the Constitution is a suicide pact.

The willingness to weigh the practical consequences of decision is the pragmatic approach to law, and if it is sound then the Supreme Court was not acting illegitimately in bringing a concern with avoiding disorder to bear on the decision of the constitutional issues in *Bush v. Gore,* just as it would not have been acting illegitimately had it given President Clinton a temporary immunity from suit by Paula Jones in order to spare the nation the spectacle of a President brought low by a sex case.[32] It would have been nice had the majority Justices in *Bush v. Gore* articulated the practical concerns that justified the boldness of their constitutional innovations. But judges are shy about the pragmatic grounds of their decisions. The Court did not have time to craft a rhetorically adroit opinion that would have explained these grounds without inviting charges that it was being "political" in straying outside the narrowest formalist grounds of decision.

---

32. See Richard A. Posner, *An Affair of State: The Investigation, Impeachment, and Trial of President Clinton* 225–228 (1999), discussing *Clinton v. Jones,* 520 U.S. 681 (1997).

Liberals detest *Korematsu,* but not because it allowed pragmatism to trump principle; rather because of suspicion of the military and a sense of shame about the history of the nation's mistreatment of East Asians (who, we recall from Chapter 1, could not even become American citizens until well into the twentieth century). I mentioned affirmative action, but consider now, as an even closer liberal counterpart to *Korematsu* because it too involved a national emergency, *Home Building and Loan Association v. Blaisdell,*[33] the case that fileted the contracts clause in the Constitution. In 1933, in the depths of the Depression, Minnesota passed a law that gave relief to debtors by declaring a moratorium on foreclosures. Although Article I, section 10, clause 1 of the Constitution provides that "No State shall . . . pass any . . . Law impairing the Obligation of Contracts," and Minnesota's law did precisely that, the Supreme Court upheld the law. The Court reasoned ingeniously that "the policy of protecting contracts against impairment presupposes the maintenance of a government by virtue of which contractual relations are worth while—a government which retains adequate authority to secure the peace and good order of society."[34] This is a fancy way of saying that a state can impair the obligation of contracts, notwithstanding the constitutional provision (a provision aimed at debtor relief laws, which had flourished after the Revolution, frightening the commercial class and providing impetus to the enactment of the Constitution), provided it has a compelling reason to do so.

The symmetry between *Korematsu v. United States* and *Home Building and Loan Association v. Blaisdell,* on the one hand, and *Bush v. Gore,* on the other, is not perfect. In the earlier cases the Court had used pragmatic considerations to override constitutional principles, the equal protection of the laws and the nonimpairment of contracts respectively. In *Bush v. Gore* the Court used such consid-

---

33. 290 U.S. 398 (1934).
34. Ibid. at 435.

erations to enlarge the equal protection principle or, in my preferred grounding of the decision, to create a new principle—that Article II, section 1, clause 2 of the Constitution constrains state judicial interpretation of the state legislature's scheme for selecting Presidential electors—just as in *Clinton v. Jones* the Court had been asked (but refused, in retrospect mistakenly) to create, for pragmatic reasons, a new Presidential immunity from suit. But the difference between pragmatic contraction and pragmatic expansion of constitutional principle is not fundamental. Think of Holmes's famous example of how the ancient law of deodands, which affixed criminal responsibility to inanimate objects that caused human injury (and so a wagon wheel that broke loose and killed a person might be tried and executed for murder), was adapted to allow a person who had a legal claim against the owner of a ship to sue the ship itself.[35] The reason was practical: "the ship is the only security available in dealing with foreigners, and rather than send one's own citizens to search for a remedy abroad in strange courts, it is easy to seize the vessel and satisfy the claim at home, leaving the foreign owners to get their indemnity as they may be able."[36] Or think of how the warrant clause of the Fourth Amendment, originally designed to limit the use of search warrants—regarded as engines of abuse because officers executing a search could set up the warrant as a defense to a suit against them for trespass[37]—became the device by which the Supreme Court imposed on law enforcement authorities a prima facie duty to obtain a warrant before conducting a search, in order to interpose a judicial officer between the police and the citizen.

---

35. Oliver Wendell Holmes Jr., *The Common Law* 25–30 (1881).

36. Ibid. at 28.

37. See, for example, *United States v. Mazzone,* 782 F.2d 757, 759 (7th Cir. 1986); Telford Taylor, "Search, Seizure and Surveillance," in Taylor, *Two Studies in Constitutional Interpretation* 23–43 (1969). The amendment merely forbids general warrants and unreasonable searches and seizures. It does not require obtaining a warrant (which is issued by a magistrate, a judge, or some other judicial officer) before making a search or seizure.

In none of the cases that I have discussed did the Court come right out and say, "we're deciding the case on pragmatic grounds." Holmes and Jackson are about the only Justices in the history of the Supreme Court who had the rhetorical skills to acknowledge the pragmatic grounds of their constitutional interpretations without appearing lawless. But only by positing pragmatism as the hidden ground of decision can some of the most notable decisions of the Supreme Court be explained and defended. *Bush v. Gore* may be such a decision.

The four dissenting Justices did the Court no service by accusing the five-Justice majority of having impaired public confidence in the impartiality of the judiciary. Such an accusation, however heartfelt, is what is called fouling one's own nest. It also has an element of self-fulfilling prophecy: by telling the world that the decision would undermine public confidence in the courts, the dissenters made it more likely that it would indeed undermine public confidence in the courts. That was a gratuitous blow to the Court's prestige, hardly justifiable by a possible deterrent effect on future "activist" impulses of the majority, the dissenters themselves being widely regarded as activists for liberal causes. The majority decision, it is true, also damaged the Court's prestige, at least in the short run; but it did not do so gratuitously—it averted a potential crisis.

Consciously or not, the dissenters were reminding the public that all the Justices had a conflict of interest of sorts in ruling on a case that would decide who would become President (more precisely that *might* decide this, since Bush might have become President anyway by virtue of Republican control of the Florida legislature and the U.S. House of Representatives, even if Gore had won the recount). Judges are not indifferent to who their colleagues are, and specifically to whether they have colleagues who agree with them on the big issues that come before their court; and as there may be vacancies on the Supreme Court in the next four years, the current Justices are unlikely to be indifferent to who the next President is. Judges are also concerned lest their handiwork be undone by their successors; they would like their successors to have values similar to their own. But all this is as true of the four liberal Justices as it is of the five conservative ones. For the four to insinuate that the five had impure motives is to live in a glass house and throw stones.

Under the "rule of necessity" a court all of whose members are afflicted with a conflict of interest can decide the case anyway if otherwise it could not be decided at all. It is on this basis that federal judges, including the Justices of the Supreme Court, hear and decide cases involving federal judicial salaries.[38] The rule of necessity was not strictly applicable to *Bush v. Gore* because the Court did not *have* to decide the case for it to be decided; it could have allowed the Florida supreme court to have the last word. Moreover, the rule assumes rather than eliminates a conflict of interest, which in the case of *Bush v. Gore* will forever cast a shadow over a decision that in other circumstances might have garnered considerable professional support. If I am right that the Court was in a no-win situation—that damage to public respect for the judiciary was inevitable once Gore decided to bring the courts into the process of Presidential selection rather than to accept the machine recount or the decisions of the county canvassing boards—judges' ire should be directed not at each other but at him.

Only the naïve believe that ideology plays no role in constitutional adjudication at the Supreme Court level. There is a difference, however, between political ideology and partisan politics,[39] and it has been many years since the Justices have been accused of voting in cases along party lines. That is precisely the accusation leveled in liberal circles against the majority Justices in *Bush v. Gore*

---

38. *United States v. Will,* 449 U.S. 200 (1980).

39. See generally Richard A. Posner, *The Federal Courts: Challenge and Reform,* ch. 10 (1996).

(the parallel charge has been made in conservative circles against the Florida supreme court), and it is based in part on the fact that the Justices seem, as we have seen, to have been voting *against* their ideological proclivities (for which ordinarily they would be complimented!). But this is true only in part. Close beneath the surface of the legal issues in the postelection litigation are intertwined issues of personal responsibility, demotic power, governmental paternalism, and judicial discretion that divide left and right.

Most of the punchcard votes in Florida that the tabulating machines refused to count were rejected because of voter error. The voter had not followed the directions, although they should have been clear to anyone who could read at a high school, or maybe even an elementary school, level. Illiterates are permitted to vote, but some conservatives may think it rather an excess of democracy for illiterates to hold the electoral balance of power. One recalls Justice O'Connor's remark at the oral argument on December 11: "Why isn't the standard the one that voters are instructed to follow, for goodness sakes? I mean, it couldn't be clearer. I mean, why don't we go to that standard?"

On the other side of the ideological divide, liberals point out that Bush won on a technicality, Gore having won the popular vote nationwide, having lost the popular vote in Florida largely perhaps because of a lousy voting technology that discriminated however unintentionally against black voters, and being on top of all that the undoubted second choice of most of Nader's supporters, who gave their candidate 97,000 votes in Florida.[40] Although the Justices could not have known on December 12, they could have sensed—and would, we know from Chapter 2, have been correct to sense—that a majority of the people who cast votes in the 2000 Florida Presidential election thought they had voted for Gore.

---

40. Buchanan and the Libertarian Party candidate, Browne, together received only 38,000 votes; presumably Bush would have been the second choice of most of these voters. The other Presidential candidates received only a smattering of votes.

Small-d as well as capital-D democrats will add that the Congress—which would have ended up selecting the President if the Supreme Court had kept its hands off—is a more democratic institution than the Court. The Florida supreme court's invocation of the "people power" provision of the Florida constitution, however inadequate a description of the goals animating our representative democracy, doubtless struck a chord with populist Democrats; and the disproportionate disenfranchisement of black voters would have distressed Democrats on ideological as well as partisan grounds.

A conservative might think the Democrats were urging that the Florida voters whose ballots had been rejected be relieved from their errors through the beneficent intervention of government officials who would try to guess what the voters would have done had they followed directions. Government would ascertain and effectuate the popular will. An election is a formal procedure, a statutory artifact, rather than a public opinion poll. When Gore's attempt to overturn the election was thwarted by a Republican elected official (the Florida secretary of state), Gore's supporters turned to the state courts, appealing to freewheeling interpretive principles that aggressive judges use to override even the clearest expressions of legislative intent. The use of the "people power" clause of the state constitution to revise the state election law was a conservative's nightmare of constitutional free interpretation. "All power to the people" is not a conservative slogan.

One way to put the case for Gore was that he had won the election as it might have been conducted in different circumstances, notably with more user-friendly ballots. That hypothetical election might be a closer approximation to the popular will than the actual election was. But the actuality of the actual election is reassuring in much the same way that we find it reassuring to know that the only statutes that can be enforced are statutes that have actually been enacted, as distinct from the statutes that would have been enacted had there not been some discreditable obstacle of some sort in the way of the will of the people. It is the same reassurance we derive from knowing that the allocation of Representatives across states is determined by a census—that is, an actual head count, imperfect as it is, rather than by statistical sampling.[41] Like the census, an election is a count, not a statistical projection. We rightly sense that analytical techniques used to improve the results of actual counts, whether of heads or of votes, lend themselves to potentially sinister manipulation. We think in short that formalities—such as counting votes according to an objective standard based on rules adopted before (subject only to minimal later interpretation) rather than after the election to which they are to apply—have an important role to play in the practice of representative democracy and are not to be criticized on the basis that they occasionally generate outcomes that clash with democratic ideals. That is a paradox rather than a failure of democracy.[42] The rules of Presidential succession, hence the rules governing the elections that determine that succession, have to be clear; but any clear rule will create occasional discrepancies between its terms, which determine its scope and application, and its objective. Form and substance are in tension; conservatives tend to lean toward the former.

Hostility to Rousseauan democratic exuberance (the elevation of substance over form) may not sort well with an embrace of judicial activism, which is also the elevation of substance over form and which is arguably illustrated by *Bush v. Gore* itself. But that is as much a problem for liberals (who tend to voice enthusiasm for populist democracy while at the same time advocating democracy-limiting interpretations of constitutional rights) as it is for conser-

---

41. *Department of Commerce v. United States House of Representatives,* 525 U.S. 316 (1999).

42. That disagreement over the nature or meaning of American democracy may be at the root of the divided vote in *Bush v. Gore* is also argued in Richard H. Pildes, "Law, Order, and Democracy," in *The Vote.*

vatives. Anyway my point is only that there were reasons, whether good or bad, besides the party identity of the litigants, for conservative Supreme Court Justices to want to reverse the Florida supreme court and liberal Justices to affirm it. And there was sufficient play in the legal joints to enable either side to write a professionally respectable opinion justifying its preferred outcome; mere limitations of time may have prevented either side from actually doing so.

Do I believe, therefore, that *Bush v. Gore* would have been decided the same way if the parties had been reversed, that is, if Bush had been challenging the certification of Gore as the winner of the popular vote in Florida? I doubt that any of the Justices has so debased a conception of the judicial office as to try *deliberately* to swing the election to his preferred Presidential candidate. But the undeniable interest that a judge, especially a Justice of the U.S. Supreme Court, has in who his colleagues and successors will be is likely to have alerted the Justices to features of *Bush v. Gore* that might otherwise have eluded them. The conservative Justices may have been more sensitive to arguments based on Article II and the equal protection clause than they otherwise would have been, and the liberal Justices more sensitive to the weaknesses of those arguments than they otherwise would have been. It is because judges who have different values and experience are sensitive to different features of a case that diversity of backgrounds is a valid consideration in judicial selection.[43]

Liberals find it easier to attack the U.S. Supreme Court for *Bush v. Gore* than to defend the Florida supreme court, and conservatives find it easier to attack the Florida supreme court than to defend the U.S. Supreme Court, but the symmetry is not quite perfect. True, the justices of the Florida supreme court are Democrats, but they had a smaller stake in the outcome of the Presidential election

---

43. Cf. Richard A. Posner, *The Problems of Jurisprudence* 447–448 (1990).

than the Justices of the U.S. Supreme Court did, because the President does not appoint state judges. They faced a less acute conflict of interest, and so it is perhaps not surprising that they were less supportive of Gore than the conservative Justices of the U.S. Supreme Court were of Bush. Three of the seven justices of the Florida supreme court broke ranks and dissented from the court's December 8 decision. And earlier the court had refused Gore's plea to extend the time for the recounts beyond November 26. The court also affirmed the dismissal of the suits challenging the absentee ballots in Seminole and Martin Counties. Had those ballots been discarded, as the plaintiffs in those suits urged, Gore would have taken a commanding lead over Bush. But had the court ordered those ballots discarded it would have been contradicting the "count-every-vote" spirit of its recount decisions.

What is clear, however, though not necessarily to be attributed to partisanship, is that the Florida court committed a series of grave legal errors in both recount decisions, as well as tactical blunders in failing to respond promptly to the Supreme Court's request for clarification of the November 21 decision and in allowing itself to be outsmarted by the Court in the matter of the deadline for the recounts. Most striking is the sheer imprudence of the Florida supreme court, which could so easily have averted needless turmoil and its own humiliation by applying the election law as written and thus upholding the secretary of state's refusal to extend the statutory deadline. There would probably have been no contest proceeding had that deadline stuck. But if there had been a contest, and if the Florida supreme court, in reviewing Judge Sauls's decision in that proceeding, had adhered to the principles of administrative law, the decision would have been upheld and the recounts not restarted.

The justices of the Florida supreme court should not be criticized too harshly. They labored under the same time pressures as the U.S. Supreme Court Justices, and with fewer resources to cope with those pressures. The lower-court Florida judges who played important roles in the litigation, Nikki Ann Clark (the trial judge in the *Seminole County* case, involving absentee ballots), Terry Lewis, and Sanders Sauls, should not be criticized at all. They outperformed their superiors in the Florida judiciary.

To wrap up my discussion of the judicial performance in the postelection cases, I must consider the possible bearing of the "political questions" doctrine, to which I alluded very briefly earlier in this chapter. The doctrine teaches that there are some constitutional questions that federal courts simply will not answer, because the questions are "political" in a special sense—it has to be a special sense, since most of the constitutional questions that courts do answer are "political" in a general sense. Although the doctrine is a century and a half old,[44] its boundaries remain unclear.[45] At one extreme, it might be regarded as a doctrine of pure prudence: courts will not enforce constitutional rights if to do so would seriously impair judicial prestige or authority. The formlessness of such a construal of the doctrine is not the only objection to it; nor that it invites bullying of the courts. Another objection is that it is otiose, that the tools of constitutional interpretation are sufficiently flexible to enable the courts to avoid interpretations that make the Constitution a straitjacket.

At the other extreme, the doctrine may simply remove from judicial consideration questions that the Constitution has assigned to the nonjudicial branches of government to answer definitively. *Nixon v. United States*[46] illustrates the doctrine understood in this sense. A federal judge who had been impeached by the House of Representatives and tried and convicted by the Senate complained about the Senate's use of a committee to conduct the evidentiary

---

44. *Luther v. Borden,* 48 U.S. (7 How.) 1 (1849).
45. See Laurence H. Tribe, *American Constitutional Law,* vol. 1, 365–385 (3d ed. 2000), for a helpful discussion.
46. 506 U.S. 224 (1993).

phase of his trial, a shortcut that Nixon argued violated the constitutional provision concerning impeachment trials. The Court invoked the political questions doctrine to hold that there is no judicial power to review impeachment decisions. The decision is best understood as an exercise in constitutional interpretation. The constitutional text contains no suggestion that the courts are to review impeachments; and given that judges are one of the classes of impeachable officials, it would be anomalous to empower them to reverse convictions by the Senate in trials of impeachment. But when an issue can thus be resolved by interpretation, the political questions doctrine does no work.

In between the extremes is the idea that the doctrine identifies a class of constitutional questions that, though the framers' intent may be obscure, are not amenable to judicial resolution because the relevant considerations are beyond the courts' capacity to gather and weigh; the answers the questions demand simply are not legal answers, answers a court might give without ceasing to be a court.[47] The case usually thought to have originated the doctrine, *Luther v. Borden,* was such a case. Rather than adopt a new constitution after the break with England, Rhode Island had continued to use its colonial charter as its constitution. Restive citizens convened a constitutional convention not authorized by the charter. The convention adopted a new constitution to which the charter government refused to submit, precipitating rebellion and the establishment in 1841 of a rival state government. The Supreme Court refused to decide which of the two competing governments was the legitimate one. It would have been very difficult to gather and assess, by the methods of litigation, the facts relevant to such a

---

47. As noted in the *Nixon* case, this conception of the doctrine is related to the conception of it as a doctrine of textual interpretation. "The concept of a textual commitment to a coordinate political department is not completely separate from the concept of a lack of judicially discoverable and manageable standards for resolving it; the lack of judicially manageable standards may strengthen the conclusion that there is a textually demonstrable commitment to a coordinate branch"; ibid. at 228–229.

decision.[48] It would have been even more difficult to formulate a legal concept of revolutionary legitimacy to guide the decision. So the Court left the matter to the President, to whom Congress had delegated the duty of resolving it.

There is at least a passing resemblance to the situation that would have confronted the Supreme Court if, having abstained in November and December from intervening in the election deadlock, it had been asked in January to choose between competing slates of Florida electors, were Congress stymied. The Court might have been asked whether electoral votes can be counted as votes if cast after December 18, whether electoral votes certified by a state's governor can be counted as votes if the state courts have ordered him to certify other electoral votes and have held him in contempt for his refusal to do so, and whether a state legislature can appoint Presidential electors if the outcome of the popular election in the state is still being disputed in the courts. These are in the first instance statutory rather than constitutional questions, but the Constitution lurks in the background by virtue of the various provisions in Article II that we have discussed, some of which sit uneasily beside Title III.

Once a dispute over electors lands in Congress, it is arguable, by analogy to the *Nixon* case, that judicial jurisdiction ceases. The responsibility for counting electoral votes is lodged firmly in Congress by Article II and the Twelfth Amendment (which in this respect is identical to Article II), and there is no suggestion of a right or power of judicial review and no hint of a standard that a court reviewing Congress's decision on which electoral votes to count might steer by. There would thus be a strong argument for invoking the political questions doctrine. If so, this becomes an additional argument for the Court's intervening when it did, before the dispute over Florida's electors reached Congress.

---

48. 48 U.S. at 41–42.

But if the ultimate decision on whose slate of electors to accept is Congress's, not the Supreme Court's, shouldn't the Court have left the resolution of the dispute over Florida's electoral votes to Congress in the first place? It did. The Court did not command Congress to count the electoral votes that Florida had submitted back on November 26. Congress could have refused to count them, thereby either giving the Presidency to Gore or tossing the decision to the House of Representatives, depending on how the phrase "a majority of the whole number of Electors appointed" in the Twelfth Amendment is interpreted (see Chapter 3). The Court's intervention made it easy for Congress to sidestep the dispute. But it did not *prevent* Congress from stepping in to resolve it, a resolution the Court would probably have deemed judicially unreviewable by reason of the political questions doctrine. The dissenting Justices in *Bush v. Gore* thus were incorrect in arguing that the Court, in terminating the Florida recount, had displaced Congress's authority to resolve disputes over electoral votes. Of course as a practical matter, with the recount stopped and so the popular vote totals in Florida up in the air, there was very little basis for challenging the Bush electors in Congress when the electoral votes were counted in January. But if the dissenters were concerned merely or mainly with the symbolic finality of Congress's decision on the counting of electoral votes, they should have considered the bearing of *Luther v. Borden*. Had Congress felt strongly enough, it could have refused to count Florida's electoral votes. That it did not is some evidence that the country was content with the Court's resolution of the dispute.

I criticized the conception of the political questions doctrine as a doctrine of prudence; and this criticism may seem at war with my endorsement of pragmatic adjudication. "Pragmatic" as an adjective for anything to do with the judicial process still causes shudders. It seems to open up vistas of judicial willfulness and subjectivity and to mock the rule of law; it seems to equate law to prudence, and thus to be Machiavellian. All that pragmatic adjudication need mean, however—all that I mean by it—is adjudication guided by a comparison of the consequences of alternative resolutions of the case rather than by an algorithm intended to lead the judges by a logical or otherwise formal process to the One Correct Decision, utilizing only the canonical materials of judicial decision making, such as statutory or constitutional text and previous judicial opinions. The pragmatist does not believe that there is or should be any such algorithm. He regards adjudication, especially constitutional adjudication, as a practical tool of social ordering and believes therefore that the decision that has the better consequences for society is the one to be preferred.

Systemic consequences are not excluded. The pragmatic judge does not squint myopically at the consequences of the case at hand, oblivious to the possible consequences of his decision for future cases. He recognizes that the needs of the future, along with the limitations of judges' knowledge, may rule certain consequences out of consideration, such as a preference for one Presidential candidate over another. It would be exceptionally foolish—and, even to a pragmatist, plainly lawless—for a Supreme Court Justice who happened to feel passionately about the issue of abortion rights to allow his passion to influence a decision, such as *Bush v. Gore,* that might determine the winner of a Presidential election in which the candidates had expressed opposing views on such rights. But given the importance of the Constitution as a framework for orderly government, and the threat of disorder posed by a struggle between branches of a state government over the selection of the electors of the President, it was appropriate for the Supreme Court, in deciding what if anything to make of the "Manner directed" clause of Article II or the equal protection and due process clauses (in relation to the electoral process) of the Fourteenth Amendment, to consider the consequences for the orderly process of Presidential succession. John Harrison has defended the legality of the Reconstruction amendments to the Constitution, which turns in part on the legitimacy of the southern state governments that ratified the amendments, by reference to "the overwhelming need to identify with certainty the effective government of a state"[49]—or, I add, of the United States.

Had the "Manner directed" clause been unavailable as a ground for decision in *Bush v. Gore*—had the tatterdemalion equal protection ground been the only federal hook with which to hoist the Florida litigation into the Supreme Court—the systemic costs of the Court's intervention would have been higher. That the Article II ground did not command a majority is a blow to the perceived legitimacy of *Bush v. Gore,* but not a fatal one; the decision may have been right for a reason that only a minority of the Court perceived.

Analysis of systemic consequences provides further support for the Article II rationale. The "Manner directed" clause is about one thing only, and that is the appointment of Presidential electors. A decision interpreting the clause has no implications for other constitutional issues. In contrast, a decision based on equal protection or due process, and focused not on the appointment of electors as such but on disparities in voting power, has implications for a much broader range of electoral issues, implications the Justices were in no position, given the pressure of time under which they were laboring, to weigh in a responsible fashion. There was a public relations advantage to getting two liberal Justices "on board" a ruling that the Florida supreme court had acted unconstitutionally. But the advantage did not require the conservative Justices to agree with the ground embraced by the liberals. There would still have been seven votes against the Florida court's December 8 decision if five had based the decision on Article II and two more on the Fourteenth Amendment.

---

49. John Harrison, "The Lawfulness of the Reconstruction Amendments," 68 *University of Chicago Law Review* 375, 458 (2001).

Pragmatism expands the bounds of the possible for judges; it does not eliminate those bounds. I offer two more examples from Lincoln's conduct of the Civil War. The first is his action in defying a writ of habeas corpus issued by Chief Justice Roger Taney on the application of a Maryland resident who had been seized and detained by the Union army on suspicion of being implicated in treason and rebellion.[50] The Constitution authorizes habeas corpus to be suspended in time of rebellion, but by Congress,[51] not the President. Lincoln's was an unconstitutional act validated by a higher source of justice than the U.S. Constitution, namely national survival. The governing maxim was *silent enim leges inter arma,*[52] and is the antithesis of a legal maxim.[53]

Some Unionists wanted Lincoln to cancel the 1864 Presidential election,[54] a measure that might have appealed to Machiavelli. That would have been a mistake, and unlike the contretemps with Taney would have created a very bad precedent. It would have been another unconstitutional act, but one the bad effects of which would have exceeded the good ones.

I place *Bush v. Gore* with the Emancipation Proclamation and *Korematsu,* rather than with *Ex parte Merryman,* because it is a case in which the constitutional text (Article II, section 1, clause 2) could be stretched—indeed, rather easily, it seems to me—to enable a national crisis to be averted by constitutional means, albeit a much less ominous crisis than in the earlier examples.

---

50. *Ex parte Merryman,* 17 Fed. Cas. 144 (Cir. Ct. D. Md. 1861) (Taney, C.J., in chambers). See Carl B. Swisher, *The Taney Period* (vol. 5 of the *Oliver Wendell Holmes Devise History of the Supreme Court of the United States*) 844–854 (1974). Other unconstitutional acts committed by Lincoln at the outset of the Civil War are discussed in Jill Elaine Hasday, "Civil War as Paradigm: Reestablishing the Rule of Law at the End of the Civil War," 5 *Kansas Journal of Law and Public Policy* 129, 130 (1996).

51. U.S. Const. art. I, § 9, cl. 2.

52. "Law stands mute in the midst of arms"—Cicero.

53. Though Lincoln would not have agreed. He held a concept of "adequacy constitutionalism," whereby the President had vastly enlarged war powers in times of acute national emergency. Hasday, "Civil War as Paradigm," at 131–132.

54. Ibid. at 134.

Pragmatism is just one possible approach to constitutional interpretation; it would be unpragmatic to call it The Right Approach. There are respectable schools of jurisprudence according to which *Bush v. Gore* could be shown to be unprincipled, even usurpative. But can liberals enroll in any of those schools without repudiating much of the constitutional law forged by the Supreme Court in the Warren and Burger eras? I don't think so.

The Lawyers

The lawyers on both sides of the election litigation have been criticized by normally astute observers for a variety of tactical blunders.[55] For example, it is pointed out that by pressing for an extension of the period for submission of the counties' vote totals, Gore compressed the contest period so tightly that it would have been difficult to complete the contest litigation even if the Supreme Court had not intervened. Gore also failed to request a statewide hand recount during the protest period or to request that overvotes as well as undervotes be hand counted, to propose a uniform recount standard, or to deny that December 12 was the deadline for Florida to appoint its Presidential electors. Bush is criticized for having been the first to sue (he brought an unsuccessful suit in federal district court,[56] based on the arguments that he later made in the Supreme Court when he appealed from the Florida supreme court's decisions), thus weakening his position that the state's election officials, not the courts, should decide who won the election. He is also criticized for having resisted a limited hand recount

---

55. See, for example, Michael W. McConnell, "Two-and-a-Half Cheers for *Bush v. Gore*," in *The Vote;* David Barstow and Adam Nagourney, "Gore's Critical Mistake: Failure to Ask for a Statewide Recount," in Correspondents of the *New York Times, 36 Days: The Complete Chronicle of the 2000 Presidential Election Crisis* 331 (2001); William Glaberson, "Boies's Concession on 'Deadline' Proved Fatal," in ibid. at 334.

56. That was the *Siegel* suit, which I cited in note 1 to Chapter 3.

under a uniform standard that would probably have confirmed his lead and so enhanced the legitimacy of his ultimate election to the Presidency.

I believe that none of these criticisms is sound, and that—surprisingly, given the pressure of time and the fact that most of the lawyers involved in the litigation had no previous experience with election litigation—no clear errors, legal or tactical, were committed by either side if an ex ante perspective is taken, as it should be, since anyone's performance can be improved with the aid of hindsight. For example, in retrospect it is apparent that Bush gained nothing from his suit in federal district court to stop the recounts; but he lost nothing either,[57] and the risk of a harmless loss was well worth running. And in retrospect it is apparent that Gore should not have limited his recount requests to four counties, but I shall argue that the limitation was reasonable when made.

In part the critics of the lawyers' tactics have gone astray by adopting too narrow a conception of a lawyer's role in litigation. Most of the critics are law professors, and thus lawyers, and it is a professional deformity of lawyers to take a narrow, a legalistic, view of their role. But the lawyer's role is not to win the case, as such; it is to protect and advance his client's interests. That may sometimes require winning small, or even losing, and often it requires risking loss; for tactics singlemindedly aimed at maximizing the likelihood of a legal victory will often defeat the client's ultimate goals. The clearest example of such a mistake in the postelection litigation would have been a decision by Gore's lawyers not to protest the machine recount (which, after the addition of the late-arriving overseas ballots, gave Bush a 930-vote lead) but instead to move

---

57. More precisely, he lost little, for he did take a public relations hit from being the first candidate to turn to the courts for help. The accusation was correct, but misleading. In demanding recounts, Gore was initiating a legal process. He could have refused the initial machine recount; and hand recounts were conducted only because he filed protests with several county canvassing boards, initiating administrative proceedings that were bound to and did end up in the courts when they did not give him the relief he was seeking. The protests were the ground floor of the litigation.

directly into the contest phase, which Gore could have done as early as November 15. That was the first day after the deadline for the counties to certify their vote totals (minus the late overseas ballots) to the secretary of state, and if there is no protest that certification is the starting gate for filing a contest suit.[58] Gore lost twelve days by protesting the counties' vote totals.

The criticism of Gore's protracting the protest phase ignores two things. One is that if Gore had overcome Bush's lead then, the political momentum would have shifted in his favor, while the legal burden of proof would have been expected to shift from him to Bush. Gore could not know—no one could know—that the Florida supreme court would jettison settled principles of administrative law and so give no weight to the election officials' vote count. The general expectation concerning the contest proceeding was as stated by Professor Paul Rothstein, a Gore supporter:

> It [the contest proceeding] . . . is tougher for Gore than the protest stage. This contest stage—he's got a strict burden of proof. It's an uphill climb. The presumption is against him. The presumption is in favor of the validity of the count that Secretary of State Harris of Florida certified tonight [November 26], and . . . Gore's going to have to mount a full evidentiary attack in which particular ballots are going to be brought in and argued and statistics are going to be applied. . . . I think the court's inclination will be [to say that] "There really isn't enough time to do this full evidentiary hearing and, Mr. Gore, you can't really meet the burden of proof anyway."[59]

Second—and more interesting because it is such a clear illustration that legal advantage is not the only thing a good lawyer seeks—a failure to protest the county vote totals, and the consequent certification of Bush on November 18 as the winner of the popular vote by 930 votes, would probably have caused Gore to concede the election right then and there. There is an analogy to

58. Fla. Stat. §§ 102.111(1), 102.168(2).
59. *Fox Special Report with Brit Hume*, Nov. 26, 2000, Transcript #112601cb.254.

the dilemma that faced President Clinton when his relationship with Monica Lewinsky first burst into public view in January of 1998. Dick Morris advised the President that if he acknowledged having lied about his relationship with Lewinsky in his deposition in the Paula Jones case, his position would be untenable; his supporters would abandon him, and he would be forced to resign. It took time for people to accustom themselves to a President who had committed perjury in an effort to conceal an adulterous relationship in his White House office with a young White House employee. Clinton bought the necessary time by a campaign of lies and slanders. Similarly, though not because there was anything scandalous afoot, it took time for the public in 2000 to accustom itself to a protracted postelection struggle to determine who the next President would be. At first it seemed unthinkable that the resolution of the deadlock could be postponed for more than a few days. As a former chairman of the Democratic National Committee said only three days after the election, "So I think the facts matter. I think the American people are very reasonable people. Our Constitution is strong. *We can wait a few more days.*"[60] If on November 18, the eleventh day after the election, Katherine Harris had certified Bush the winner by almost a thousand votes, it would have been difficult for Gore to retain the support of influential Democrats for litigation challenging the certification. Even on November 20 it seemed that "as a matter of practical politics, I think, once the secretary of state does that certification, that a person who tries to contest it is going to look like a sore loser."[61] When on November 26, after a ruling favorable to Gore by the Florida supreme court, Harris certified Bush the winner by a much diminished margin,

---

60. *CNN Street Sweep*, Nov. 10, 2000, Transcript #00111000V61 (remark of David Wilhelm) (emphasis added). Speaking just two days after the election, former President Jimmy Carter opined: "My guess is that this process [determining what the will of the Florida voters was] is going to take several days"; *The NewsHour with Jim Lehrer*, Nov. 9, 2000, Transcript #6894.

61. *Fox Special Report with Brit Hume*, Nov. 20, 2000, Transcript #112002cb.254 (remark of Paul Rothstein).

the nation had schooled itself to patience, to allowing Gore to complete the contest proceeding. The compression of that proceeding was the price he had to pay for keeping his hopes alive. The analogy is to a cancer patient's decision to undergo a potentially fatal medical treatment in order to avert the certainty of a swift death.

As for Gore's failure to seek a statewide recount, the compelling reasons for that decision did not include the danger that he might have lost the recount; given his parlous state, that would have been a danger worth embracing[62] had there been a net legal or political advantage to be gained. But there did not seem to be. For one thing, there is no procedure under Florida law for a statewide protest. Protests have to be filed county by county. Gore had no politically attractive basis for protesting the election results in most of the state's counties, especially those that use the marksense method, and they are the majority. I emphasize the qualification "politically attractive." We know from Chapter 2 that in counties in which marksense ballots are counted at the county rather than the precinct level, marksense ballots can produce recoverable overvotes—notably, overvotes created by the voter's marking and writing in the same candidate's name, which the scanners that count marksense ballots are programmed to reject even though the voter's choice of candidate is plain. But remember that the challenge to the election outcome had begun with complaints about the butterfly ballot, which was a punchcard ballot, and had rapidly shifted to punchcard ballots in general. To broaden the challenge to include the other principal voting technology in use in Florida (as throughout the nation), implying that virtually the entire U.S. system of voting was rotten, would have lacked plausibility, especially when marksense technology was being touted as the superior

---

62. As powerfully argued in Brian C. Kalt, "The Endless Recount: Some Thoughts on Optimal Recount Strategy and Al Gore's Plan in the 2000 Florida Presidential Race" (Michigan State University–Detroit College of Law, March 2001).

alternative to punchcard technology! It would have marked Gore as desperate, unreasonable, a sore loser. Canvassing boards in many of the marksense counties would probably have refused to conduct a hand recount, and then Gore would have had to bring more lawsuits, with uncertain consequences—except delay.

Moreover, had Gore filed protests in every county, county canvassing boards controlled by Republicans would have hurried the recount if they thought it would yield a net gain for Bush and dragged their heels if they thought it would yield a net gain for Gore. In counties where the canvassing board was controlled by Democrats, the Republicans would have filed suits designed to slow down the recounts. As a result, Bush's lead would have steadily mounted, while the time for beginning a contest proceeding— which in the event of protests is not until "the *last* county canvassing board empowered to canvass the returns certifies the results of that particular election following a protest"[63]—would have been delayed indefinitely. Which means that if Gore had sued to delay recounts in counties in which a recount was likely to favor Bush, he would have been playing into Bush's hands.

It does not follow that because a statewide hand recount was not in Gore's interest it must have been in Bush's interest. Not at all. *Any* hand recount was potentially fatal to Bush, and not only because the results were unpredictable and he had more to lose from the gamble (namely the Presidency) than he had to win (namely an increased margin of victory).[64] In addition—and this also explains why his lawyers never proposed specific criteria to guide a hand recount—any acknowledgment of the propriety of a hand recount would have damaged, probably fatally, Bush's ace in

---

63. Fla. Stat. § 102.168(2) (emphasis added).

64. According to the Democratic "bible" of election challenges, "if a candidate is ahead, the scope of the recount should be as narrow as possible, and the rules and procedures for the recount should be the same as those used election night"; Timothy Downs, Chris Sautter, and John Hardin Young, "The Recount Primer" 5 (Aug. 1994, available from Sautter Communications, Washington, D.C.).

the hole, namely the willingness of the Florida legislature to appoint a slate of electors pledged to him if he lost the recount. If he had wavered in his position that hand recounts were illegitimate and those recounts had given the popular vote lead to Gore, it would have been difficult for the legislature to have fielded a slate of electors against the popular vote winner; it would have seemed like a pure power play. Bush's position had to be that the entire recount process was illegitimate, demanding and justifying extraordinary legislative intervention whatever the recounts showed. Gore was thus on safe ground in offering to abide by the results of a statewide recount if Bush would do likewise; Bush was sure to refuse the offer.

But if it was not in Bush's interest to propose a specific standard to guide the recounts that Gore had demanded, must it not have been in Gore's interest to propose one? No. If he proposed any standard tighter than what the Broward County canvassing board had used, he could not pocket the 582 votes that the Broward recount had given him. But if he proposed the Broward standard, he would have to describe and defend it, and merely to describe it would be to demonstrate its irremediable subjectivity, while to defend it would be impossible. (The unfortunate term "dimple" makes it difficult as a rhetorical matter to insist that all "dimpled" chads, not to mention "pregnant" chads, be counted as votes.) Better to go with "clear indication" of the voter's intent, undefined, but with the unvoiced understanding that Broward's use of an unclear-indication standard was okay. When David Boies, in his oral argument for Gore in the U.S. Supreme Court on December 11, refused to particularize "clear indication" of the voter's intent, he avoided a trap. Had he endorsed the Broward standard, he would have strengthened the equal protection argument against the Florida supreme court's recount order. But had he endorsed a tighter, a more objective, standard, he could not have justified pocketing the critical 582-vote net gain that the Broward

County recount had generated for Gore. Even to endorse uniformity in principle would have been risky, because it would take time to establish a uniform standard, and Gore was almost out of time.

The most questionable decision by either side was Gore's decision not to seek a recount of overvotes as well as of undervotes. The decision was due in part to a deficit of information,[65] and in part perhaps to a bit of timely disinformation by the Republicans. At first most people just could not see how a ballot containing votes for two or more candidates for the same office could possibly be recovered as a vote for any of the candidates. The possibility that a voter might punch the chad of a candidate and then write that candidate's name in the write-in space seemed too goofy to be worth investigating. As I mentioned in Chapter 2, Democrats learned that there might have been a number of such overvotes for Gore in Duval County. But they may have learned this too late to request a recount there. And because the county had gone for Bush, they may have feared that a thorough canvass might turn up more overvotes for Bush than for Gore. An additional factor was that the Republicans from the start had argued that it was irrational to count undervotes but not overvotes. The reaction of Democrats was that the Republicans were just trying to throw a monkey wrench into the works, since in all likelihood few if any overvotes could be recovered as countable votes. It would be natural to think that if your opponent asked that some class of ballots be recounted, it could not be in your interest to accede to his request. It might have been a brilliant stroke for the Democrats had they acceded to the Republicans' demand to extend the count to overvotes, but even great lawyers are not infallible. Later, when it

---

65. Like Bush, Gore was "going by the book": "Avoid taking a position on a particular set of facts until the effect on the entire recount can be projected"; Downs, Sautter, and Young, "The Recount Primer," at 5. Conversely (and a point well illustrated by Gore's strategy), "If a candidate is behind, the scope [of the recount] should be as broad as possible, and the rules for the recount should be different from those used election night"; ibid.

became clear that overvoted ballots were a potential treasure trove for Gore, it was too late for the Democrats to reverse field, because counting another 110,000 ballots would have been infeasible in the limited time available at the contest stage.

Another reason for Gore not to seek a recount of overvoted ballots was that he had cause to believe that a recount of undervoted ballots alone, in the four counties in which he had requested hand recounts, would yield him more than enough additional votes to overcome Bush's lead. He cannot be criticized for having failed to foresee that the Miami-Dade canvassing board would abandon its recount and that the Palm Beach board would use relatively conservative criteria for recovering votes from undervoted ballots. Both boards were dominated by Democrats. They could not be expected to let Gore down. The cost in delay and confusion of adding a search for recoverable overvotes exceeded the expected benefits of racking up additional votes for Gore that it seemed he would not need.

Brian Kalt (who believes that Gore's recount strategy was mistaken) disagrees, pointing out that Gore's hopes for these county recounts depended on the courts' accepting dimpled chads as legal votes, and this could not be assumed. But Kalt's major criticism is that while Gore may have been justified in confining his protest to four counties, once the process entered the contest stage he should have gone for broke and sought a statewide recount.[66] I doubt that this was feasible. Time was rapidly running out for Gore when the contest trial before Judge Sauls began on December 2. Gore was desperate to complete the trial in one day, or at most two days. This would have been impossible had Gore been required to present evidence that would raise serious doubts about the accuracy of the vote totals in other counties, especially marksense counties. He was in a box.

---

66. Kalt, "The Endless Recount."

No doubt a microscopic examination of the litigation record would reveal mistakes. But often it is difficult to distinguish a mistake from a sound tactic. Let me give just one example. One of Bush's witnesses at the contest trial before Judge Sauls was the former IBM engineer who had developed the punchcard voting technology. On cross-examination, one of Gore's lawyers confronted the witness with a patent application that the witness had filed for a new and improved punchcard voting technology, listing various deficiencies in the old (such as a propensity for chad buildup in the tray under the ballot) that might make it difficult for the voter to punch through the ballot. The language of the application contradicted the witness's testimony at the trial. Bush's lawyer could have tried to pull the sting by conducting redirect examination of the witness, eliciting from him (as should not have been difficult to do) an acknowledgment that in applying for a patent an inventor is required to establish the utility as well as the novelty and nonobviousness of his invention and so has an incentive to disparage the previous technology, and also that the fact that a technology is improvable does not mean that it is defective. There was no redirect examination, however, and my guess is that it was avoided because it would have riveted the court's attention on the issue of defects in the punchcard voting machines and have opened the witness to a further round of cross-examination ("recross examination," it is called). And who can know what the witness, already flustered by the surprise appearance of his patent application, would have conceded under further cross-examination?

The Professorial Commentators

For the second time in only three years, a momentous legal dispute of an intensely political character riveted the attention of the American public. The first time it was a multifaceted dispute arising from President Clinton's affair with Monica Lewinsky—a dispute (really a series of disputes) that involved the law of perjury and of obstruction of justice more generally, sexual harassment law, the independent counsel statute, criminal contempt, the proper use of grand juries, the impeachment provisions of the Constitution, and much else besides. The complexity of the dispute, its political importance, and the public fascination with it created both a demand for and a ready and abundant supply of "real-time" commentary by "public intellectuals," prominently including law professors. I was and remain highly critical of the quality and disinterest of that commentary.[67]

The legal dispute that arose out of the 2000 Presidential election deadlock was also multifaceted, complex, fascinating, and intensely political, and it also elicited a flood of real-time commentary by public intellectuals, prominently including law professors. Law professors in fact played an even bigger role in the election controversy than in the impeachment controversy. The law was both more central to the election controversy and more complex (with its layers of statutory and constitutional provisions—the Florida election code, Title III, the provisions of the U.S. Constitution relating to Presidential elections, the Fourteenth Amendment, administrative law), and the litigation proceeded at such a breakneck pace that persons without legal training had great trouble getting a handle on it. Once again, the commentary by public intellectuals was seriously deficient in quality and disinterest. I have discussed some of this commentary elsewhere[68] and will not repeat that discussion here. I want to focus on a different though overlapping issue: not the deficiencies of academic public intellectuals, as such, who commented publicly on the election controversy, but the deficiencies of a number of the constitutional-law scholars who commented on it.

---

67. See Posner, *An Affair of State,* at 233–245; Richard A. Posner, *Public Intellectuals: A Study of Decline,* chs. 3, 10 (Harvard University Press, forthcoming).

68. Ibid., ch. 3.

Beginning within a couple of days after the election, and continuing until the public's interest evaporated with Gore's concession speech on December 13, the many professors of constitutional law who were willing to take a public position on the deadlock and the deadlock litigation were frequent guests on radio and television talk shows; frequent signatories of open letters, petitions, and newspaper advertisements; and frequent authors of op-ed pieces and, occasionally, longer articles in newspapers or magazines. (The articles continued to appear after the electronic media had lost interest.) A few constitutional law professors, such as Laurence Tribe and Charles Fried, were professionally involved in the litigation, as counsel for various parties. They are experienced lawyers, and they played their lawyer roles with aplomb, though with no greater aplomb than did the nonprofessorial lawyers, such as David Boies and Theodore Olson. My interest is in the nonparticipating academic lawyers—the kibitzers.[69]

A number of these criticized the Supreme Court's interventions in the election deadlock, and particularly its culminating decision of *Bush v. Gore,* with unusual sharpness.[70] The vehemence, the

---

69. Some of these lawyers did play peripheral participatory roles in the litigation.

70. See, for example, Neal Kumar Katyal, "Politics over Principle," *Washington Post,* Dec. 14, 2000, p. A35 ("lawless and unprecedented"); Akhil Reed Amar, "Should We Trust Judges?" *Los Angeles Times,* Dec. 17, 2000, p. M1 ("as activist a decision as I know"; not worthy of "respect"); Anthony G. Amsterdam, "The Law Is Left Twisting in the Wind," *Los Angeles Times,* Dec. 17, 2000, p. M5 ("abandonment of any pretense at behaving like a court of law"; "sickening hypocrisy and insincere constitutional posturing"); Rosen, "Disgrace"; Herman Schwartz, "The God That Failed," *Nation,* Jan. 1, 2001, p. 5 ("the rule of law has taken a terrific beating from the Supreme Court. Basic principles of adjudication have been trampled on"); Cass Sunstein, "What We'll Remember in 2050," *Chronicle of Higher Education,* Jan. 5, 2001, p. B15 ("illegitimate, undemocratic, and unprincipled"; Supreme Court "discredit[ed] itself"); Richard D. Friedman, "'Bush' v. 'Gore,'" *Commonweal,* Jan. 12, 2001, p. 11 ("egregious," "sleight-of-hand trick," "perhaps the most imperial decision ever by the United States Supreme Court"); Randall Kennedy, "Contempt of Court," *American Prospect,* Jan. 1–15, p. 15 ("scandal," "outrageousness," "Gang of Five, "hypocritical mishmash"; "the Court majority acted in bad faith and with partisan prejudice"); Jamin Raskin, "Bandits in Black Robes: Why You Should Still Be Angry about *Bush v. Gore,*" *Washington Monthly,* March 2001, p. 25 ("quite demonstrably the worst Supreme Court decision in history, *Bush v. Gore* changes everything in American law and politics. . . . *Dred Scott* was, by comparison, a brilliantly reasoned and logically coherent decision"); Michael J. Klarman, "*Bush v. Gore* through the Lens of Constitu-

emotionality, of these attacks to one side, many of them were one-sided, superficial, hyperbolic, and precipitate, just as many law professors' "real-time" reactions (in radio and television appearances) concerning the unfolding drama and impending crisis had been hasty, one-sided, sometimes poorly informed, and (particularly in predicting the course of the litigation) surprisingly inaccurate. Reading the transcripts of interviews of these academics on radio and television, the open letters and newspaper advertisements that they signed, and their op-ed pieces and longer articles (especially but not only those that appeared in the immediate heat of combat, before Gore's concession bought time for reflection), one learns several disquieting facts about the current state of constitutional law in the academy.[71]

One is that some professors of constitutional law do not know the Constitution—that is, the document, as distinct from its enormous accretion of case law—very well;[72] they are like Talmudists who have forgotten the Bible itself. That the "Manner directed" clause of Article II, one of the pivots of the election litigation, might have implications for a contested Presidential election; that the Constitution does not provide a clue to how a Hayes-

---

tional History" (forthcoming in *California Law Review*) ("the *Bush* [*v. Gore*] result can be explained only in terms of the conservative majority's partisan political preferences"; "*Bush v. Gore* reveals partisan preferences trumping law"). Terrance Sandalow, former dean of the Michigan Law School, called the stay that the Supreme Court issued on December 9 "incomprehensible . . . an unmistakably partisan decision without any foundation in law" (quoted in Linda Greenhouse, "Collision with Politics Risks Court's Legal Credibility," *New York Times* (late ed.), Dec. 11, 2000, p. A1), and of *Bush v. Gore* itself stated that "the majority's decision can only be justified on the basis of the party that they favored, the man they wanted to be president, not on the basis of judicial philosophy"; *ABC World News This Morning*, Burrelle's Information Services, Dec. 14, 2000. The Kennedy, Rosen, and Sunstein papers are reprinted in *Bush v. Gore: The Court Cases and the Commentary* (E. J. Dionne Jr. and William Kristol eds. 2001).

71. I have made similar criticisms of academic constitutional law before. See Richard A. Posner, *Overcoming Law*, pt. 2 (1995); *Problematics of Moral and Legal Theory*, at 144–185; "Introduction," in *Frontiers of Legal Theory* 1 (2001).

72. "It is entirely possible, indeed it is probable, that a law student can complete a constitutional law course without actually having read the Constitution"; Brannon P. Denning and Glenn H. Reynolds, "Studying Constitutional 'Incidents'" (Southern Illinois University and University of Tennessee Schools of Law, 2001).

Tilden type of deadlock (the type of deadlock that occurred in the 2000 election) might be resolved; that much of Title III of the U.S. Code, which does provide some clues (though not enough) might be unconstitutional; that one clearly constitutional provision of Title III, section 1, which designated November 7 (in 2000) as the date for selecting each state's Presidential electors, would probably forbid conducting a revote in Palm Beach County, necessarily at a later date, to eliminate the effect of the butterfly ballot; that the Electoral College is not a deliberative body; and that state statutes that require the state's electors to vote for the winner of the state's popular election may be unconstitutional—these things, if one may judge from the early commentary, came as a surprise to a number of professors of constitutional law (though not to all, a qualification to be kept in mind throughout this part of the chapter).

Several of our most distinguished constitutional theorists, in an advertisement published in the *New York Times* shortly after the election, urged—without discussion of the feasibility or legality of the measure—that serious consideration be given to having Palm Beach County revote for President. The advertisement states that "there is good reason to believe that Vice President Gore has been elected President by a clear constitutional majority of the popular vote."[73] It is elementary constitutional law that a majority of the popular vote has no constitutional significance in a Presidential election; only the vote of the Electoral College (or of the House of Representatives if the Electoral College fails to produce a majority

---

73. "The Election Crisis," *New York Times* (national ed.), Nov. 10, 2000, p. A29. The organizers claim that 3,488 persons have signed the "petition" (as they describe the advertisement). See http://www.eccc2000.org/, visited Feb. 27, 2001. Among the signatories listed are Bush Won, Pol Pot, Loonycat Fuckwad, This Is Simply a Farce, Comrade Al Gore, and DIE, pinko scum! The failure of the organizers to screen the signatories is notable, and the analogy of the inclusion of these phony names to vote fraud irresistible.

vote for one of the candidates) counts. The term "constitutional majority of the popular vote" is gibberish.[74]

The suggestion to conduct a revote in Palm Beach County, though seconded by Professor Tribe[75] before his retention by Gore to assist with the litigation, was a bad one, quite apart from the question of its legality (Title III made November 7 *the* Presidential election day), and it was quickly dropped by the Gore forces. It was true that the butterfly ballot had confused voters. But it had been designed by the Democratic election supervisor for the county and approved by both parties. To have ordered a revote against such a background would have created an enormously destabilizing precedent. In future elections any loser could press for a revote on the ground that the very ballot design that he had sponsored or approved was confusing. And think of the mechanics of such a revote in a Presidential election. A new election day would have to be scheduled. A new ballot would have to be designed and approved, printed, and distributed to the polling places, which would have to be reopened and restaffed. With Palm Beach County determining the Presidency, frenzied campaigning and insanely energetic turnout efforts could be anticipated. Tribe argued that "a corrective election could be limited to people who voted the first time around, and those voting could be required to submit sworn affidavits that they will vote for whichever candidate they had intended to vote for on Election Day." But there would be no way

---

74. Michael Sandel (a political philosopher rather than a law professor) argues that the fact that Gore received more votes nationwide than Bush should make a difference "for the way senators should think about the confirmation process"; Bush's mandate to govern is "fragile," and "impaired," by virtue of his loss of the popular vote; "The Right to Judge a Nominee's Ideology," *New York Times* (late ed.), Jan. 14, 2001, § 4, p. 17. That is akin to saying that if a tennis player wins in the final round at Wimbledon by a score of 0–6, 6–4, 1–6, 6–4, 6–4, his title is "impaired," is "fragile," because while winning a majority of the sets, his opponent won more games (24 versus 19, in the example).

75. Laurence H. Tribe, "Let the Courts Decide," *New York Times*, Nov. 12, 2000, § 4, p. 15.

to verify the truthfulness of such affidavits. And who would be deciding on such measures, on the structure of the revote? The parties would not agree. Where in Florida or federal law would authoritative, or for that matter any, guidance be found for structuring so unique a corrective of a supposedly botched Presidential election? And would the nation accept the idea of a vote in one county in the United States—a vote held after the outcome of the election in the rest of the country was known—to decide who would be President?[76] Tribe is an able and experienced advocate, not an ivory tower stargazer. But the suggestion to conduct a revote in Palm Beach County was "academic" in the worst sense.

There has been much handwringing by academic (as by other) critics of *Bush v. Gore* over the racial impact of Florida's punchcard voting systems. But while the vast majority of constitutional law professors are political liberals highly solicitous of the interests of black Americans and cognizant of the long history of franchise discrimination against them, none of these professors seems to have been aware before November 7 of the disproportionate effect of the punchcard ballot in disenfranchising eligible black voters. The punchcard ballot has been in widespread use in American elections since the 1960s, and its racial impact (which is not limited to Florida) has long been known, though not well publicized.[77] So limited was the acquaintance of the professorial commentators with the actual administration of elections that they overlooked the possibility that a voter's intention might be clearly ascertainable in a significant number of overvoted ballots; probably they had never heard of an "overvote." That the systematic though not deliberate disenfranchisement of black voters, poor voters, voters

76. Compare *Foster v. Love,* 522 U.S. 67, 73 (1997), remarking "the distortion of the voting process threatened when the results of an early federal election in one State can influence later voting in other States, and with the burden on citizens forced to turn out on two different election days to make final selections of federal officers in Presidential election years."

77. John Mintz and Dan Keating, "A Racial Gap in Voided Votes: Precinct Analysis Finds Stark Inequity in Polling Problems," *Washington Post,* Dec. 27, 2000, p. A1.

with limited experience, new or occasional voters, and voters with reading difficulties might be due to the choice of voting systems had not occurred even to those academics who teach their students, and write for their colleagues, about the constitutional issues created by racial gerrymandering, poll taxes, and literacy tests.

The basic reason that the constitutional problems stirred up by the 2000 election caught professors of constitutional law unawares is that what these academics mainly know about the specific activities which that law regulates is what is contained in opinions of the U.S. Supreme Court. Not that they are old-fashioned doctrinalists. They are deeply interested in what history and political theory have to contribute to the understanding and critique of constitutional law. They are theorists as well as lawyers. Nevertheless a constitutional problem, however serious, that does not leave its traces in the pages of the *United States Reports* is unlikely to appear on the academic radar screen. For his *theoretical* bearings the modern constitutional law professor is apt to range far beyond legal materials, but for the database from which to draw applications of that theory he is content with what he can find in the Supreme Court's opinions.[78]

A fixation on case law is not a deformity peculiar to constitutional law professors. But it is especially noticeable in them because of the extraordinary breadth of modern constitutional law, and it can occlude an awareness of serious but merely *potential* constitutional issues.[79] Among the subjects that law regulates are public welfare, homosexual rights, discrimination against women, racial discrimination (including affirmative action), tenure contracts of civil servants, political patronage, pornography, education, hate

---

78. Cf. Neal Devins, "How Constitutional Law Casebooks Perpetuate the Myth of Judicial Supremacy," 3 *Green Bag* (second series) 259 (2000); Gerald N. Rosenberg, "Across the Great Divide (Between Law and Political Science)," ibid. at 267.

79. J. M. Balkin, "Agreements with Hell and Other Objects of Our Faith," 65 *Fordham Law Review* 1703, 1729–1738 (1997).

speech, police conduct, election districting, advertising, judicial and administrative procedure, abortion, public officials' immunities from federal suits, term limits of public officials, roadblocks, school discipline, drug testing of public employees, taxation of interstate commerce, standing to sue in federal court, loitering and panhandling, public support of religion, medical treatment of prison inmates, book purchases by public libraries, immigrants' rights, legal representation of indigent criminal defendants, defamation, zoning, eminent domain, indecent Web sites, and nude dancing. Many of these subjects have nothing to do with each other; they belong to different domains of fact and social scientific theory. Yet a professor of constitutional law is expected—or maybe just expects himself—to be able to discuss all of them. Which he does, but by drawing on a knowledge base that is essentially limited to the constitutional law decisions of the Supreme Court, a thin gruel, since the Justices lack systematic knowledge of these subjects also. Many of the Court's opinions are not even written by the Justices but instead by their law clerks, almost all of whom are recent law school graduates, fledglings. If the lawyers who brief and argue these cases know more about the real-world settings of the cases, as indeed many of them do, than the Justices, they aren't telling, because they fear to overstep the conventional boundaries of forensic relevance and decorum. Or if they are telling, their expert knowledge is not being reflected in the Court's opinions.

There are exceptions, of course, to the underspecialization of constitutional law professors. One thinks of Lawrence Lessig, who is profoundly knowledgeable about the Internet, and Michael McConnell, who is profoundly knowledgeable about religion. Others could be named. But the generalization holds. What professors of constitutional law mainly know, outside of theory, is what is to be found in Supreme Court opinions. The resulting knowledge deficit showed in the professorial commentary on the election deadlock. Although there is a large body of Supreme Court case law dealing with the electoral process, virtually none of it deals with election administration. Voting technology, though known to professors in their capacity as voters, is not known to them in their capacity as professors of constitutional law. That particular technologies might discriminate against particular classes of voters was a thought that had not occurred to the professoriat because it had not been the subject of a decision by the Supreme Court. That Title III of the United States Code might be unconstitutional came as news too, since its constitutionality had never been the subject of such a decision. The manifest imperfections, from the standpoint of both democratic theory and orderly election administration, of the Electoral College had barely been glimpsed either, and for the same reason. (The critical literature on the Electoral College is substantial, but it is mainly the work of political scientists; the contributions of law professors have been modest.)[80] And likewise the mysterious mention of state legislatures in Article II, section 1, clause 2. One searches the constitutional law treatises and casebooks, and for that matter the election law treatises and casebooks, in vain for traces of awareness of the problems that bubbled over in the wake of the deadlocked 2000 election.[81]

Compounding the unpreparedness of the professoriat to opine on an issue that has not previously surfaced in Supreme Court case law is the intensely political character of that law. The age and

---

80. There are exceptions, however, such as Alexander Bickel's book, discussed in the next chapter, and Victor Williams and Alison M. MacDonald, "Rethinking Article II, Section 1 and Its Twelfth Amendment Restatement: Challenging Our Nation's Malapportioned, Undemocratic Presidential Election System," 77 *Marquette Law Review* 201 (1994).

81. Daniel H. Lowenstein, "Election Law as a Subject: A Subjective Account," 32 *Loyola of Los Angeles Law Review* 1199, 1202 (1999); Samuel Issacharoff and Richard H. Pildes, "Not by 'Election' Alone," 32 *Loyola of Los Angeles Law Review* 1173, 1174 (1999). The authors of one of the leading election law casebooks, *The Law of Democracy* (1998), have rushed to make amends; see Samuel Issacharoff, Pamela S. Karlan, and Richard H. Pildes, *When Elections Go Bad: The Law of Democracy and the Presidential Election of 2000* (2001). They describe the book as a "special supplement" to their casebook (ibid. at 4), acknowledging that "*The Law of Democracy* focused more on institutional arrangements than on the nuts-and-bolts of casting votes and having them counted"; ibid. at 2.

brevity of the Constitution, the momentous character of many of the issues that are litigated under it, and the practical finality of most Supreme Court decisions on issues of constitutional law invite, enable, and even compel the Justices to base many of their constitutional decisions on contestable personal values and ideological preferences. Constitutional doctrine—the product largely of judicial decisions rather than of the ancient and often opaque text—lacks coherence because it reflects the changes in political outlook that follow inescapably from changes in the Court's membership. This lack of coherence leaves the professoriat, like the Court itself, free to pick favorites from a rich menu of inconsistent doctrines and decisions and to pronounce those favorites "the law." An incoherent, deeply politicized body of case law cannot supply the legal professoriat with the nourishment it needs in order to make up for an intellectual diet starved of fact. Because professors of constitutional law do not command the full range of subjects encompassed by modern constitutional law, in addressing the subjects within that range that elude their professional understanding they naturally tend to react on the basis of their politics or ideology. The politicization of constitutional law is reflected in, and fosters, the politicization of the academic commentary on that law. If the critics are right that *Bush v. Gore* is a political decision, the Justices can reply to the critics, with equal truth, *tu quoque:* your criticisms are politically motivated.

If the conservative Justices were out of character in their solicitude for equality of voting power and their skepticism about a state court's interpretation of a state statute, the liberal academic critics of *Bush v. Gore* were out of character in their solicitude for Congress as a democratic decision maker[82] and for the prerogatives of state

---

82. The inattention of liberal constitutional lawyers to the democratic legitimacy of legislatures is the theme of Jeremy Waldron, *Law and Disagreement* (1999).

courts, in their skepticism about expansive notions of equal protection, and in their doubts about the legitimacy of a constitutional decision that lacked firm moorings in precedent or original intent.

The politicization of academic constitutional law has been exacerbated by the leftward drift of its practitioners. The reasons for that drift are a topic for another day. The drift itself is unmistakable, so that when Professor Rosen, the shrillest academic critic (barring only Alan Dershowitz)[83] of the Supreme Court's decision in *Bush v. Gore,*[84] adduced, as evidence that the decision was "a transparent mask for a predetermined political result," the fact that "few conservative commentators even attempted to defend the legal reasoning of the decision," he neglected to add that there are very few conservative academic commentators on constitutional decisions.[85] The pitiless criticisms of *Bush v. Gore* make an illuminating contrast to the academics' response to bad opinions in decisions whose result they like. When professors of constitutional law sympathize with the decision but find the opinion unsatisfactory, they search for "alternative justifications."[86] So frantic has the search for an alternative justification for *Roe v. Wade* become that I have described the case as "the Wandering Jew of constitutional

---

83. See, for example, *CNN Breaking News,* Nov. 14, 2000, 8 P.M., Transcript #00111438V00, p. 9; *Rivera Live,* CNBC News Transcripts, Nov. 14, 2000; Somini Sengupta, "The Florida Secretary of State: A Human Lightning Rod in a Vote-Counting Storm," *New York Times* (national ed.), Nov. 20, 2000, p. A17; *ABC: Good Morning America,* Burrelle's Information Services, Dec. 13, 2000.

84. Rosen, "Disgrace."

85. Jeffrey Rosen, "In Lieu of Manners: As Respect for Authority in All Its Forms Erodes, Americans Turn to the Courts to Tell Them How to Live Their Lives. What Happens When We No Longer Respect the Courts?" *New York Times Magazine,* Feb. 4, 2001, pp. 46, 50. An irony arising from the fact that Rosen is the legal affairs editor of the *New Republic* is that—with or without his knowledge, I do not know—the editor of that journal, having asked me to write an article about the election litigation for the *New Republic,* then refused without explanation to publish it.

Bruce Ackerman has also remarked that "the silence of leading conservative academics [about *Bush v. Gore*] is deafening"; Ackerman, "The Court Packs Itself In," *American Prospect,* Feb. 12, 2001, p. 48.

86. William K. Kelley, "Inculcating Constitutional Values," 15 *Constitutional Commentary* 161, 170–172 (1998).

law."[87] Few professors of constitutional law will be searching for alternative justifications for *Bush v. Gore*.[88]

The leftward drift has deflected professorial attention from the structural provisions of the Constitution (such as those regulating the election of the President) to the provisions that create individual rights against government, leaving the professoriat unprepared to address the issues thrown up by the Florida deadlock. The structural provisions are less interesting to the civil libertarian, the civil-rights advocate, and the environmental activist. The vital importance of clarity in those provisions, so that the framework of government is not open to truly debilitating partisan challenge and manipulation (imagine the sheer distraction from other legislative tasks if Congress had to decide in every session how many Senators each state should be allotted), is apt to be overlooked, and with it the tradeoff between certainty and substantive justice. Elections are part of the framework and so belong to the domain of formal justice. They are not actualizations of the popular will.

The leftward drift of the constitutional-law professoriat has also deprived that professoriat of the vitalizing effects of vigorous debate. The left-liberal reflex reaction to *Bush v. Gore* will not be widely challenged in the academy, though the decision is no more vulnerable to criticism than many of the cases that liberals cherish. As John Stuart Mill pointed out in *On Liberty*, the defenders of a position become flabby when they have no attackers to put them on their mettle. They forget the arguments for their position because no one is pushing them to argue for it. Surrounded by the like-minded, browsing comfortably in a herd, implicitly defining a narrow channel of left liberalism as the mainstream, many profes-

---

87. Posner, *Overcoming Law*, at 180. The due process clause of the Fourteenth Amendment was the ground of the Court's decision. Alternatives proposed have included the equal protection clause of the Fourteenth Amendment and the First, Ninth, and Thirteenth Amendments. See ibid. at 179–182.

88. But in fairness it should be noted that some of the liberal critics of *Bush v. Gore*, such as Terrance Sandalow and Jeffrey Rosen, are also critics of *Roe v. Wade*.

sors of constitutional law have become dogmatically complacent. Their conversational community is an echo chamber. They utter as truisms what a detached observer would recognize as prejudices. The organizer of a newspaper advertisement by law professors excoriating *Bush v. Gore,* the distinctly left-liberal Margaret Jane Radin of Stanford Law School, was quoted as saying that "law professors are generally quite conservative, and we [so implicitly including herself in the conservative category] don't do things like this frequently."[89] For her to call herself conservative is to situate herself in a political community unrepresentative of a nation in which 50 million people voted for George W. Bush for President. Bill Clinton and Al Gore are both well to her right.

The advertisement itself, "554 Law Professors Say: By Stopping the Vote Count in Florida, the U.S. Supreme Court Used Its Power to Act as Political Partisans, Not Judges of a Court of Law,"[90] is simplistic. The Justices in the majority were partisans, the advertisement explains, because "it is not the job of a federal court to stop votes from being counted. . . . By stopping the recount in the middle, the five justices acted to suppress the facts. . . . By taking power

---

89. David Abel, *"Bush v. Gore* Case Compels Scholars to Alter Courses at US Law Schools," *Boston Globe,* Feb. 3, 2001, p. A1. I may be doing her a disservice. She may mean only that most law professors are "conservative" with regard to methods of publicizing their views rather than politically conservative. But that would be wrong too. Law professors have long been active on the paid ad/open letter/mass petition front. *Two thousand* of them participated in a public campaign to block the confirmation of Robert Bork as a Supreme Court Justice (Neal Devins, "Bearing False Witness: The Clinton Impeachment and the Future of Academic Freedom," 148 *University of Pennsylvania Law Review* 165, 166–167 [1999]), and hundreds lent their names to advertisements opposing the impeachment of President Clinton. See Posner, *Public Intellectuals,* ch. 3. See also Ward Farnsworth, "Talking out of School: Notes on the Transmission of Intellectual Capital from the Legal Academy to Public Tribunals," 81 *Boston University Law Review* 13, 14 n. 2 (2001).

90. *New York Times* (national ed.), Jan. 13, 2001, p. A7. The number signing the ad has since risen to 673; see "Law Professors Denounce Supreme Court Ruling," http://www.the-rule-of-law.com, visited Feb. 26, 2001. Not all of these, by any means, are professors of constitutional law; their action in nevertheless signing the ad is consistent with Alexander Bickel's quip that "every lawyer nowadays—or at least every academic lawyer—seems to have two specialties: his own, and constitutional law"; Alexander M. Bickel, unpublished book review of Adolf Berle, *Three Faces of Power,* Alexander M. Bickel Papers, Yale University, Sterling Memorial Library, Series III, Box 24, Folder 0169. I am indebted for this reference to Brannon Denning.

from the voters, the Supreme Court has tarnished its own legitimacy." If ballots were forged, it would certainly be the job of the courts to stop them from being counted. And votes are not facts. Nor is the question of who won the popular vote in Florida a question of fact; it is a question of law. If the recount was unlawful, the winner of the recount would not be the winner of the election even if he was in some sense the more popular candidate.

Adding one's signature to the advertisement was a gesture of solidarity masquerading as a statement of professional expertise. We saw in Chapters 2 and 3 how complex are the statistical and legal issues that bear on a responsible evaluation of the deadlock and its resolution by the Supreme Court. How many law professors who subscribed publicly to the Democratic position that the Republicans "stole" the 2000 election through an act of judicial usurpation had studied these issues in sufficient depth to have a responsible opinion? If as I believe the answer is very few, what does this tell us about the professionalism of academic constitutional law?[91]

Or about its sobriety. So out of sympathy is the legal professoriat with Republicans and conservatives, and particularly the Republican conservatives on the Supreme Court, that a decision which—by sweeping away the last obstacle to the election as President of a man whose favorite Supreme Court Justices are Scalia and Thomas—postpones still further the day when the Court will once again be staffed by the likes of William Brennan and Thurgood Marshall is perceived not as a dubious or even clearly mistaken decision but as an outrage, a usurpation. Radin calls it "akin to a coup d'etat. It was beyond the pale and went against all legal precedents. It was a naked power grab."[92]

---

91. For a similar criticism, see Farnsworth, "Talking out of School."

92. Quoted in Abel, "*Bush v. Gore* Case Compels Scholars to Alter Courses." Professor Rosen, remarking what he considers "the inherent polarization that results when social and political disputes are legalized," says that in *Bush v. Gore* "liberal and conservative Supreme Court justices, like Republicans and Democrats throughout the

Similar hyperbole graces an article, quite typical of the academic commentary on *Bush v. Gore,* by Bruce Ackerman in the *London Review of Books.*[93] "Coup" is in the title; and we know that Ackerman takes the word seriously in this context, for he has urged that because *Bush v. Gore* "is a blatantly partisan act, without any legal basis whatsoever," a betrayal of "the nation's trust in the rule of law," the Senate should refuse to confirm any nominations by Bush to the Supreme Court should there be vacancies during his Presidency.[94] The *London Review* article does not substantiate Ackerman's harsh assessment of *Bush v. Gore* or justify his proposed remedy, a form of civil disobedience. He describes Republican demonstrators as a "Republican mob" that "successfully intimidated them [the members of the Miami-Dade County canvassing board] into calling it [the hand recount] quits,"[95] though the members of the board denied being intimidated by this handful of middle class rowdies (there were no arrests) and Jesse Jackson had already begun stirring up trouble on the other side with demagogic charges of racism. The "mob" characterization, moreover—contrary to the thrust of Ackerman's article—supports the view that the Supreme Court really did head off an ugly crisis. And in the next paragraph he undermines the claim of successful intimidation by speculating, plausibly enough, that the antipathy of Cuban-Americans (an influential segment of the Miami community) to the Clinton-Gore administration that the Elián Gonzalez affair stirred up may have played a significant role in the canvassing board's decision to abandon the recount.

---

country, behaved like polarized molecules, aligning themselves even more dramatically in the direction in which they were only tentatively leaning on Election Day"; Rosen, "In Lieu of Manners," at 51. But Rosen, whose article on the decision referred to Justice O'Connor as "addled" and "preening" ("Disgrace," at 20), was one of the molecules.

93. Bruce Ackerman, "Anatomy of a Constitutional Coup," *London Review of Books,* Feb. 8, 2001, p. 3.

94. Ackerman, "The Court Packs Itself In." Katyal, "Politics over Principle," appears to agree with Ackerman's proposal.

95. Ackerman, "Anatomy of a Constitutional Coup," at 3, 5.

Ackerman argues that "after one of the most boring campaigns in history, Americans were sleepwalking their way to the ballot box—when crisis hit after it was supposed to be all over."[96] So the deadlock *was* a crisis, though if so then the earlier it was resolved the better, and therefore the Supreme Court should be thanked for stepping in. But a more interesting point is that if Bush and Gore are really Tweedledum and Tweedledee, why should Ackerman think it so important that Bush not be allowed to make any Supreme Court appointments? In fact the electorate was not so apathetic as Ackerman suggests, especially the fraction of it (which includes himself and the other professors of constitutional law) that considers it terribly important whether a President prefers Clarence Thomas or Thurgood Marshall for the Supreme Court. Ackerman describes the campaign as "boring" presumably to reassure his readers that his indignation at *Bush v. Gore* is not a partisan reaction, that he is above the fray. That is hard to credit. Liberals were very concerned about the consequences of the election for judicial and executive appointments, as we learned when President Bush appointed John Ashcroft as Attorney General; and Ackerman is proudly and forthrightly liberal.

He describes Katherine Harris, Florida's secretary of state, as "egregious," "brazen," a "well-dressed flunky" (to go with the "well-dressed mob"—surely an oxymoron), adding that she should have disqualified herself from ruling on any issues involving the 2000 election and left the necessary rulings to be made by career officials in the department of state. A key ruling—which if sustained by the Florida supreme court, as it should have been, would probably have ended the electoral battle on November 18—was made not by Harris but by Clayton Roberts, the director of the division of elections in the department of state. It was he who ruled that "error in the vote tabulation" does not include voter error (to

---

96. Ibid. at 3.

which most undervotes and overvotes are due), but is limited to miscounting properly voted ballots. Should he have disqualified himself? (Not that anyone asked him to disqualify himself.) If so, how low would one have to delve in the division of elections to find a modestly dressed responsible career official? Because Harris is a Republican and Republicans presumably run in all Florida elections, must she relinquish all control over the division of elections, even though the supervision of elections is the secretary of state's most important duty?

Ackerman argues that Bush's loss of the nationwide popular vote is bound to make him a weak President. There are no signs of that so far, though it is early days. John Kennedy was a popular President who almost certainly would have been reelected had he not been assassinated, yet no one knows whether he really won the popular vote in 1960. It depends, as I pointed out in Chapter 1, on how one classifies the votes cast for the unpledged Democratic electors in Alabama. The argument that a President who did not win the popular vote should be treated as the loser, at best an accidental President, overlooks among other things that if Presidents were elected by nationwide popular vote, candidates would campaign differently; if both Bush and Gore had been gunning for a popular vote majority, it is impossible to determine who would have gotten it. Shortly before the election it was believed that Bush might gain a popular vote majority and Gore a majority of the electoral votes. If that was Bush's perception, he must have redoubled his efforts to win electoral votes, and the popular vote be damned. To call the winner of the popular vote for President the "real" winner, to accord *constitutional* status to the winner of the popular vote, and to question the legitimacy of the candidate who won the electoral vote and so became President are further examples of changing the rules of the game after the game has been played.

Ackerman argues that the 2000 Presidential election deadlock could have been painlessly resolved in the same manner as the

Hayes-Tilden election deadlock of 1876 was resolved, that is, by the appointment of an ad hoc commission in which Supreme Court Justices would play the decisive role. Painlessly? The resolution of the 1876 deadlock was not painless—why otherwise did Congress enact Title III a decade later to resolve such deadlocks in an entirely different fashion? Ackerman does not consider whether current norms of judicial conduct would permit federal judges to be cast in such an extrajudicial role, or explain why, if Justices ought to play the decisive role in the ad hoc commission, the decision cannot be left to the Supreme Court that they compose.

In contrasting the close 5–4 vote in *Bush v. Gore* with the more robust 7–2 vote that gave us *Roe v. Wade,* Ackerman neglects to acknowledge the 7–2 vote in *Bush v. Gore* for the proposition that the recount ordered by the Florida supreme court on December 8 was a denial of equal protection. The likeliest outcome of the remand that Justices Souter and Breyer wanted would have been abandonment of the recount when it became clear that it could not be completed, subject to appropriate judicial review, by December 18. The Hawaii "precedent" on which Ackerman relies for the argument that votes cast after that date can still be counted is unpersuasive. As I pointed out in Chapter 3, Hawaii's tardy votes were irrelevant to the outcome of the electoral vote in the 1960 election. So they could be counted merely as a courtesy—and (as Ackerman neglects to mention) they were counted on the explicit understanding that doing so would *not* set a precedent for future elections.

Aware, despite his sunny view of the Hayes-Tilden solution, that the appointment of a Bush-pledged slate of electors by the Florida legislature could have caused chaos when Congress met to count electoral votes on January 6, Ackerman argues that the U.S. Supreme Court should have enjoined Florida's governor, Jeb Bush, from certifying such a slate. No one asked the Court to do this, however, or even attempted to make Jeb Bush a party to the suit;

nor would there have been any legal basis for such an injunction if he had been a party. Given the likelihood that the contest litigation would prevent Florida from meeting the December 12 safe harbor deadline, or even the final deadline of December 18, the legislature would have been only prudent to appoint a backup slate of electors. Ackerman may be right that Florida would be deemed to have made a "final choice" on November 7, notwithstanding that the identity of the chosen would not have been revealed until the conclusion of litigation more than a month later; and we recall from Chapter 3 that a final choice is conclusive on Congress—if this provision of Title III is constitutional. But Ackerman's position is not so clearly correct that enjoining the Florida legislature from appointing a backup slate would have been an appropriate exercise of the equitable powers of a federal court.

If I seem to be one-sided in criticizing only the liberal critics of the Supreme Court's interventions in the election deadlock and not the Court's conservative defenders as well, it is not because I have any sympathy for the approaches typically taken by conservatives to issues of constitutional interpretation. (I am not an "originalist" or a "textualist.") It is not even because there are so few conservative professors of constitutional law. It is because the tiny conservative legal professoriat has been so measured, indeed so diffident, in its defense of the Court.[97] The reason is that—whether it is a bad decision or, as I believe, a rather good one—*Bush v. Gore* is an activist decision. It forges new doctrinal ground. The Court thrust itself boldly into the center of a political struggle. The five most conservative Justices gave an expansive reading to the equal protection clause. The three most conservative Justices dusted off a forgotten provision of the Constitution (the "Manner directed" clause of Article II) and gave it a meaning very likely unintended

---

97. See, for example, Michael W. McConnell, "Two-and-a-Half Cheers for *Bush v. Gore,*" in *The Vote: Bush, Gore & the Supreme Court* (Cass R. Sunstein and Richard A. Epstein eds. 2001), http://www.thevotebook.com.

by the Constitution's framers, whom conservative lawyers and judges tend to venerate to the point of idolatry. The decision deals a blow to states' rights by overriding a state supreme court's interpretation of its own state's statute. Conservative law professors might be pleased with the outcome, but they could not be expected to offer a full-throated, let alone strident, defense. (Liberals, in their anger, may have overlooked the possibility that the "restraintist" posture which they have affected in criticizing *Bush v. Gore* may cramp them when next they are summoned to advocate or defend liberal judicial activism.) There was conservative vilification of the Florida supreme court, conservative aspersions on the legitimacy of its positions parallel to the liberal aspersions on the legitimacy of *Bush v. Gore*. But the aspersions were cast by politicians and columnists rather than by academics.

An especially curious feature of the professorial reaction to *Bush v. Gore* remains to be noted: anger that the decision threatens to unmask the "noble lie" of law-school teaching of constitutional law. Professor Stephen Wermiel "for years . . . [has] lauded the judiciary in his classes for its independence," but remarks that *Bush v. Gore* "'has made me really stop and reconsider how zealously I want to challenge my class to think about the Supreme Court being an institution above regular politics. . . . That makes it a soul-searching moment, maybe even a defining moment, for many constitutional law professors.'"[98] Professor Heather Gerken says that the decision "'has certainly led me to question my confidence in the courts. It's going to be a challenge to persuade students that the law does matter and that it's not all one big political game.'"[99] Maybe these are rhetorical flourishes. If meant seriously, they are startling in two respects. First, it argues a considerable naïveté to believe that it took *Bush v. Gore* to knock the scales loose at last

---

98. Quoted in Abel, *"Bush v. Gore* Case Compels Scholars to Alter Courses."
99. Ibid.

from the professors' eyes. There has never been a period in U.S. history in which the Supreme Court has not decided a significant fraction of its constitutional cases on grounds that could easily be described as political. The idea that *Bush v. Gore* is a quantum leap beyond the normal practice of political adjudication cannot be sustained. Second, the remarks I have quoted imply that these professors, though finally disillusioned about the Supreme Court, will try to hide this hideous truth from their students. In other words, they will deliberately conceal the truth as they perceive it about the Court from graduate students whose ability to operate successfully as lawyers requires a realistic rather than a fairy tale understanding of how courts operate in the politically charged sphere of constitutional law. An issue of academic ethics lurks here.

The inadequacies of the professorial reaction to *Bush v. Gore,* and to the deadlock more broadly, ought to make law professors more forgiving of the inadequacies of the Supreme Court's opinions in that case. Anyone with judicial experience knows—and those without it should have enough imagination to be able to guess—that judges faced with a completely unfamiliar case involving a high degree of factual as well as legal uncertainty and complexity cannot be expected to produce a good judicial opinion in a few days, any more than professors of constitutional law were able to produce good commentary on the decision in *Bush v. Gore* in a few days or a few weeks. Intuition is an important resource of an experienced judge, and all the current Justices of the Supreme Court have extensive judicial experience, most before as well as since their appointment to the Court. An experienced judge may sense what the right decision in a case is before being able to articulate the path of reasoning that leads from the lawyers' arguments and the other conventional materials of legal advocacy to that decision. Five Justices in *Bush v. Gore* sensed that the Florida supreme court was embarked on a path that impaired rather than promoted constitutional values. History may reject the academic criticism of the decision and conclude that those Justices wrought better than they knew. The challenge to the rest of the society is to reform the process of Presidential election so that the Supreme Court will never again be placed in so fraught a position. That is the subject of the next chapter.

Chapter 5

Consequences and Reforms

IT IS too early to say what the consequences of the 2000 election deadlock, and of the manner in which it was resolved, will be. It is reasonably clear that had Gore not sought a hand recount or other relief after the machine recount confirmed Bush's lead in Florida, or had the Florida supreme court refused to interfere with Katherine Harris's rulings, the near tie in the Florida popular vote would have had only two consequences. One would have been to accelerate the movement away from the punchcard voting method, widely regarded as outmoded yet still in use in more than a third of the nation's precincts.[1] The other would have been to awaken dormant criticisms that the Electoral College is an undemocratic institution, since Gore unquestionably won the popular vote nationwide. The bitter and protracted legal struggle touched off by Gore's refusal to accept the result of the machine recount has done

---

1. Even Katherine Harris has now recommended replacing all punchcard systems in Florida with marksense systems; Florida Department of State Press Release, March 2001, http://www.dos.state.fl.us/press/oss/elecreform.html. At this writing, committees in both houses of the Florida legislature have approved bills that would do that.

at least short-term damage to race relations in the United States, has tarnished Bush's victory, and has fomented criticism (especially in academic circles) of the Supreme Court as having shown its partisan colors. At this writing, none of these consequences looms very large. Nor would they have been mitigated (they might even have been aggravated) had the Court held aloof from the struggle and allowed it to be resolved if need be by Congress in January—or later. The Court would not have escaped criticism had it washed its hands of the entire mess, Pilate-like, to protect its prestige.

My guess (and not only mine[2]) is that history's verdict on *Bush v. Gore* will depend significantly, though improperly, on the success of Bush's Presidency. If it is a success, most Americans, given their lack of interest in theoretical issues such as political legitimacy and judicial restraint, will be uninterested in criticisms of the judicial decision that may have been responsible for Bush's becoming President. If his Presidency is adjudged a failure, that failure will become an influential talking point for critics of the decision. Of course the Court could not know how Bush would do as President; and should he do badly, it would not follow that Gore would have done better. Whatever criticisms can fairly be lodged against the Court, failing to pick the better Presidential prospect is not one of them. But history is not the story of fairness; judgment based on hindsight predominates, and liability frequently is strict. If things go badly for Bush, many people will blame the Court for having helped him become President. If they go well, the Court will bask in reflected glory. All that will "save" the Court from being blamed or praised for Bush's Presidency will be a consensus, should it ever emerge, that Bush would have been confirmed as the winner of the popular vote in Florida even if the Supreme Court had not intervened.

---

2. Jack M. Balkin, "*Bush v. Gore* and the Boundary between Law and Politics" (forthcoming in *Yale Law Journal*); Michael J. Klarman, "*Bush v. Gore* through the Lens of Constitutional History" (forthcoming in *California Law Review*).

The conventional wisdom is that *Bush v. Gore* will make it harder for Bush to appoint conservatives to the Supreme Court, should there be vacancies during his term of office. I am dubious. What will make it hard for Bush is that the Court is closely divided between conservatives and liberals, that the Senate is evenly divided between Republicans and Democrats, and that interest groups that are influential with most Democratic and some Republican Senators feel passionately about a number of the issues that are likely to be resolved by the Court in coming years. *Bush v. Gore* will give opponents of conservative judicial appointments a rallying point. They will argue, with support from the liberal critics of the decision, that it has unmasked conservative Justices as partisans not to be trusted to apply the law in an evenhanded manner. If the public is impressed by the argument, it will strengthen the political support of opponents of conservative appointments. I doubt that the public will be impressed.

All that is for the future. So far the principal consequence of the legal struggle has been to strengthen the felt need for electoral reform, up to and including the Electoral College. We have learned not only that the Electoral College is undemocratic (more precisely, malapportioned)—which everyone knew—but also that the constitutional and statutory procedures for the election of the President by the Electoral College are incomplete, unclear, and unreliable. Had the Supreme Court not stepped in, something quite like chaos might have ensued when Congress met on January 6 to count the electoral votes. It will not do to say that because the last deadlocked Presidential election took place 124 years before this one (the Hayes-Tilden election of 1876), we have 124 more years in which to think of ways to prevent a repetition. In the 34 Presidential elections since 1868 (the date of the first post–Civil War Presidential election), there have been two deadlocks. That is a nontrivial 6 percent of the Presidential elections in this period. Realism counsels assigning a similar probability of deadlock to the

Presidential election four years from now—or maybe a higher probability, since, with the growing professionalization of political campaigning, close elections may become more frequent. The better both parties are at gauging voter sentiment, appealing to voters, and assembling winning coalitions, the likelier they are to fight to a near tie.

I focus first on Electoral College reform and then turn to the reform of election administration, with particular reference to ballot design and to the question whether to institute a national ballot for federal elections.

Electoral College Reform

There are two quite different kinds of criticism of the Electoral College. The first is that it is undemocratic, and that this is bad. The second (which the Florida experience has made salient) is that it is an unreliable device for selecting the President.[3]

It is undemocratic in two ways. The first and obvious one is that it is malapportioned, because each state gets two electoral votes, regardless of the state's population, in addition to votes equal to the state's delegation in the House of Representatives. Malapportionment is a common feature of democratic governments, the U.S. Senate being the most conspicuous surviving example in the United States now that the Supreme Court has required that state senators be elected from districts of equal population. But the undemocratic character of malapportionment is masked when each malapportioned district elects a different official. No one bothers to add up the number of votes that all the Republican and all the Democratic senatorial candidates receive in

---

3. Until the 2000 election, this factor was not given sufficient weight in the debates over reforming or abolishing the Electoral College. See, for example, Paul A. Freund, "Direct Election of the President: Issues and Answers," 56 *American Bar Association Journal* 773, 775 (1970). Some scholars, however, recognized the problem. See, for example, Michael J. Glennon, *When No Majority Rules: The Electoral College and Presidential Succession* (1992).

an election and compare the totals; and if the votes were aggregated, the interpretation would be difficult, since the sum of the votes for each party would not be the votes received by a single candidate. Nor are votes in the Senate translated into the number of voters who voted for those Senators who prevailed in the Senate vote, because those voters did not vote for particular bills. The mask is stripped off malapportionment when the popular vote is for electors pledged to a particular candidate, whose name, indeed, appears on the ballot, so that the aggregate popular vote for each candidate is immediately computed and reported. The malapportionment of the Electoral College is thus transparent—one has only to compare a candidate's percentage of the electoral vote with his percentage of the popular vote—especially in elections in which the popular vote winner loses in the Electoral College.

Despite the closeness of the 2000 election, there is no doubt that Gore really did win the popular vote, in the sense that, had the entire nationwide vote been recounted by an infallible counter using the best criteria for determining whether a ballot should be counted as a vote, Bush would not have overcome Gore's lead. Nationwide about 2 percent of all the ballots cast were not counted as votes for one reason or another. Suppose, very optimistically, that the infallible counter would have recovered half of these as votes. Suppose further, rather pessimistically, that 1 percent of the 100 million votes that were recorded for one Presidential candidate or another were not counted carefully. On these assumptions, 2 million votes cast in the 2000 election would be in play. To overcome Gore's lead of 540,000 votes, Bush would have to be awarded 1,270,001 of the 2 million votes, which is almost two-thirds—an unrealistic expectation given the election outcome and the absence of any theory that would point to Bush as the wildly disproportionate favorite of the voters whose votes got botched. Florida's experience suggests that Democratic voters are more likely than Republican ones to spoil their ballots.

The fact that the Electoral College is undemocratic is not decisive against it any more than the fact that the Senate is malapportioned, or that federal judges are not elected at all, need be thought a flaw in our system of government. Ours is not a pure democracy, and we know from Chapter 1 that pure democracy is as undesirable as it is unattainable. But it is not all that easy to come up with a convincing justification for the Electoral College. From a 1787 political standpoint it was an ingenious—but not necessarily a principled or, had it not been for political imperatives, even a sensible—device for achieving two purposes important to the framers. These were (1) preserving the balance among the states that had been struck in the design of the Congress (2) without confiding the election of the President to the Congress, a method of achieving objective (1) that would have weakened the Presidency unduly.

The invention of the Electoral College also reflected concerns about the administrability of a nationwide popular election that have no current validity; equally anachronistic concerns, rooted in a preference for deferential democracy, that the President's status and dignity would be seriously compromised were he directly elected by *hoi polloi* who should in any event entrust their "betters" with momentous political choices such as the choice of the President; and also expectations, which have proved unfounded, that the contingent election procedure ordained by the Constitution— election of the President by the House of Representatives (the most democratic component of the governmental structure created at Philadelphia in 1787) if no candidate received a majority of the electoral votes—would be used as or more frequently than the normal method.[4] The framers did not foresee political parties, let

---

4. Lawrence D. Longley and Alan G. Braun, *The Politics of Electoral College Reform*, ch. 2 (1972); Neal R. Peirce and Lawrence D. Longley, *The People's President: The Electoral College in American History and the Direct Vote Alternative* (rev. ed. 1981); Shlomo Slonim, "The Electoral College at Philadelphia: The Evolution of an Ad Hoc Congress for the Selection of a President," 73 *Journal of American History* 35 (1986). But remember that since each state's delegation would have one vote, the contingent procedure

alone a two-party system, which would make it rare for one of the Presidential candidates to fail to obtain a majority of the Electoral College. The two-party system doomed any hope that the Electoral College would choose the "best" person to be President,[5] since the choice would be limited to the candidates picked by the parties. (The electors could pick the better, but not the best.) Another way to put this is that a party system is already a system of indirect election, making indirect election via the Electoral College otiose. And when there are only two major candidates, both will pitch their appeal to the median voter and so are likely to be much alike, leaving the Electoral College with little scope for choice quite apart from the limited number of choices.

Even in the absence of parties, the type of indirect election envisaged by the creators of the Electoral College did not make a lot of sense.[6] The implicit theory was that the public at large is more competent to pick individuals who can pick a President well than to pick the President directly. But if this is so, then the people will not be exercising a political judgment at all. It is unclear whether they are any better at picking a good President-picker than at picking a good President. But even if they are, they are likely to want to exercise a political judgment rather than be content with picking other people to exercise such a judgment; and then electors will compete by pledging themselves to a particular candidate—which means that instead of electors being the people most competent to pick the President, they will be the people most loyal to the candidate and therefore *least* likely to exercise an indepen-

---

is not actually very democratic, as was discovered in 1824 when Andrew Jackson lost the Presidential election in the House even though he had received both the most popular votes and the most electoral votes.

5. It was because the framers assumed that different electors would have different ideas about who would be the best person to be President, as well as because they assumed that very few Americans would have a national reputation, that they thought it would be difficult for one person to gain a majority in the Electoral College, and therefore many or even most Presidential elections would be decided by the House of Representatives.

6. John Stuart Mill, *Considerations on Representative Government*, ch. 9 (1870).

dent judgment. So indirect election is likely to decay into a clumsy form of direct election, which has in fact been the history of the Electoral College. Recall from Chapter 1 that one of the reasons for abolishing the indirect election of Senators was that the election of state legislators was being influenced by the electorate's preferences regarding the U.S. Senatorial candidates among whom the legislators would be choosing.

But as I pointed out in discussing the "Manner directed" clause of Article II of the Constitution, finding new functions for old, even anachronistic constitutional provisions is a familiar technique of government; and there has been no dearth of efforts to rationalize the Electoral College in terms of modern conditions unforeseen by the framers. I shall mention six.

(1) Reversing the traditional criticism that the Electoral College is malapportioned in favor of voters in small states,[7] Alexander Bickel and others have argued that the Electoral College overweights the votes of minorities, because minorities are concentrated in the big (by population) states, and big states, rather than small ones, are advantaged by the Electoral College.[8] And in fact proposals to abolish or reform the Electoral College were opposed in 1979 by blacks and by Jews "arguing that the voting strength of black and Jewish voters is maximized under the Electoral College system because both groups are concentrated in urban areas of the large electoral vote states."[9]

It is not clear why it would (as Bickel thought) be good for the nation for minorities to have more voting power than they would

---

7. A criticism widely repeated in the wake of the 2000 election. See, for example, Bruce Ackerman, "Anatomy of a Constitutional Coup," *London Review of Books,* Feb. 8, 2001, pp. 3, 4.

8. Alexander M. Bickel, *Reform and Continuity: The Electoral College, the Convention, and the Party System,* ch. 2 (1971).

9. Congressional Quarterly, Inc., *Guide to U.S. Elections* 354 (3d ed. 1994). See also Robert M. Hardaway, *The Electoral College and the Constitution: The Case for Preserving Federalism* 25 (1994).

have if the Electoral College did not exist. But Bickel appears to have been correct that, at least if other things are equal, the Electoral College favors the big states rather than the small ones—though only because all but two minor states award all their electoral votes to whoever receives a plurality of the popular vote for President in their state. Given the winner-take-all allocation of electoral votes in all the other states, if Bush won Montana by one vote that marginal voter would have swung 3 electoral votes while if Gore had won Florida by one vote that voter would have swung 25 electoral votes, thus exercising more than eight times the voting power of the Montanan. Of course there are more than eight times as many voters in Florida as in Montana, which dilutes the influence of swing voters in the more populous state. But state outcomes are likely to be closer to the national outcome the more populous the state is.[10] This is partly because the larger the population, the more likely it is to be representative of the nation as a whole and partly because, if there are any economies of scale in campaigning, candidates will devote disproportionately more resources to campaigning in the most populous states, and their efforts will tend to produce a tighter race in those states, so a smaller percentage of the voters will be able to swing the outcome.

Another reason that the greater voting power of the swing voter in the big state is not fully offset by the greater number of voters is statistical. The probability of a tie decreases with the number of votes cast, but it decreases more slowly, namely by the square root of the number of votes. This is the elementary statistical proposition that the standard deviation from the mean of a sample is inverse to the square root of the sample size. It follows that vot-

---

10. In support of this conjecture, I note that the winning percentages of the Presidential candidates in 1988, 1992, 1996, and 2000, both by state and by Florida county, were negatively correlated with the population of the state or Florida county, as the case may be.

ing *power,* being the probability *per vote* of influencing the outcome of a close election, increases with the size of the electorate.[11] Compare two states, one with a population of 100 and the other with a population of 10,000. In each state, 51 percent of the voters prefer Bush to Gore. But there is some probability that because of a last-minute change of heart by swing voters, Bush will lose or tie. In the smaller state, assuming a normal distribution, there is a 95 percent probability that Bush's actual vote will fall between .46 and .56—and if it is less than .50, he will lose. In the larger state, assuming the same distribution, the 95 percent confidence interval runs from .515 to .505. This is a tenfold reduction in variance (because 10 is the square root of 100). There is that much less likelihood that swing voters will cause an upset. But if they do cause an upset, the effect on the national election will be 100 times greater because of the winner-take-all rule for allocating electoral votes.

The increase in voting power in Presidential elections as a function of state population can be quantified. One study arrays the voting power of the voters in each state on a scale from 1 (Montana) to 2.663 (California).[12] By weighting the composition of the voting population of each state by the state's voting power score, the authors of the study are able to conclude that the Electoral College not only confers "a net large-state advantage and a disadvantage to states with 3 to 21 electoral votes,"[13] but also "advantages Hispanic origin, foreign born, Jewish, and urban voters as well as inhabitants of the Far West," while disadvantaging "rural and black voters, as well as inhabitants of the Mountain, Midwestern, Southern, and Eastern states." In sum, "urban citizen-voters

---

11. Steven J. Brams, *The Presidential Election Game* 107–133 (1978), esp. 107–109 and n. 27. The theory has been criticized on various grounds. See, for example, Howard Margolis, "The Banzhaf Fallacy," 27 *American Journal of Political Science* 321 (1983).

12. Lawrence D. Longley and Neal R. Peirce, *The Electoral College Primer 2000* 151–152 (tab. 22).

13. That is, all the states with 21 or fewer electoral votes, since no state has fewer than 3 electoral votes.

have above average voting power in the electoral college, while rural voters, on the other hand, are relatively disadvantaged by the present electoral college."[14]

This problem would disappear if every state awarded electoral votes in proportion to a candidate's popular vote. But that is something the states are unlikely to do voluntarily. It is no accident that all but two minor ones allocate all their electoral votes to the winner of the popular vote, no matter how slight his margin. Because winning the popular vote is much more valuable to the winning candidate in a winner-take-all state, states get more attention from the candidates if they use that system.

Voting power depends on a host of factors besides winner take all, such as turnout,[15] the likely effect of one's votes on the outcome of other elections besides the election of the President (who is after all not the only official that people vote for), and whether one is a swing voter (that is, how political preferences are distributed across the state's population). Throughout the 2000 election campaign, for example, Gore had a commanding lead in New York and California, and Bush a commanding lead in Texas. The nation's three most populous states were not seriously in con-

---

14. Longley and Peirce, *Electoral College Primer 2000*, at 155, 157. Recalling the opposition of blacks to abolition of the Electoral College, we see that there is room for disagreement over whether they would be benefited or harmed by the abolition. This is an example of the difficulty of measuring voter power.

In light of the passage quoted in the text from Longley and Peirce (and see Nelson W. Polsby and Aaron Wildavsky, *Presidential Elections: Strategies and Structures of American Politics* 247 [10th ed. 2000], which also argues that abolition of the Electoral College would benefit rather than harm the South), it is ironic that Professor Amar should have written that the intended and the actual beneficiaries of the Electoral College are "white Southern males"; Akhil Reed Amar, "The Electoral College, Unfair from Day One," *New York Times* (late ed.), Nov. 9, 2000, p. A23. Amar's article advocates the abolition of the Electoral College without mention of any consideration pro or con other than what he considers the Electoral College's racist origin and continuing racist impact. That is what might be called playing the race card. What is correct is that until the election of 1860, the constitutional structure, including the Electoral College, gave the Southern states disproportionate influence in the federal government. See, for example, James M. McPherson, "Southern Comfort," *New York Review of Books,* April 12, 2001, pp. 28, 31.

15. Eric R. A. N. Smith and Peverill Squire, "Direct Election of the President and the Power of the States," 40 *Western Political Quarterly* 29 (1987).

tention and their voters were therefore largely ignored (though Bush made some play for California votes).

(2) These complications make it impossible to equalize voting power across all eligible voters. Whether abolishing the Electoral College would, by erasing some of the inequalities in voting power, bring about a net increase in equality of voting power is unknown, and perhaps unknowable. Abolition might actually—this is the second argument for retention—reduce equality. The big-state advantage conferred by the Electoral College under the winner-take-all regime tends to offset the small-state advantage conferred by the structure of the Senate. We have in effect offsetting—rather than, as usually assumed, reinforcing—malapportionments.

(3) It is sometimes argued that Presidential candidates would concentrate even more heavily (implicitly, too heavily) on big states if the Electoral College were abolished, especially if the alternative were to move from winner take all to proportionate allocation of each state's electoral votes (though that might well require a constitutional amendment too, as we shall see). This is not a persuasive argument. Abolish the college and state boundaries become irrelevant.

(4) What does seem likely, however, and potentially worrisome, if the Electoral College were abolished, is that each candidate would focus more than at present on encouraging turnout in areas in which he was already popular, since the political preferences of nonvoters tend to be similar to those of voters.[16] The more

---

16. Raymond E. Wolfinger and Steven J. Rosenstone, *Who Votes?* 108–114 (1980); Stephen Earl Bennett and David Resnick, "The Implications of Nonvoting for Democracy in the United States," 34 *American Journal of Political Science* 771 (1990). Ron Shachar and Barry Nalebuff, "Follow the Leader: Theory and Evidence on Political Participation," 89 *American Economic Review* 525, 529, 543–544 (1999), presents evidence that nonvoters are more likely to favor Democratic candidates. Contrary evidence, however, is noted in Bennett and Resnick, "The Implications of Nonvoting," at 795.

lopsided the preference for a candidate in a particular area, the more intensely he would seek to increase turnout in that area. As a result, there would be a greater tendency than at present to preach to the converted, as it were, and less to appeal to swing voters. This would have a polarizing effect, which most students of American politics would consider a bad thing. Not all: some would like to see more ideological conflict and less preoccupation with personality and scandal. Personally I prefer our current "postideological" politics, but I cannot begin to defend that preference within the compass of a book on election deadlocks and their resolution.

(5) Abolishing the Electoral College might have an undesirable regional consequence. The geographic configuration of the United States in relation to the distribution of the nation's population makes it impossible for a candidate whose appeal is limited to a particular region (provided "region" is not too broadly defined) to win the Presidency, however strong his appeal in that region. That is, no one whose popularity was confined to the South, the West, the Pacific Coast, the Middle West, or the Northeast could assemble enough electoral votes to win, given our two-party system. A candidate has to have some transregional appeal, though not necessarily a truly national appeal; in the 2000 election Bush carried only one state, New Hampshire, in the Northeast, and Gore only one in the West, New Mexico, and none in the South. Thus, to the extent that regions have different political cultures (which in fact they still do), the Electoral College counteracts political polarization. For those who put a high value on political peace, this is a third advantage of retaining that archaic institution, though one closely related to the second; together they form an "antipolarization" rationale for retaining the Electoral College.

(6) The last advantage of retention is highlighted by the 2000 election. Were Presidents elected by popular vote, a nationwide recount might have been unavoidable in 2000 (and in a number of

previous Presidential elections as well, such as those of 1876, 1880, 1884, 1888, 1960, 1968, and 1976, in all of which the popular vote was very close)[17] because Gore's popular vote margin was so slight. He received 51 million votes and Bush 50.5 million,[18] a difference of 0.5 percent. If a plurality of the popular vote were what elected a President, a margin this small would have incited calls for a national recount on the same grounds that Gore argued for a Florida recount. Even though under a post–Electoral College, pure-popular-vote regime the Presidential election would presumably still be administered by the states, no state could refuse the demand for a recount on the ground that the election in that state had not been close. The state would no longer be a relevant entity for purposes of determining the winner of the election. Each candidate would be trolling for votes everywhere in the country.

Suppose Gore had won the popular election by one vote, but in New York his margin was a million votes. Nevertheless, if Bush could in a recount pick up one net vote in New York, he would erase Gore's lead, so it would be worthwhile for Bush to seek a recount there. The example is extreme, but the reality is stark enough. Gore's margin in the nationwide popular vote averaged fewer than eight votes per precinct. There is little doubt that if Bush's people nosed around heavily Democratic precincts throughout the nation they would come up with colorable arguments about voter and tabulation errors—not to mention outright fraud, which remains common,[19] especially with regard to absentee ballots—that might have made the difference (though it would have been a long shot, given Gore's popular-vote margin), while Gore might have been eager to shore up his lead by also hunting for

---

17. See Longley and Peirce, *Electoral College Primer 2000,* at 177–187 (app. a), for a complete list of the national vote totals in all the Presidential elections through the 1996 election.

18. David Stout, "The 43rd President: The Final Tally: Gore's Lead in the Popular Vote Now Exceeds 500,000," *New York Times* (national ed.), Dec. 30, 2000, p. A11.

19. See references cited in Chapter 2.

votes all over the country. A national recount would be an expensive nightmare. The risk of protracting the period of deadlock and precipitating a rancorous battle in Congress in January would be greater than under the present system, which localizes the deadlock to one or conceivably a few states.

So there is a case for retaining the Electoral College after all—though not a case the framers of the Constitution would have recognized. I have yet to mention the most undemocratic feature of the Electoral College, however, and this will take us directly to a consideration of the second class of criticisms, that the Electoral College is an unreliable device for determining the winner of a Presidential election. Its most undemocratic feature is that the Constitution requires neither that Presidential electors be elected by popular vote, nor, if the state chooses that method of picking electors, that they cast their electoral votes in conformity with the wishes of the voters who elected them. The Constitution leaves the manner of selecting the electors to each state's legislature, as we know; and it places no limitations on the electors' choice among candidates.

It is true that all states now select their Presidential electors by popular vote, and as no state is about to abandon that approach it would be pedantic to complain that the Constitution does not require it and that Congress could not by statute require it (more on that shortly). The practical concern, rather, is that electors are not bound to cast their votes for the candidate to whom they are pledged. In an election as close as that of 2000, the defection of a tiny handful—in 2000 of only 3—of the 538 electors could swing the election. Bush's margin in the electoral vote was 271 to 266 rather than 267 because one of Gore's electors decided to abstain in protest against the District of Columbia's not having statehood. Had three of Bush's electors voted for Gore, the vote would have been 269 to 268 in Gore's favor. Gore would have had a plurality, but not a majority, of the appointed electors, so the House of Representatives would have chosen the President.

No defection by electors has yet swung an election (out of more than 21,000 electoral votes cast since the first Presidential election, only 10 have violated explicit pledges,[20] which is no surprise, since electors are handpicked by the candidate for their loyalty). The likelihood of its ever happening is even less than the statistics imply. That Gore elector who defected would not have done so if it would have cost Gore the election! But the possibility that runaway electors might swing an election cannot be excluded. The 2000 election has sensitized us all to the possibility that small probabilities can become frightening actualities.

Many states have passed laws requiring electors to honor their pledge to the candidate who selected them, but even if these laws are constitutional,[21] the refusal of an elector to comply with the law would have the same effect on the electoral vote as it would if he were legally free to vote his pleasure (unless Congress decided not to count his vote).[22] And it is doubtful that the laws *are* constitutional.[23] The only authority the Constitution grants the states with regard to Presidential electors is authority for the state legislature to determine the manner in which the electors are appointed, not the manner in which they vote. A law that makes the elector a mere rubber stamp of the popular vote is contrary to the notion of indirect election that is at the heart of the Electoral College; the voter *becomes* the elector under such a law. It would likewise be unconstitutional, I believe, for Congress to pass a law requiring

20. Longley and Peirce, *Electoral College Primer 2000,* at 24. Their figure is nine, but there was one more in the 2000 election: the Electoral College member pledged to Gore who abstained.

21. An issue left open in *Ray v. Blair,* 343 U.S. 214, 228–230 (1952), which held only that a state could allow political parties to extract a pledge from the electors whom they slated.

22. Recall from Chapter 3 that section 15 of Title III requires that an electoral vote be counted only if "regularly given," a term of undetermined meaning.

23. See David P. Currie, *The Constitution in the Supreme Court: The Second Century, 1888–1986* 371 (1990).

that electoral votes be cast in conformity with the state's popular vote. Nothing in the Constitution authorizes Congress to eliminate the system of indirect election that the Electoral College creates.

I do not say that the Supreme Court would hold laws that require electors to stand by their pledges unconstitutional. The fact that such laws have been in force for many years without being questioned, and their utility in averting potential election disasters, are practical arguments for brushing aside merely "logical" objections to their constitutionality; and *Ray v. Blair,* though distinguishable, provides some support. But most states do not have such laws, and those that do cannot actually prevent an elector from violating his pledge even if they could lawfully punish him for doing so. In any case the freedom of electors to defy the popular vote is only one of the concerns with the Electoral College's reliability as a method of determining the choice of President without precipitating the kind of chaos that the Supreme Court may have averted in *Bush v. Gore.* Another concern, of course, is the failure of the Constitution to prescribe a method for resolving disputes over electors.[24]

The fact that the electoral votes are counted in the presence of both houses of Congress[25] implies, as I noted in the last chapter, that Congress is authorized to resolve, with or without judicial review (probably without, if my analysis in that chapter of the political questions doctrine is correct), disputes over whose votes should be counted. Congress took a crack at this in Title III, with very imperfect results, as we have seen. The law could be improved, but the problem is organic rather than accidental. The short time between the election and the inauguration, the necessity under the conditions of modern U.S. government for a transition period before inauguration in order to enable the President-elect to organ-

---

24. Others are discussed in Glennon, *When No Majority Rules;* see especially ch. 4.
25. U.S. Const. art. II, § 1, cl. 3; and 12th Amendment.

ize the new administration and so hit the ground running on Inauguration Day, the fact that the "old" Congress takes a Christmas recess and the new one is not sworn in until after the first of the year, and the structure of Congress with its two houses and hundreds of members and poor reputation for statesmanship—all these things taken together make a credible, expeditious resolution of a dispute over electors unlikely. Title III did not accomplish much; and anyway there is nothing to prevent the two houses of Congress, when they meet together in January to count the electoral votes, from ignoring Title III, especially given its dubious constitutionality.

We need a constitutional amendment. For it to have any chance of adoption, it should focus on resolving disputes over electors and preventing "runaway" electors, rather than on abolition of the Electoral College. Runaway electors have historically been rare, as I have noted. But they could wreak havoc in a close election, and it is time to shut them down—a more urgent and feasible goal of constitutional reform than abolishing the Electoral College in the name of democracy. Not that abolition is an entirely quixotic long-term goal, despite the assumption that the small states—more plausibly the big ones—will oppose it and the fact that a constitutional amendment requires ratification by three-fourths of the states and so can be blocked by one more than one quarter of them. There was a serious push in 1969 and 1970 to abolish the Electoral College in favor of a nationwide popular vote with a runoff if no candidate received at least 40 percent of the vote. The proposal passed the House by the requisite two-thirds vote but failed in the Senate.[26] The objection to abolition has less to do with considerations of feasibility than with the fact that, as we have seen, a convincing case for abolition has not yet been made.

---

26. Bickel, *Reform and Continuity,* at 10–11; Longley and Braun, *Politics of Electoral College Reform,* ch. 5.

Of particular pertinence to this book is the fact that the democratizing and dispute resolution goals of Electoral College reform are in conflict,[27] so that doing away with the Electoral College (and even some lesser reforms of the Electoral College) would exacerbate the problem of disputed Presidential elections. Consider the superficially attractive reform of requiring that each state's electoral vote be divided among the Presidential candidates in proportion to their share of the popular vote. This would reduce the likelihood that the popular vote winner would lose in the Electoral College, as well as eliminate the big-state advantage that the winner-take-all system confers. But it would increase the likelihood of deadlocks. Under the winner-take-all system, the only possible deadlock is a 50–50 split in the popular vote in the state. Under a proportional system, every vote combination on which the allocation of an electoral vote turned would be a candidate for deadlock and recount. Suppose a state has 10 electoral votes. Under the proportional system, if a candidate got 10 percent of the votes, he would get one elector; 20 percent, two; and so on. It might be uncertain whether he had gotten just 10 percent, uncertain whether he had gotten just 20 percent, and so on. There would be 10 potential vote combinations rather than one on which a recount would be necessary in order to determine which candidate had obtained an electoral vote.

What may be both feasible and helpful would be a constitutional amendment that did just two things. The first would be to require that each state's electoral votes be cast for the winner of the popular vote for President in their state.[28] With the electors thus bound, there would be no need for electors at all—a welcome sim-

---

27. Part of the more general conflict between the desirability of clear structural provisions in a constitution and the desire for substantively just outcomes. See John Harrison, "The Lawfulness of the Reconstruction Amendments," 68 *University of Chicago Law Review* 375, 457–461 (2001).

28. This has been proposed repeatedly. See Longley and Braun, *Politics of Electoral College Reform*, at 43–49.

plification of the Presidential selection process that would eliminate, for example, such problems as what to do when electors die or
become disabled after the election but before the Electoral College
vote. There would still be electoral votes under the proposed
reform, but they would be computed automatically from the popular vote in each state and the state's determination of how to allocate electoral votes among candidates (whether winner take all
or proportionately). Second, the amendment would require—
confirming the interpretation of Article II, section 1, clause 2 of the
Constitution that I defended in Chapters 3 and 4—that the winner
of the popular vote in each state be determined in the manner
directed by the state's legislature by statute passed *before* the election (implicit I think in Article II, but good to make explicit),
subject to obligatory, rather than discretionary, review by the U.S.
Supreme Court to determine the conformity of the state's determination of the winner with the legislature's directions. Contesting
the result of the popular vote election in a state would still be possible, but there would be a streamlined, disciplined, and unquestionably constitutional method of resolution. The only difference
so far as the resolution of the 2000 election deadlock is concerned,
had the suggested amendment been in effect, would be that Bush,
having lost the contest proceeding in the Florida supreme court,
would have had a right to insist that the U.S. Supreme Court review
the Florida court's decision for conformity to the Florida election
law. The Supreme Court would not have had discretion to refuse to
hear the appeal; and it would have been obliged to determine
whether the Florida court was applying or revising the election
statute, as well as to consider any other constitutional challenges to
that court's resolution of the contest. This would lay to rest the
curious notion that the Florida supreme court was a more appropriate body to rule on issues that might determine the outcome of a
Presidential election than the Supreme Court of the United States.
But this particular reform would doubtless be blocked by Demo-

cratic opposition to any measure that would tend to legitimize the Supreme Court's intervention in the 2000 election.

Nonconstitutional Reforms

I turn finally to the question of nonconstitutional reforms.[29] They should not be limited to changes in law. The time has come to phase out punchcard voting. Extravagant numbers have been tossed around in the press concerning the cost of replacing the punchcard voting and tabulating machines—numbers as large as $9 billion for the nation as a whole. These estimates cannot be credited; in fact they seem absurdly exaggerated.

The cost of replacing all the punchcard voting systems in the nation with marksense systems can be estimated with the aid of cost figures provided by marksense manufacturers. There are roughly 80,000 precincts (distributed across more than 3,000 counties) in the nation, of which 37 percent use punchcard technology, as shown in Table 8.[30] The marksense software costs about $50,000 per county (with a nominal additional charge) and the cost of each marksense optical scan (tabulating) machine is about $4,500. If it is assumed based on their percentage of precincts that punchcard systems are in 37 percent of the nation's counties, or roughly 1,000 counties, then the total marksense software cost (assuming no volume discounts!) for those 1,000 counties would be a little over $50 million. We want precinct rather than county counting, and there-

---

29. A thorough canvass of possible reforms would not ignore the experience of foreign democracies, but systematic information about that experience is not easy to come by. Some information can be found in "Vote Counting in Comparative Perspective," http://www.usc.edu/dept/polsci/gillman/comparativevotecounting.html (visited March 23, 2001). In addition, the Independent Institute for Democracy and Representative Government is assembling global data on electoral systems. As far as I have been able to determine, most countries use old-fashioned paper ballots and count them by hand.

30. The source for the data in this table is Eric A. Fischer, "Voting Technologies in the United States" (Congressional Research Service, Report for Congress, RL 30773, Jan. 11, 2001), http://www.cnie.org/nle/rsk-55.html (tab. 1).

—— Table 8

Voting Systems in Use in the United States

System	Percentage of precincts	Percentage of population
Punchcard	37.4	34.3
Votomatic	33.4	31.0
Datavote	4.0	3.3
Marksense	24.7	27.3
Lever	21.8	18.6
Electronic	7.3	9.1
Mixed	5.9	9.1
Paper	2.9	1.6

fore a marksense scanner in every precinct—or rather several scanners, to avoid long queues by voters on election day. Assume we want four per precinct, for a total cost, therefore, of $18,000. If that figure is multiplied by the number of precincts that have punchcard systems today, the result is an estimate for the total cost of the needed marksense scanners of $533 million (0.37 × 80,000 × $18,000), which when added to the $50 million estimated software cost totals $583 million—not $9 billion. And the $583 million is a capital cost, which, to give a true picture of the burden on the public finance of the states, ought to be amortized over the life of the machines, reducing the annual cost to a level that would be a minute burden. Nor need the money be spent all at once. It can be spread over the almost four years to the next Presidential election. We may thus be speaking of an annual average expenditure per state to replace punchcard with marksense systems of less than $3 million ($583 million divided by 4 years divided by 50 states) to replace all the punchcard voting and tabulating machines in the nation with marksense machines. Of course, there are other costs besides the cost of purchasing the hardware and the software—training costs, the costs of spares, the costs of the ballots themselves, shipping costs, and so on. But these, the running costs of the marksense systems, are unlikely to exceed the running costs of the punchcard systems. And remember that the capital cost, the not quite $3 million a year, should be amortized over the life of the machines. I conclude that cost should not be an obstacle to the abandonment of the punchcard technology.[31]

Granted, there are objections to the marksense system, and even to precinct counting. Some voters mark the marksense ballot incorrectly, and the scanner does not count it as a vote; but the scanner can be programmed to reject undervotes as well as over-votes, thus giving the voter a second chance. This is provided that there are scanners in the polling place, as I assumed in my cost estimates. There should be scanners there, enabling votes to be counted (or rejected) on the spot, but it must be acknowledged that counting votes at the precinct creates additional opportunities for fraud and error, especially when the precinct phones in its vote totals to the county election office.[32] There are no panaceas; a tricky issue, which I have not attempted to resolve, is whether the scanners should be programmed to reject undervoted ballots (as distinct from completely blank ones), since that would slow down the voting a lot—a great many voters do not bother to vote for all the offices on the ballot. But on balance marksense voting with precinct counting would be a significant improvement over the punchcard system.

There has been much discussion of electronic voting (and we see in Table 8 that it already has a nontrivial market share of U.S. voting systems), including voting over the Internet. But there are also well-founded concerns about the security of electronic voting, especially Internet voting, which is still in the discussion stage.

---

31. I do not know what it would cost to place marksense tabulating machines in every precinct that already uses the marksense technology, because I do not know how many marksense counties count votes at the county rather than at the precinct level.

32. Roy G. Saltman, *Accuracy, Integrity, and Security in Computerized Vote-Tallying* § 3.6 (National Bureau of Standards Special Publication 500-158 Aug. 1988).

Internet communications are insecure without (and possibly even with) elaborate encryption protocols.[33] The fundamental objection, however, is to *anything* new, because it is bound to have bugs, and we cannot afford to have a Presidential election botched because of an insufficiently tested and proven technology. That is why the marksense method, first used in the 1980s and in growing use throughout the country, is the most promising alternative to the punchcard system. Statistics from Florida and other states indicate that undervotes and overvotes are at least three times more frequent with punchcard voting than with the marksense method. These are raw statistics, which do not correct for other differences between counties that use the different systems. And we recall from the regressions in Chapter 2 that when other differences are held constant, the punchcard method does not increase the incidence of overvotes (in most though not all of my regressions), and may even reduce that incidence, though it does increase the incidence of undervotes substantially. What does increase the incidence of overvotes, however, and again substantially, is counting votes at the county rather than the precinct level, because when the votes are shipped off to the county election office rather than being counted at the precinct level the voter has no chance to revote. The marksense method with the scanner programmed to spit back a ballot that contains an overvote solves this problem; I do not know whether this solution is even feasible in a punchcard voting system.

The alternative to technological reform is reform of state election codes; the alternatives are not mutually exclusive. The Florida and Texas codes (both discussed in Chapter 3) illustrate opposite, but equally unsound, approaches to the problem of electoral deadlock. The Florida code is open-ended, delegating (until the Florida

---

33. For a thorough analysis of the problems and potential of Internet voting, see Internet Policy Institute, "Report of the National Workshop on Internet Voting: Issues and Research Agenda" (Internet Policy Institute March 2001).

supreme court in effect rewrote it) broad authority to the state election officials to interpret, particularize, and apply the code. This approach is unsatisfactory, because the officials are political animals and so can be expected to use their discretionary authority to aid the candidates of their own parties. The Florida election officials' interpretations of the code were reasonable, as we saw, but the widespread suspicion that their *motivation* was political is understandable, to say the least. The Texas code, in contrast to the Florida code, is highly specific, right down to the level of prescribing precise criteria for the recovery of votes from spoiled punchcard ballots. As I read the code (see Chapter 3), it permits a candidate in any close election to insist on a full hand recount, in which dimpled chads are to be counted as votes so long as the counters are satisfied that the voter's intent can be discerned from the ballot. The code's precision is thus illusory. Discretionary authority is not extinguished or even curtailed, but merely shifted to the lowest level of election officialdom, the local canvassing board.

If the punchcard technology is to be retained, either the administration of elections, right down to the hand recounting of spoiled ballots in close elections, must somehow be vested in officials of unquestioned neutrality—which may well be an impossible prescription at the state level (even U.S. Supreme Court Justices are not spared imputations of partisan bias)—or the criteria for recovering votes from spoiled punchcard ballots must be narrowed to the point at which subjectivity is so far reduced that the political sympathies of the counters are no longer likely to swing elections. If I were legislating, I would permit the counting of undervotes only in cases in which the chad is dangling (thus excluding trichads and dimpled chads) and the counting of overvotes only in cases in which the overvote consists of the combination of a punched chad (whether fully punched or dangling) for a candidate with the writing of the same candidate's name (or the name of the candidate's running mate) in the write-in space or elsewhere on the ballot. This approach is inferior to replacing the punchcard machines because it will exclude the recovery of votes from people who because of reading difficulties, inexperience, or sheer clumsiness are unable to produce a recoverable vote under the standard set forth. There is no justification for disenfranchising these people (see Chapter 1) if the need to do so can be eliminated with a technological fix that is cheap and reasonably secure. Marksense with precinct counting fits this bill.

A state legislature that trusts its courts, or some alternative dispute resolution mechanism, can avoid a repetition of the 2000 election fiasco in its own state by specifying a final, conclusive method for resolving disputes over the appointment of the state's electors. One of the better arguments against *Bush v. Gore* is that Florida had done just that, by entrusting the resolution of election disputes to the Florida judiciary. The counterargument was the unrealism of supposing that the legislature had actually foreseen and embraced the possibility that the state's supreme court would use the vague "people power" provision of the state constitution, or the justices' own Rousseauan or Rousseauesque version of democratic theory, to rewrite the election code that the legislature had painstakingly enacted, by shifting control over elections from the election officials to the judges and thus throwing a Presidential election into turmoil and jeopardizing the state's right to cast its electoral votes. But if a state statute were to provide clearly that the resolution by the state's highest court (or some other body of dispute resolvers) of any dispute over the state's Presidential electors would be final, any challenge to that resolution based on the "Manner directed" clause of Article II would fail.[34]

One hopes that the states will take either of the suggested paths of reform, the technological or the legal (or both), without

---

34. David P. Currie, *The Constitution in Congress: The Federalist Period, 1789–1801* 291 (1997).

prodding or coercion by the federal government.[35] But it may be too much to hope for. Incumbents may oppose *any* reform—having won with the existing voting technology, they may be afraid to take a plunge into the unknown by changing it. They may even think it favors them[36]—and that may be right. My concern with resistance by incumbents is supported by the fact that the inadequacies of election administration, including the disproportionate number of undervotes and overvotes generated by punchcard voting systems, have been well known for a very long time,[37] yet little has been done to ameliorate them. The movement away from punchcard technology, and from poorly designed election statutes, may be glacial.

One of the much-discussed reforms, a national ballot for Presidential elections, would be a mistake. It might also be unconstitutional, unless voluntarily adopted by every state, as invading the prerogative of the state legislatures conferred by the "Manner directed" clause of Article II. Article I, section 4 authorizes Congress to regulate the "Manner" of congressional elections. But there is no provision authorizing Congress to regulate the manner of Presidential elections (as distinct from the power that it may have, by virtue of its responsibility to count electoral votes, to resolve disputes over electors); it is the state legislatures that have been given that power

---

35. There is no dearth of thoughtful discussion. See, for example, the Jan. 31, 2001, testimony of Texas secretary of state Henry Cuellar, available at http://www.sos.state.tx.us/elections/testimony.shtml, visited Feb. 7, 2001, before the elections committee of the Texas house of representatives, suggesting a number of possible amendments to the state's election code. Cuellar suggested among other things that the legislature might consider making a "pattern" of dimples a precondition to counting dimpled ballots. Cf. Palm Beach County's "three dimples" rule, discussed in Chapter 2.

36. See, for example, John Mintz and Dan Keating, "A Racial Gap in Voided Votes: Precinct Analysis Finds Stark Inequity in Polling Problems," *Washington Post,* Dec. 27, 2000, p. A1.

37. "Almost everyone agrees that states generally must do a better job" in election administration; Jeanne Richman and Robert Otis, "State Control of Election Administration," in *Issues of Electoral Reform* 117, 118 (Richard J. Carlson ed. 1974). With specific reference to punchcard voting, see Roy G. Saltman, *Effective Use of Computing Technology in Vote-Tallying* 15–32, 70–71 (U.S. Dept. of Commerce, National Bureau of Standards, March 1975).

by Article II. So Congress may not be able to coerce the states into adopting this reform. A constitutional amendment might be necessary to accomplish this, though conceivably Congress could use the power granted it by section 5 of the Fourteenth Amendment (the power to enact legislation enforcing the other provisions of the amendment) to decree a national ballot in order to assure equal protection of the (voting) laws. Congress could just pay the states to induce them to adopt a uniform ballot for Presidential elections, through grants in aid conditioned on the states' adopting the national ballot. The constitutional authority would be the power of Congress to promote the "general Welfare,"[38] a term surely broad enough to include Presidential elections, even if ultimate authority to determine the manner of appointing Presidential electors resides with the state legislatures.

An intensely practical objection to the national ballot is that because Presidential elections coincide with elections for state and local officials, the voter would have to be given two ballots unless the state knuckled under and adopted the national ballot, merely adding the candidates for state and local office. This would be a substantial displacement of state authority; but the alternative of giving the voter two ballots would confuse many voters, slow up the voting and counting processes, and generate additional errors in counting. Another objection is to prematurely nationalizing the Presidential ballot issue, the kind of mistake many people think the Supreme Court made in deciding *Roe v. Wade* in favor of a federal right of abortion rather than leaving the regulation of abortion to the states. Just as *Roe* propelled abortion to the top of the national policy agenda by identifying it as an issue to be decided at the national level, so a national ballot would become a focus of political dispute over the conduct and result of Presidential elections. The parties would fight over every feature of the ballot and

---

38. U.S. Const. art. I, § 8, cl. 1.

the counting mechanism, and the loser in the Presidential election would blame the ballot and its designers for his loss. (Just imagine the consequences if Congress had adopted the butterfly ballot for use throughout the nation in the 2000 Presidential election!) The electoral process would become a cockpit of partisan wrangling, and public faith in the reliability of the process would be eroded. An advantage of our federal system is that many contentious issues can be diffused across a multitude of different state systems rather than becoming a magnet for high-visibility nationwide political strife. Federalism also facilitates experimentation, something we very much need in a period of rapid technological change that may affect the choice among voting technologies. The downside of federalism is that the quality of public administration is generally poorer at the state and local levels than at the national level. Our ramshackle electoral system attests to that. It is curious, by way of a minor example, that the Palm Beach election officials adopted the butterfly ballot without first testing it on a sample of potential voters.

The most difficult issue of nonconstitutional reform is what to do with the Electoral Count Act (Title III). Even if my suggested constitutional amendment were enacted and electors (but not the Electoral College) thus were banished from the scene, there could still be deadlock when Congress met to count the electoral votes— and this quite apart from the possibility of a tie in the Electoral College or a failure of any candidate to obtain a majority of the electoral votes. I am thinking rather of an 1876- or 2000-style dead-lock—that is, one resulting from a dispute over which electoral votes to count. Suppose that instead of litigating the issue of recounts, Bush had procured from the Florida legislature the appointment of a slate of Bush-pledged electors and that as a result Congress on January 6 had been confronted with rival Bush and Gore slates. Title III does not speak clearly to this issue. Bush could argue that the electoral votes submitted by the Gore slate on

December 12 (assuming the contest proceeding would have been resolved by then and would have given Gore the lead in the popular vote) had not been "regularly given." Recall from Chapter 3 that while compliance with section 5 of Title III (the safe harbor provision) precludes a challenge to the appointment of the state's *electors* if they are appointed by December 12, section 15 requires their electoral *votes* to be counted only if those votes are "regularly given," whatever that means. The dispute would wind up in the lap of Congress, with nothing to guide its members' decision.

We should endeavor to keep Congress out of the picture, so far as that is possible to do. It is a large, unwieldy, undisciplined body (actually two bodies), unsuited in its structure, personnel, and procedures to legal dispute resolution and—if only because the new Congress does not meet until January—not to be relied upon to produce a *timely* resolution of a dispute over who is to become President. The alternative of allowing the lame-duck Congress to resolve the dispute, in November or December, is not attractive.

I suggest a simple solution. Let Title III be amended to make the safe harbor deadline the final, absolute deadline for the appointment of a state's electors.[39] If a state failed to appoint electors by the deadline, its electoral votes would not be counted, period, and since electors would not have been appointed, winning the electoral vote would require only a majority of the electoral votes cast by those states that had made the deadline. If this seems abrupt, the statute could provide that if a state seemed unlikely to make the deadline because the outcome of the popular election in the state was in dispute, the candidates could turn to the courts, just as they did in November 2000, and the courts would accelerate their processes to make sure there was a final decision by the deadline, which is what they did in 2000.

---

39. Or for the determination of the state's electoral votes, if electors have been abolished by constitutional amendment.

Problems can be imagined that my proposed solution—basically a ratification and regularization of the solution the courts backed into in the 2000 election litigation—will not solve. But the incompleteness of the proposal is not a fatal flaw. Title III cannot prevent Congress when it meets to count the electoral votes from adopting an ad hoc solution to an unforeseen problem. The constitutional power to count the votes is the power ultimately to resolve disputes for which provision has not been made.

Conclusion

THE DRAMA that culminated in the Supreme Court's decision in *Bush v. Gore* is depicted in some quarters as a defeat of democracy, a thwarting of the popular will. The winner of the popular vote nationwide—who might well have prevailed in the Electoral College too had Florida used up-to-date voting machines, or even if a single county in Florida had designed a less confusing ballot (Palm Beach County, site of the infamous butterfly ballot)—was robbed of the victory that a manual recount would have given him. He was robbed, the argument continues, by a bare majority of that least democratic of major American political institutions, the Supreme Court of the United States, whose members are appointed for life and so never have to face the voter. As a result, the argument continues, President Bush has lost democratic, and the Supreme Court political, legitimacy.

There are elements of truth in this picture, but it is grossly overdrawn. Al Gore was indeed the fair winner of the nationwide popular vote; and if Florida's most populous counties had employed a more user-friendly voting methodology he might well have won the popular vote in Florida as well, and with it the Presidency. Many people refuse to think any more deeply about the election and its aftermath. That refusal is dogmatic and simpleminded. Among the important things that it overlooks is that American democracy is an institutionally complex and historically determined set of laws and practices rather than a simple mapping of preferences onto votes. If, as political scientists doubt, there is some method of actualizing the popular will in a large and complex polity such as the modern United States, it is not to be found in the Constitution or in the laws of the states. Our system of representative democracy, with indirect election of the President through the device of the Electoral College, is a pragmatic method of ensuring accountability of officials and a smooth and peaceful succession of them. It is not a failed stab at realizing a theorist's democratic ideal, or at approximating the deliberations of a faculty meeting or a university senate—which is the implicit conception of democracy held (unsurprisingly) by many academic students of democracy.

The question presented by the deadlocked election in Florida is not whether Gore was the people's preference but whether he had a legal right to overturn the election results by means of a hand recount of selected ballots, using criteria that, by allowing "dimpled chads" to be counted as votes, would have enabled Democratic-dominated canvassing boards to recover votes for Gore from ballots that the voter had spoiled by failing to follow instructions. Without the highly subjective criteria employed by Broward County's canvassing board, it is highly unlikely (as we saw in Chapter 2) that a hand recount of the undervoted ballots would have enabled Gore to overcome Bush's lead. A hand recount of overvoted ballots might have done the trick, but it was not sought by Gore—in fact was opposed by him and sought by Bush.

Whether to conduct a hand recount in the counties selected by Gore was a question in the first instance of Florida law. That law made clear that decisions on whether and how to recount votes were committed to the discretionary authority of state and local election officials, with only limited judicial review. The decisions made by these officials were reasonable and so should have been upheld by Florida's supreme court. Countywide recounts are authorized by the state's election code only when there is an error in the tabulation of the vote, and the election officials were for a number of reasons on solid ground in refusing to classify an error by the voter as an error in the tabulation (that is, the counting) of the votes. The voter casts the vote; he does not count it. The Florida supreme court, grievously misapplying the Florida election code in a quixotic effort to enforce the state constitution's "all power to the people" provision, repeatedly overturned the election officials' reasonable decisions.

The question for the Supreme Court was whether in doing so the Florida supreme court was violating federal as well as state law. This was and is a most difficult question, and only a dogmatist could be certain of the answer. The answer that I am inclined to give— because I think it is the best answer, not because I think it is the One Right Answer—is that the Florida court had violated the clause of Article II of the federal Constitution that commits the "Manner" of appointing Presidential electors to the "Legislature" of each state. Florida's legislature had spoken in the state election code. The Florida supreme court so far deformed the code—primarily though not only by abrogating the discretionary authority that the code unmistakably grants to state and local election officials—as to have arrogated the legislative function to itself. In the guise of interpretation, the court became the legislature; its opinions became the election code. There was no basis in the Florida election code for any of the hand recounts after the initial sample recounts failed to disclose a defect in the design, maintenance, or operation of the tabulating machinery. Bush really had won Florida by 930 votes—

for remember that votes are legal artifacts, not simple one-to-one measures of democratic preference.

For reasons that are unclear, the U.S. Supreme Court flinched from embracing Article II as the ground of its decision of December 12, 2000, in *Bush v. Gore,* reversing the Florida supreme court and ending the electoral deadlock. A majority of the Justices decided that the criteria (or rather lack of criteria) for the recount prescribed by that court in its decision of December 8 were so arbitrary that the recount would deny the voters of Florida the equal protection of the laws. This ground was doubtful for a number of reasons, not least that it implied a remedy—sending the case back to the Florida court with instructions to adopt uniform criteria for the recount—different from the one the Court adopted, which was to declare that the resumption of the recount would violate Florida law. Had the Court held that the recount violated Article II, and so could not be redeemed by tinkering with the recount criteria, the remedy would have followed directly from the holding.

The interpretation of Article II that I defend, and in particular the application of that interpretation to the opinions of the Florida supreme court, are, to repeat, not inevitable. They persuade me; they will not persuade everyone. In particular they will not persuade legal thinkers who are passionate liberals or, more interestingly, who do not believe that pragmatic considerations should play a larger role in the decision of constitutional cases than history and precedent. The foundation of my interpretation of the "Manner directed" clause of Article II, and of my defense of its application to Bush's challenge to the Florida supreme court, is my conviction that the clause can and should be regarded as a means of heading off interbranch struggles over Presidential electors that could spark political and constitutional crisis when Congress meets in the January following the Presidential election to count the electoral votes. This is a pragmatic concern. Some critics of the

Court's decision, including the dissenting Justices in *Bush v. Gore,* made light of the belief that intervention by the Court was necessary to avert a political and constitutional crisis. Either they thought that calmer heads would prevail in the contestants' camps and negotiate a solution or they thought that a congressional free-for-all would be more democratic than a judicial resolution. Or, believing that the recount would soon be abandoned under pressure of time, they may have wanted to strike a symbolic chord for the populist principle (which had become the Gore mantra) of "count every vote."

No one can say they were wrong to dissent. Apart from predictive uncertainty, and rival jurisprudential approaches between which no choice can be made on objective grounds, there were value judgments in play that also could not be evaluated objectively, that were matters of intuition and temperament rather than of logic or measurement. On one side was a preference for order—for an orderly transition, an orderly succession, an avoidance of protracted partisan wrangling, of an awkward interregnum, and of a diminished Presidency. On the other side was a preference for a more populist, perhaps even carnivalesque, but certainly less orderly and legalistic conception of American democracy—specifically one more forgiving of voter errors due to the inexperience of new voters, who in the 2000 Florida election were disproportionately black, and to the literacy problems of some voters, also disproportionately black. My statistical analysis in Chapter 2 confirms the suspicion that blacks were placed at a disadvantage by punchcard technology and (a distinct and underemphasized point) by the decision of most counties to have the precinct polling places ship the ballots off to the county election office for tabulation rather than tabulating them at the precinct level and just reporting the results to the county office.

The decision in *Bush v. Gore* (and the anterior five-to-four decision of the Supreme Court to stay the recount ordered by the

Florida supreme court) has provoked an avalanche of criticism. Some of it has been directed at Gore's lawyers. I argued that these criticisms are misdirected. The lawyers on both sides performed admirably, in sharp contrast to the lawyers' performance in that other recent political melodrama, the Clinton impeachment. The Supreme Court, however, can be criticized—for adopting the wrong ground of decision (equal protection rather than Article II), for Justice Scalia's effort to justify the stay publicly, for the inflamed rhetoric of some of the dissenting opinions, and for the less than convincingly argued majority and concurring opinions. What these criticisms overlook is the haste with which the Court was forced to act. Not only were the legal issues immensely complex (as we glimpsed in Chapter 3), but they were issues unfamiliar to the Court from its previous decisions. The Court had days to produce opinions over which it normally would have labored for months.[1] The conflict of interest inherent in deciding a case that might determine who would be appointing colleagues and successors of the judges deciding the case was, if not unavoidable, no more disagreeable than the alternative of allowing the Florida supreme court to decide the election in defiance of the federal Constitution.

The refusal to make allowances for the time pressures that deformed the U.S. Supreme Court's product is conspicuous in the criticisms of *Bush v. Gore* by law professors. The precipitance, inaccuracy, superficiality, partisanship, and anger of many of the professorial critics are notable. I attribute this donnybrook of professional criticism to several factors: that academics, unlike journalists, are not experienced in reacting to current events in real time; that most constitutional law professors identify strongly with the Democratic Party, and indeed with its liberal wing; and that professors of constitutional law tend to be underspecialized. This

---

1. The Court could have issued just its decision, with the notation that opinions would follow, and taken its time over the opinions, but this would simply have prolonged the agony.

underspecialization renders them ill equipped, despite their intelligence, to comment off the cuff about highly specialized, indeed esoteric, legal issues, such as the meaning of the "Manner directed" clause of Article II, the procedures of the Electoral College, or the details of Florida's election code or the federal Electoral Count Act—let alone the operational problems associated with particular voting technologies. A lack of expert knowledge fosters evaluations based on politics and emotion.

Some of the anger of the Court's academic critics may also be due to a dawning recognition that activist decisions (and, right or wrong, *Bush v. Gore* is undoubtedly activist, in adopting a bold, novel, and expansionary interpretation of federal judicial authority over the electoral process) are as much a weapon of the right as of the left, and that the left's uncritical approbation of liberal activist decisions such as *Roe v. Wade* has disarmed the academic left against the activism of a conservative Supreme Court. During the chief justiceship of Earl Warren, and to a lesser extent that of Warren Burger, the Court, wielding the mighty weapon of constitutional interpretation, engineered a breathtaking expansion in the power of the federal courts over the other branches of government. At first the legal academy protested, invoking the then-orthodox principle that courts should play a modest role vis-à-vis the elected branches of government. In time the protests diminished. The attractiveness to most academics, especially those who reached maturity in the 1960s and later, of the results of the Court's liberal decisions during the Warren and Burger eras overwhelmed concerns with the risks of judicial aggressiveness. If *Bush v. Gore* reminds constitutional theorists of these risks, credible criticism of the decision on the basis of them will require the theorists to reexamine their commitment to an activist constitutional jurisprudence.

More interesting and important than the travails of the academic lawyer, and more manageable than efforts to predict the consequences of *Bush v. Gore* for the reputation of the Supreme Court and the success of the Bush Administration, is the issue of reform. The pragmatic theory of democracy that I embrace, chilly as it may seem in comparison to idealistic conceptions, provides solid nonideological support for user-friendly voting technologies that make it easier for people who have difficulty in complying with voting instructions, because of limited education or intellectual ability, to cast a valid vote. Political elections are not faculty seminars. They are means of ensuring the accountability of the rulers to the ruled. Among the ruled in the United States are people who are very poorly educated, and even illiterate or barely literate. They are not well informed about political matters, but they are not completely ignorant; and though some may be the dupes of a cynical self-appointed leadership, they probably have a better idea of, as well as a greater solicitude for, their interests than the rest of the electorate does. They ought not to be prevented from voting by a de facto literacy test, which is what punchcard voting technology amounts to, and, to a lesser extent, marksense technology as well when the votes are counted at the county rather than the precinct level.

Punchcard technology ought to be replaced by marksense technology, and marksense ballots should be counted at the precinct level to enable as many spoiled ballots as possible to be revoted. These reforms are possible at modest cost. At the same time, states should establish procedures for the prompt and authoritative adjudication of election challenges; the federal Electoral Count Act should be amended to establish a definitive deadline for the submission of electoral votes and to provide for mandatory review by the U.S. Supreme Court of state decisions resolving challenges to those votes; and the Constitution itself should be amended to require that electoral votes be cast in conformity with the popular vote for President in each state and the Presidential electors themselves eliminated. More ambitious reform schemes are premature.

The modest legal and technological measures that I have proposed should be feasible, though incumbents may oppose them. If adopted, these measures will greatly reduce the likelihood of another Presidential election fiasco, while at the same time expanding the suffrage. At little cost we shall have more—and more orderly—democracy.

Index

Ackerman, Bruce, 209 n. 85, 213–17, 228 n. 7
activism, judicial, 175, 179, 217–18, 258
Adams, John Quincy, 45, 141, 165
administrative law: judicial review of exercise of discretion, 100–104, 106–7, 118–20, 123, 191; remedy for failure of official to exercise his discretion, 103
Albright, Madeleine, 138
Amar, Akhil, 200 n. 70, 231 n. 14
Amsterdam, Anthony, 200 n. 70
arbitration, labor, 112–13
Arendt, Hannah, 26
aristocracy, 27; in democratic theory, 15, 17; founders' aristocratic conception of Presidency, 31

Balkin, Jack, 169–70
ballot: absentee, 93, 98, 181, 234; Australian, 37; butterfly, 7, 61 n. 20, 70, 82–88, 193, 249; county-counting versus precinct-counting, 51–52, 70–82, 88, 90–91, 193, 241–46, 256; defective, 94, 107 n. 29, 131; electronic, 243–44; forged, 212; marksense (optical scan), 51–52, 72–74, 193–94, 197, 241–44, 246; military, 93, 98; national ballot for President, 247–49; overvoted, 8, 50 n. 4, 52, 60–61, 66–82 passim,
121, 124–25, 193–97 passim, 204, 244–46; paper, 37, 51 n. 6, 241 n. 29, 243 (tab. 8); party, 37; punchcard, 7–8, 29, 51–53, 56–90, 94–103 passim, 122, 193–98 passim, 204, 221, 241–47, 256; spoiled, 2, 68 n. 30, 70–76, 87; undervoted, 8, 50–52, 66–82, 121, 243–46
Beckstrom v. Volusia County Canvassing Board, 107 n. 29
Bickel, Alexander, 207 n. 80, 211 n. 90, 228
Blacker, McPherson v. See McPherson v. Blacker
Blair, Ray v. See Ray v. Blair
Blaisdell, Home Building and Loan Association v. See Home Building and Loan Association v. Blaisdell
Boardman v. Esteva, 107 n. 29
Boies, David, 80 n. 43, 133, 195, 200
Borden, Luther v. See Luther v. Borden
Breyer, Stephen, 79 n. 43, 144–45, 168–69, 216
Broward County recount, 8, 10, 50–66 passim, 73, 95, 119–31 passim, 136, 195–96
Buchanan, Patrick, 7, 82–83, 85, 177 n. 40
Burr, Aaron, 38–39

Burroughs v. United States, 142

Bush v. Gore, 92, 128–33, 141–49, 162–63, 167–80, 188–89, 246, 255, 257–59; as activist decision, 217–18, 258; critical comments of law professors on, 199–219, 257–58; dissents in, 141, 144–47, 175–76, 185, 256; likely consequences of, 221–22; remedy ordered by, 132, 150–52, 156, 255. *See also* Constitution (U.S.), "Manner directed" clause of Article II

Bush v. Palm Beach County Canvassing Board, 92 n. 1, 109–15, 157

Bush, Jeb, 141, 216

Butterworth, Robert, 95, 101 n. 23, 104

Carter, Jimmy, 193 n. 61

census, 179

chad. *See* ballot, punchcard

Clark, Nikki Ann, 182

Clinton v. Jones, 172 n. 32, 174

Clinton, Bill, 142, 172; affair of with Monica Lewinsky, 192, 198–99

conflicts of interest: of Florida election officials, 104; 214–15, 245; judicial, 151, 175–80, 256; rule of necessity, 176

Congress, authority of to count electoral votes, 144–45, 184–85, 236–37; authority of to regulate Presidential elections, 20 n. 26, 236–38, 247–48; as dispute resolution body, 145, 238, 250. *See also* Title III of U.S. Code

constitution (Florida), 107, 113, 116, 141, 178, 246, 254; as just another election statute, 112

Constitution (U.S.): Article V, 154; contracts clause, 173; democracy in, 17; due process clause of Fourteenth Amendment, 130–32; equal protection clause of Fourteenth Amendment, 123, 128–32, 151–52, 167–68, 187, 248; general-welfare clause, 248; guarantee clause of Article IV, 154; habeas corpus, 188; "Manner directed" clause of Article II, 29 n. 26, 109–14, 123, 151–61, 186–87, 217–18, 236, 240, 246–48, 254–55; Reconstruction amendments to, 187; reserved powers of states, 110–11; right to vote, 131–32, 164; section 5 of Fourteenth Amendment, 248; slave counted as three-fifths of free person, 35 n. 35; structural versus rights provisions of, 210; voting-related provisions of, 31–34, 134–136, 153–54, 157–58; war

powers, 172, 188. *See also* Electoral College; *specific amendments*

constitutional law: academic, 4–5, 199–219, 257–58; activist, 175, 179, 217–18, 258; conservative commentators on, 209, 217–18; interpretation, 154–55, 182–83, 217; political character of, 207–8; political questions doctrine, 137, 144, 162, 182–85; politicization of academic constitutional lawyers, 208–12, 257–58; pragmatic approach to, 169–75, 185–89, 255–56; role of intuition in, 219–20; teaching of in law schools, 218–19

constitutional theory, 205

Datavote voting system, 51 n. 6, 74 n. 36

Delahunt v. Johnston, 57 n. 17

democracy: classical, 15, 24; direct versus representative, 15–16, 24–26; relation of market economy to, 26–29; plebiscitary, 16–17; populist conception of, 29, 178–79, 256; pragmatic, 28–29, 100, 253, 259; pure versus limited, 25–26, 226; representative, 15–29, 179, 253; spirit of American, 29, 100; U.S. Constitution's theory of, 17. *See also* voting

Denning, Brannon, 201 n. 72, 211 n. 90

Dershowitz, Alan, 209

District of Columbia, 41

Duval County, overvotes in, 80, 196

Dworkin, Ronald, 86–87

election administration, 44–47, 204–5; foreign, 37 n. 45, 241 n. 29; hand counting versus machine counting, 53–54, 86, 96–97; legal reform of, 244–51; politics of, 246–47; technological improvement of, 241–47. *See also* ballot; voting

election law: academic, 206–7; contest versus protest proceedings, 93–94, 96, 105, 117–20, 189–94. *See also* Florida election code

election statistics, Florida, 6–9, 48–49, 117, 121, 147–48

elections: increase in types of official appointed by, 38; indirect versus direct, 34–36, 41, 227–28, 236–37, 253; 1984 election for representative from Indiana's Eighth Congressional District, 45, 144; Presidential election

day, 135 n. 79; Presidential election
of 1800, 38–39; Presidential election of
1824, 32–33, 39, 45; Presidential
election of 1876, 39, 45, 114, 139–41,
215–16, 249; Presidential election
of 1888, 38, 46; Presidential election of
1960, 40, 45, 215; Presidential election
of 1968, 45. *See also* ballot; election
administration; voting
Electoral College, 11, 18, 40; and
avoidance of nationwide recount,
233–35; big-state advantage in,
228–32; Bush's margin in, 235–36;
critical literature on, 207; criticisms
of, 224–28, 235–38; day on which
electoral votes are cast, 133–36,
142; founders' conception of, 31–34,
153–54, 156, 226–27; likelihood of
deadlock in, 223–24; modern
defenses of, 228–35; movement to
abolish, 45, 238; pledges by electors,
236–37; racial and ethnic effects of,
228, 230–31; reforms of, 238–40;
regional effects of, 233; runaway
electors problem, 45, 235–40;
structure of, 31–32; as system of
indirect election, 227–28, 236–37;
winner-take-all system, 231, 239
Electoral Count Act. *See* Title III of U.S.
Code
Eleventh Amendment, 154–55
Emancipation Proclamation, 171–72, 188
Esteva, Boardman v. See Boardman v. Esteva
Ex parte Merryman, 188
exit polls, 61, 78

federalism, 249
Federalist No. 68 (Hamilton), 30 n. 28
Fifteenth Amendment, 36, 41
Florida election code, 7–8, 104–5, 109,
124–25, 194, 244–45; contest versus
protest proceedings under, 93–94, 96,
105, 117–20, 189–94; contest remedy,
127–28, 194; defective-ballot
provision, 94, 107 n. 29, 131;
discretion granted election officials
by, 100–4, 106–7, 118–20, 123, 245,
254; key provisions (relating to
recounts) of summarized, 93–94;
overvote provision, 124–25; voter's-
intent provisions, 94, 101, 131
Florida supreme court, 124, 126–27, 142,
145–46, 152, 181–82. *See also specific
decisions*
Foster v. Love, 135 n. 79, 204 n. 76

Fourteenth Amendment: due process
clause, 130–32; enforcement clause
(section 5), 248; equal protection
clause, 123, 128–32, 151–52, 167–68,
187, 248
Fourth Amendment, warrant clause of,
174
Frey, Bruno, 16 n. 9
Fried, Charles, 200
Friedman, Richard, 200 n. 70

Gerken, Heather, 218
Gore, Bush v. See Bush v. Gore
Gore v. Harris, 92 n. 1, 118–28, 148–49,
160
Gore, Al, as winner of popular vote
nationwide, 40, 225

Harris, Gore v. See Gore v. Harris
*Harris, McDermott v. See McDermott v.
Harris*
*Harris, Palm Beach County Canvassing
Board v. See Palm Beach County
Canvassing Board v. Harris*
Harris, Katherine, 8–9, 94, 104, 221;
criticism of by Bruce Ackerman, 214
Harrison, John, 186–87, 239 n. 27
Hastert, Dennis, 137–38
Hawaii, 1960 Presidential electors
appointed by, 135–36, 216
Hayes-Tilden election (1876), 39, 45, 114,
139–41, 215–16
Herzog, Don, 28 n. 25
Holmes, Oliver Wendell, 174–75
*Home Building and Loan Association v.
Blaisdell,* 173
Honig, Bonnie, 26
House of Representatives, election of
President by, 30 n. 28, 32–33, 39, 134,
138, 143, 226

impeachment, 145, 182–83; law
professors' opposition to impeachment
of Clinton, 211 n. 89
income: effect of on county's choice of
voting system, 70, 90–91; effect of on
voting, 71, 72 n. 34, 76 n. 38, 85
intellectuals, public, 199
interpretation. *See* constitutional law,
interpretation; statutory interpretation

Jackson, Robert, 170–71, 175
*Jacobs v. Seminole County Canvassing
Board,* 92 n. 1, 98 n. 18, 181–82

Johnston, Delahunt v. See Delahunt v. Johnston
Jones, Clinton v. See Clinton v. Jones

Kalt, Brian, 193 n. 62, 197
Karlan, Pamela, 65 n. 24, 102 n. 24
Katyal, Neal, 200 n. 70, 213 n. 94
Kennedy, Randall, 200 n. 70
Kirby, James, 156 nn. 7, 8
Klarman, Michael, 126–27, 200 n. 70
Korematsu v. United States, 170–73

law schools. *See* constitutional law, academic
lawyers: litigation strategies of, 79–80, 189–92; litigation tactics of, 198; recount strategies of, 54–55, 79–80, 189–90, 193–97; role of in election litigation, 190–91
legislation, democratic legitimacy of, 208; how differs from adjudication, 159–60
legislature, meaning of word in Constitution, 153–56
LePore, Siegel v. See Siegel v. LePore
Lessig, Lawrence, 206
Lewis, Terry, 102, 104, 137, 182
liberalism, judicial, 142–43, 168–70, 175, 179–80, 189, 208–209, 258
liberty, 25, 27
Lieberman, Joseph, 6, 78 n. 40, 99
Lincoln, Abraham, 171–72, 188
literacy, 29, 37, 41, 42 n. 57, 68 n. 30, 99–100, 177; defined, 42 n. 57; effect of on voting, 72–82, 88, 177, 204–5. *See also* voting, literacy as qualification for
Love, Foster v. See Foster v. Love
Luther v. Borden, 182 n. 44, 183–85

malapportionment, 41; of Electoral College, 224–25; offsetting, 232
marksense. *See* ballot, marksense
Marshall, Thurgood, 6, 212, 214
McConnell, Michael, 100–101, 104 n. 27, 206
McDermott v. Harris, 102 n. 24
McPherson v. Blacker, 113–14, 123–24
media, election coverage by, 6; 65–67
Miami-Dade County recount, 57–60, 63–65, 73, 99, 117–19, 121–22, 124, 147, 197
Mill, John Stuart, 13, 42 n. 57, 43–44, 227 n. 6; *On Liberty,* 210
Mitchell, Oregon v. See Oregon v. Mitchell

Nader, Ralph, 6, 177
natural law, 107–8
New Republic, 152 n. 1, 209 n. 85
Nineteenth Amendment, 41
Nixon v. United States, 182–83

O'Connor, Sandra Day, 177
Olson, Theodore, 200
optical scan. *See* ballot, marksense
Oregon v. Mitchell, 29 n. 26
overvote. *See* ballot, overvoted

Palm Beach County Canvassing Board, Bush v. See Bush v. Palm Beach County Canvassing Board
Palm Beach County Canvassing Board v. Harris (first decision), 92 n. 1, 96, 104–9, 133, 148–49
Palm Beach County Canvassing Board v. Harris (second decision), 115–17
Palm Beach County: butterfly ballot used in, 7, 82–88, 203; recount, 9–10, 57–60, 62–65, 73, 117–19, 121–22, 124, 130, 197
Pildes, Richard, 179 n. 42
political parties, 19, 38, 226–27; third parties, 19; two-party system, 33, 227
political questions, 137, 144, 162, 182–85
politics, 25–26; of academic constitutional lawyers, 208–12; of election reform, 246–47; ideological versus postideological, 233. *See also* democracy; voting; Supreme Court of the United States, politics in
populism, 29, 179, 256
pragmatism, legal, 169–75, 185–89, 255–56
President: acting, 137–39; constitutional debate on how to appoint, 31–32; popular vote for, 38–40, 215, 225; rules of succession, 137–39, 179; transition, 138, 143, 237–38
Presidential electors: appointment of by legislature, 159, 195; runaway, 235–37 *See also* Electoral College
property ownership as voting qualification, 30, 34–35
public intellectuals, 199
punchcard. *See* ballot, punchcard

race: and Electoral College, 228, 230–31; voting preference by, 78–79, 88, 177–78. *See also* voting, racial and ethnic issues in
Radin, Margaret Jane, 211–12

Rakin, Jamin, 200 n. 70
Ray v. Blair, 236 n. 21, 237
"Recount Primer, The," 54 n. 11, 67 n. 28, 194 n. 64, 196 n. 65
referendum, 15–16
Reynolds v. Sims, 132 n. 70
Rhodes, Williams v. See Williams v. Rhodes
Roberts, Clayton, 94, 96, 104, 214–15
Roe v. Wade, 170, 216, 248, 258; search for alternative justifications for, 153, 167 n. 19, 209–10
Rosen, Jeffrey, 152 n. 1, 209, 210 n. 88, 212 n. 92
Rothstein, Paul, 191–92
Rousseau, Jean-Jacques, 20, 29

safe harbor. *See* Title III of U.S. Code, safe harbor provision
Sandalow, Terrance, 201 n. 70, 210 n. 88
Sandel, Michael, 203 n. 74
Sauls, N. Sanders, 117–21, 182
Scalia, Antonin, 6, 166–67
Schumpeter, Joseph, 15 n. 7
Schwartz, Herman, 200 n. 70
Seminole County Canvassing Board, Jacobs v. See Jacobs v. Seminole County Canvassing Board
Senators, how appointed, 31, 154, 228
Seventeenth Amendment, 41
Siegel v. LePore, 92 n. 1, 189 n. 56
Sims, Reynolds v. See Reynolds v. Sims
Souter, David, 168, 216
statistics: and big-state advantage in Electoral College, 229–30; regression analysis, 68–70; statistical tie, 49–50, 54; tests of significance and fit, 69. *See also* election statistics, Florida
statutory interpretation, 107–8, 110–13, 116, 124; plain-meaning rule, 108–9, 116; versus judicial usurpation, 113, 123, 254
stays of decision pending appeal, role and meaning of irreparable harm, 163–67
steel seizure case, 171–72
Strauss, David, 109 n. 34, 160–61
suffrage. *See* voting
Summers, Lawrence, 138–39
Sunstein, Cass, 120 n. 50, 160–61, 171, 200 n. 70
Supreme Court of the United States, 142–43, 146; discretionary jurisdiction of, 161; ideology in, 176–80; judicial activism in, 175, 179, 217–18, 258; Justices' impartiality, 151, 175–80;

knowledge of specific subject matters, 206; impact of oral argument on decisions by, 165; politics in, 161–63, 166–68, 176–80, 219; stay of Florida supreme court's December 8 decision, 163–67. *See also* constitutional law

tabulation (of votes). *See* voting, voter error versus tabulation error
Texas election code, 102–103, 244–45, 247 n. 35
Thomas, Clarence, 6, 167, 214
Thurmond, Strom, 138
Title III of U.S. Code (Electoral Count Act), 11 n. 3, 30 n. 28, 133–41, 144–45, 155 n. 6, 217, 236 n. 22, 238; reform of, 249–251; safe harbor provision, 114–15, 118, 132–34, 217, 249–50; and state legislature's appointing electors, 159, 217
Tribe, Laurence, 200, 203–4
Twelfth Amendment, 39, 134–35, 139, 145, 155 n. 6
Twentieth Amendment, 138–39

undervote. *See* ballot, undervoted
United States, Burroughs v. See Burroughs v. United States
United States, Korematsu v. See Korematsu v. United States
United States, Nixon v. See Nixon v. United States

Vice President: acting, 138–39; how selected, 38–39
Volusia County Canvassing Board, Beckstrom v. See Beckstrom v. Volusia County Canvassing Board
Volusia County recount, 9, 57, 94, 95 n. 12, 121 n. 53, 124
voting: by aliens, 22 n. 18, 37–38; altruistic, 42; colonial, 29–30, 34–35; corporate, 13, 22; cost of different systems, 241–42; Datavote system, 51 n. 6, 74 n. 36; determinants of choice of voting system, 90–91; by elderly, 20, 72, 81, 82 n. 47; enlargement of suffrage, 34–37, 41; error, meaning and types of, 61–62, 86–88, 94–99, 101, 107 n. 29; by felons or ex-felons, 43; fraud and other irregularities in, 37 n. 44, 39–40, 72, 89, 107 n. 29, 120, 129, 234, 243; history of, 29–41; illiteracy's effect on, 70, 72–82, 88, 177; incentive and

voting (*continued*)
motives to vote, 13–15; income effect of, 70–72, 76 n. 38, 81, 85; informed versus uninformed, 13, 19–20; Internet, 243; literacy as qualification for, 29, 37, 41–43, 259; machines, whether defective, 76–77, 87, 94–95, 198; majority, 23; as method of aggregating preferences, 12–13, 17–20; power or weight, 43–44, 228–32; racial and ethnic issues in, 36, 38 n. 47, 41, 70, 72–82, 88, 177–78, 204–5, 256; recounting punchcard votes, 56–67, 96–97, 195–96; revoting as remedy for butterfly ballot, 83, 85, 202–4; role of in democracy, 28–29; sale of votes, 22–23; as solution to succession problem, 23–24, 100; turnout, 14–15, 20, 37, 78 n. 40, 232–33; universal suffrage as goal, 41–44; voter error versus tabulation error, 61–62, 86–88, 94–99, 101; Voting Rights Act of 1965, 41, 44; Votomatic voting system, 51 n. 6, 74 n. 36. *See also* ballot; elections; Florida election code

Wade, Roe v. See Roe v. Wade
Warren Court. *See* liberalism, judicial
Wermiel, Stephen, 218
Williams v. Rhodes, 124 n. 56